LAUNCHING
INTO ADULTHOOD

LAUNCHING INTO ADULTHOOD

An Integrated Response to Support Transition of Youth with Chronic Health Conditions and Disabilities

edited by

Donald Lollar, Ed.D.
Oregon Health & Science University
Portland

·P·A·U·L·H·
BROOKES
PUBLISHING Cº ®

Baltimore • London • Sydney

Paul H. Brookes Publishing Co.
Post Office Box 10624
Baltimore, Maryland 21285-0624
USA

www.brookespublishing.com

Typeset by Broad Books, Baltimore, Maryland.
Manufactured in the United States of America by
Sheridan Books, Inc., Chelsea, Michigan.

All examples in the prologue and chapters of this book are composites. Any similarity to actual
individuals or circumstances is coincidental, and no implications should be inferred.

Library of Congress Cataloging-in-Publication Data
   Launching into adulthood : an integrated response to support transition of youth with chronic
health conditions and disabilities/edited by Donald Lollar.
      p.   cm.
   Includes bibliographical references and index.
   ISBN-13: 978-1-59857-102-8 (hardcover)
   ISBN-10: 1-59857-102-8 (hardcover)
   1. Youth with disabilities—Services for—United States.   2. Chronic diseases in adolescence—
Patients—Services for—United States.   I. Lollar, Donald.   II. Title.
   [DNLM: 1. Chronic Disease—rehabilitation—United States.   2. Adolescent—United States.
3. Adolescent Development—United States.   4. Adolescent Health Services—United States.   5.
Disabled Persons—rehabilitation—United States.   6. Health Policy—United States.   7. Young
Adult—United States.
WS 460 L376 2010]
HV1569.3.Y68L38 2010
362.40835'0973—dc22   2010005203

British Library Cataloguing in Publication data are available from the British Library.

2014   2013   2012   2011   2010
10   9   8   7   6   5   4   3   2   1

Contents

About the Editor and Contributors

Donald Lollar, Ed.D., is Director of the Oregon Institute on Disability & Development at Oregon Health & Science University (OHSU)'s Child Development and Rehabilitation Center. Prior to his position at OHSU, Dr. Lollar was Senior Research Scientist, National Center on Birth Defects and Developmental Disabilities, Centers for Disease Control and Prevention (CDC), Atlanta, Georgia. Dr. Lollar received his doctorate in rehabilitation counseling from Indiana University in 1971. After 25 years of clinical practice, Dr. Lollar spent 13 years at CDC working on public health science and programs to improve the health and well-being of people with disabilities, with special emphasis on children, adolescents, and their families. He has published widely in the areas of disability, public health, and youth with disabilities. Dr. Lollar has also been a member of the international task force that developed the *International Classification of Function, Disability and Health–Children and Youth Version (ICF-CY)* for the World Health Organization.

Josie Badger, M.S., started her Ph.D. work in Fall 2009 in health care ethics. She completed graduate school for rehabilitation counseling at the University of Pittsburgh in April 2009. In May 2007, she graduated summa cum laude from Geneva College, majoring in disability law and advocacy. Ms. Badger has served as president and vice president of the National Youth Leadership Network. On the state level, Ms. Badger is a founding member, President, and staff member of the Pennsylvania Youth Leadership Network. She also works with Children's Hospital of Pittsburgh on the family forum. Ms. Badger was named one of *Glamour* Magazine's Top College Women of 2006. She recently started a job as Youth Coordinator for a state grant, assisting families in health care transition.

Laurie J. Bauman, Ph.D., is Professor of Pediatrics and Director, Preventive Intervention Research Center for Child Health, Department of Pediatrics, Albert Einstein College of Medicine, New York. Dr. Bauman received her doctorate in sociology from Columbia University in 1986. She conducts theory-driven basic research and randomized trials to test the effectiveness of interventions to enhance adolescent mental health and prevent human immunodeficiency virus (HIV) and sexually transmitted disease transmission.

Susanne M. Bruyère , Ph.D., CRC, is Professor of Disabilities Studies, Associate Dean of Outreach, and Director of the Employment and Disability Institute at the Cornell University ILR (Industrial and Labor Relations) School in Ithaca, New York. Dr. Bruyère received her doctorate in rehabilitation counseling psychology from the University of Wisconsin–Madison in 1975. She has held numerous federally funded research, training, and dissemination grants focused on employment and disability policy, workplace disability nondiscrimination, and disability statistics and demographics.

Bonnie S. Essner, M.A., is a doctoral student in the Clinical Child Psychology graduate program at Loyola University Chicago. Her research and clinical interests include psychosocial adjustment in youth with chronic illness and disabilities, such as family and peer relationship features associated with positive social and emotional outcomes; variables associated with pain expression and pain management; activity limitations; and activity involvement in youth with chronic health conditions.

Valerie Fletcher, M.T.S., is Executive Director, Institute for Human Centered Design, Boston, Massachusetts. She writes and lectures internationally about universal design. Her career has been divided between design and public mental health. She is former Massachusetts Deputy Commissioner of Mental Health. Ms. Fletcher has a master's degree in ethics and public policy from Harvard University. She is a Trustee of the Boston Architectural College.

Thomas P. Golden, M.S., CRC, is Associate Director of the Employment and Disability Institute at the Cornell University ILR (Industrial and Labor Relations) School, Ithaca, New York. Mr. Golden received his master's degree in rehabilitation counseling psychology from Syracuse University in 1992. He has held numerous federally funded research, training, and technical assistance contracts and grants focused on transition planning for youth with disabilities; social insurance and return-to-work; and disability, workplace, and community inclusion policy.

Scott D. Grosse, Ph.D., is Health Economist, National Center on Birth Defects and Developmental Disabilities, Centers for Disease Control and Prevention, Atlanta, Georgia. Dr. Grosse conducts research on public health policies, economic evaluation methods, and health outcomes and costs associated with heritable disorders associated with disability in children and adults. He has authored more than 50 articles on these topics since 2004. He received a doctorate in public health from the University of Michigan in 1996.

Bryna Helfer, Ed.D., is Senior Director of Civic Engagement, National Academy of Public Administration, Washington, D.C. She received her doctorate in special education systems change from The George Washington University in 2006. Prior to her work with the National Academy, Dr. Helfer provided leadership for United We Ride and Easter Seals Project ACTION, two national initiatives on accessible transportation. As a therapeutic recreation specialist, she has a strong interest in facilitating youth transition and community participation.

Grayson N. Holmbeck, Ph.D., is Professor of Clinical Psychology and Director of Clinical Training, Department of Psychology, Loyola University Chicago. He received his Ph.D. in clinical psychology from Virginia Commonwealth University in 1987. His research interests include the adaptation to physical disabilities and chronic illness during adolescence, pediatric psychology, and statistical applications. He is a principal investigator on grants from the National Institute of Child Health and Human Development (NICHD) and the March of Dimes for studies of young adolescents with spina bifida and type 1 diabetes.

Lisa I. Iezzoni, M.D., M.Sc., is Professor of Medicine, Harvard Medical School, and Director, Institute for Health Policy, Massachusetts General Hospital, Boston. Dr. Iezzoni is a health services researcher who has authored numerous scholarly articles and several books on risk adjustment and health care disparities for people with disabilities, among other topics.

George Jesien, Ph.D., is the executive director of the Association of University Centers on Disabilities (AUCD), which represents national networks of university-based centers and programs conducting research, interdisciplinary training, dissemination, and exemplary service model development. He has more than 30 years of experience in various capacities, including school psychologist, university faculty, and director of state and federally funded programs. Previous positions include serving as the executive director of the Joseph P. Kennedy, Jr. Foundation and the director of the Early Intervention Program at the Waisman Center of the University of Wisconsin–Madison. Dr. Jesien was awarded a Joseph P. Kennedy, Jr. Foundation Public Policy Fellowship to work with the U.S. Senate Subcommittee on Disability Policy. He has served as the president of the Division for Early Childhood at the national and state levels and received outstanding service awards at the state and national levels. Dr. Jesien received his doctorate from the University of Wisconsin–Madison in human development.

David R. Johnson, Ph.D., is Senior Associate Dean for Research and Policy, Birkmaier Professor of Educational Leadership, and Director of the Institute on Community Integration, College of Education and Human Development, University of Minnesota, Minneapolis. Dr. Johnson received his doctorate in educational policy and administration from the University of Minnesota in 1987. His research interests include studies on postschool outcomes, postsecondary education retention programs, cost–benefit analysis, and other policy-related research. Dr. Johnson serves as a principal investigator and director of numerous federal and state research, training, and demonstration projects and has published more than 100 book chapters, journal articles, research monographs, technical reports, and other products on these and other research interests.

Lauren M. Kelly, M.A., is a clinical psychology doctoral student at Loyola University Chicago. Ms. Kelly completed her master's degree in clinical psychology at Loyola University Chicago in 2008. Her research and clinical interests include psychosocial adjustment, neuropsychological functioning, and family dynamics of children and adolescents with chronic health conditions.

Paul W. Newacheck, Dr.P.H., is Professor of Health Policy and Pediatrics, University of California, San Francisco. Dr. Newacheck conducts research on children with special health care needs and access to care for vulnerable populations. He received a doctorate in public health from the University of California, Berkeley in 1989. He has authored more than 100 articles on children's health.

James M. Perrin, M.D., is Professor of Pediatrics at Harvard Medical School and Director of the MassGeneral Hospital (MGH) Center for Child and Adolescent Health Policy, Boston, Massachusetts. His research has examined asthma, middle-ear disease, children's hospitalization, health insurance, and childhood chronic illness and disabilities, with a recent emphasis on quality of life and use of primary and subspecialty care for children and adolescents with chronic illness. He currently heads the Clinical Coordinating Center (based at the MGH) for the national Autism Treatment Network. He was previously on the faculties of Vanderbilt University and the University of Rochester.

Laurie E. Powers, Ph.D., is a professor and associate dean for research at the School of Social Work and the director of the Regional Research Institute for Human Services at Portland State University, Oregon. Dr. Powers received her doctorate from the University of Oregon in 1990. Prior to joining Portland State University in 2004, she was an associate professor of pediatrics, public health, and psychiatry at Oregon Health & Science University and an assistant professor of pediatrics at Dartmouth Medical School. Dr. Powers has published extensively in research areas including self-determination, transition to adulthood, and disability.

Ruth E.K. Stein, M.D., is Professor, Department of Pediatrics, Albert Einstein College of Medicine and Children's Hospital at Montefiore, New York. Dr. Stein has worked as a clinician, health services researcher, teacher, and advocate in the areas of children with serious ongoing health conditions and child/adolescent mental health for most of her career, and she has worked on how to improve the delivery of services. She has published extensively in these areas.

Sue Swenson, A.M., M.B.A., is President of Doxa, Inc., in Bethesda, Maryland. Ms. Swenson received her A.M. in interdisciplinary humanities from the University of Chicago in 1977 and her M.B.A. in marketing management from the University of Minnesota in 1986. The mother of an adult son with developmental disabilities, she has served as U.S. Commissioner for Developmental Disabilities, as Executive Director of the Joseph P. Kennedy, Jr. Foundation, as Executive Director of The Arc of the United States, and as a Kennedy Fellow in the U.S. Senate Subcommittee on Disability Policy.

Janet L. Valluzzi, M.B.A., OTR/L, is a doctor of public health candidate at The George Washington University. Ms. Valluzzi has 20 years of experience as a licensed occupational therapist in a variety of settings. She has also served as Statistical Service Fellow for the Agency for Healthcare Research and Quality, Health Scientist for the Centers for Disease Control and Prevention, and Disability Policy Analyst for the Congressional Research Service. She is currently completing her doctoral dissertation for The George Washington University School of Public Health and Health Services. She has authored or contributed to approximately 20 publications related to disability policy, measurement, programs, and services.

Sarah von Schrader, Ph.D., is Research Associate, Employment and Disability Institute at the Cornell University ILR (Industrial and Labor Relations) School, Ithaca, New York. She received her doctorate in educational measurement and statistics from the University of Iowa in 2006. Her research interests include employment and disability, health services, and psychometrics.

Deborah Klein Walker, Ed.D., is Vice President and Principal Associate, Health Division, Abt Associates, Inc., Cambridge, Massachusetts. Dr. Walker received a doctorate in human development from Harvard University in 1978. She was on the faculty at the Harvard School of Public Health from 1976 to 1988 and was the Assistant/Associate Commissioner at the Massachusetts Department of Public Health from 1988 to 2004. Dr. Walker has authored more than 100 journal articles and 3 books on a range of issues related to child health and development, community health systems, disability and chronic conditions, program implementation and evaluation, and health outcomes and data systems.

Kathy Zebracki, Ph.D., is Lecturer, Department of Behavioral Sciences, Rush University Medical Center, and Pediatric Psychologist, Shriners Hospitals for Children, Chicago. Dr. Zebracki completed her doctorate in clinical psychology at Case Western Reserve University in 2006. Her research interests include pain, transition, and long-term outcomes in adolescents and young adults with chronic health conditions and/or physical disabilities.

Foreword

When I asked our 28-year-old son Jeffrey what is the main difference between being an adolescent with disabilities and an adult with disabilities, he replied, "It's just harder." It is harder because the structure and support that existed for him when he was younger—mainly, school and a more tightly knit pediatric medical community—are no longer there. As family, we will be here for Jeffrey as long as we're around, but living arrangements, a job, transportation, access to medical care, and a network of supporters and friends are all harder to figure out now than when he was a teenager.

No one can know what it's like to live with significant physical disabilities other than those who walk in their shoes—or in the case of our 28-year-old son, sit in their wheelchairs. But as the mother of a young man who has struggled to overcome the longest odds, I've seen and felt almost as much as a person without disabilities can, enough to know our Jeffrey, and all the other people like him, are heroes.

They never asked to be different; they never asked for the extra burdens. But day after day, no exceptions, they are called on to put forward their best effort, to exert extra energy, just to accomplish the simplest of tasks: getting dressed, brushing their teeth, fixing breakfast, studying for class, getting to work. What the rest of us take for granted is Mt. Everest for many of them.

And I've watched Jeffrey's climb become even more difficult as he's moved into adulthood. When he was little, Jeffrey had a knack for needing stitches: his curiosity and fearlessness matched up with two wheel bicycles, roller skates, and pool cues led to multiple trips to the emergency room. As a teenager, he continued to push the envelope on skis, skateboards, and even with our golden retriever.

Born with a mild case of spina bifida, his main challenges those years were learning disabilities, which he and we grappled with as they surfaced. Our biggest headaches had to do with navigating school: making sure Jeffrey's teachers understood his learning differences and took those into account. He was bright and figured out how to compensate for some of his math and abstract reasoning deficits. He was talking about becoming a doctor, or a scientist, finding a cure for spina bifida, and rapidly lining up summer internships at the Centers for Disease Control and Prevention, the National Institutes of Health, and even the Food and Drug Administration, at the ages of 14, 15, and 16, respectively. But in school, he needed accommodations in some courses that teachers weren't always willing or able to make. Invaluable was the research and explanatory material provided to us by the Spina Bifida Association of America and this book's editor, Dr. Don Lollar: through them, we learned that many thousands of other children were grappling with the same issues Jeff was.

At age 16 Jeffrey was tragically injured in surgery. He was in a coma for months and in a hospital for 6 months. He came home in November 1998 in a wheelchair, unable to walk or use his right arm, with only gross motor function in his left hand, impaired vision, impaired speech, and a devastating loss of short-term memory. (He knew exactly what had happened to him but couldn't recall whom he spoke with on the phone this morning.)

The pain we all endured as a family is indescribable. But we were determined to forge ahead, to make the best of this horrible turn of events, and to give Jeffrey every chance to lead a meaningful life. Added to the sheer force of our will, and of Jeffrey's indomitable spirit, were institutions and specialists ready to help.

The pediatric neurorehabilitation hospital where Jeffrey had spent almost 5 months as an inpatient, learning to adjust to his broken body, was planning for him to go back to school before he was ever released. Unable to return to eleventh grade, where he would have been in school, he instead attended the hospital's specialized transition program that helps children and adolescents make the difficult move from the hospital back to home, community, and school life.

For 4 months Jeff commuted every day from our home to the program. His driver and caregiver was a young woman we had met who wanted to become a doctor and who welcomed the opportunity to work with a teenager with disabilities. We had been told by a neurologist that Jeff would benefit more from having a close peer oversee his care, ideally a young person headed for medical school, rather than rotating shifts of nurses. The neurologist was so right: as I write this, all but one of Jeff's 10 former caregivers have gone on to medical school; several are practicing medicine.

After the transition program, we wanted Jeff to return to his former high school in the fall. That required preparation: testing had showed him to be at a third- or fourth-grade level when he came home from the hospital. Two of his former middle school teachers offered to tutor him. By August, he was able to do most eleventh-grade work with accommodations that his school was glad to make. Most teachers went out of their way to help Jeffrey succeed, allowing his tutor/caregiver to type papers he dictated, providing copies of class notes, and giving him extra time on tests. Two years later, in June 2001, Jeffrey graduated from high school, with his sights already set on college.

He was living at home, and community college seemed the only option. For the next 4 years, he attended a large community college. Their program to assist students with learning disabilities was no doubt stretched to its limit by Jeffrey's collection of "issues," but its staff tried to serve his needs. The main obstacles were two: 1) a rigid set of academic requirements—strict rules about test taking, for example, that probably successfully prevented cheating but were nearly insurmountable for someone with a brain injury like Jeffrey's, with a severe short-term memory deficit—and

2) some faculty members had no time or interest in working with students with special needs.

Jeffrey failed several courses in which he never really was given a chance to succeed. But he shone in others, doing well enough that after he observed his younger brother applying to colleges away from home, he announced he wanted to do the same. We found a tiny handful of schools around the United States that offered on-campus nursing care to provide the assistance Jeffrey needs with dressing, bathing, and toileting. The college we chose had been known for its outreach to students with disabilities, and when Jeffrey started there, in the fall of 2005, there were about 25 students with significant physical disabilities living together in one accessible dormitory. The sight of these young people, zooming up and down the halls in their power wheelchairs, on their way to class, or at a basketball game, brought a huge smile and tears to my eyes every time I visited.

Eventually, though, the school chose to end the special program, and by Jeffrey's fourth year on campus, he was the only student with nursing care, provided privately by us. He missed terribly the friends he had made; most had gone back to live with parents or grandparents. Some who aspired to attend graduate school could not find a place to live even after accepted, so they gave up that dream and moved home because there was no other option.

As I write this foreword, Jeffrey is in his ninth and final semester at this college—on track to graduate this winter. We never dreamed that when Jeffrey's life changed in 1998, college graduation would be in the cards for him. My husband and I know when Jeffrey rolls across the stage this May to receive his Bachelor's degree, there won't be a louder cheering section, or more tears, from any family.

At the same time, the end of school means the start of uncertainty. He's 28 years old and will have spent almost a decade in college. Jeffrey doesn't want to live at home, "with Mommy and Daddy," so that means finding a place that can handle his unique set of issues. What is the facility that can keep him safe; can provide for the basic needs on which he is utterly dependent; can see that he takes his medications; can oversee his bathing, dressing, and grooming every day; can help accompany him to work; and is located near friends and others with like-minded interests? If he lives with other adults with disabilities, will those disabilities be like his; will he be able to communicate easily; will their challenges complement his?

What about work? What job will Jeffrey be hired to do? How much supervision will he require? There is no "one-stop shopping" to find answers for any of these questions. We are just beginning to address them and are reaching out to a far-flung, still emerging network of contacts for information and suggestions. We enjoy enormous advantages because my husband and I, as longtime journalists, have met many people around the country and have experience in asking questions and pushing for answers. But what about other families who don't have that background? We are also fortunate to have the resources, because of our long careers, to do everything possible to ensure Jeffrey is in a place where he will be well taken care of.

But even with resources, it's never easy to find the right physician, physical therapist, occupational therapist, psychologist, orthotics specialist, or wheelchair repair shop, each with skills and schedules to match Jeffrey's needs. Even with resources, we know Jeffrey will need assistance with medical bills, health insurance providers, landlords, banks, lawyers, and the IRS!

He'll always need help to take care of his business and household affairs; he'll need someone who'll advocate fiercely with and for him in all of life's situations. These are the realities we face as Jeffrey moves into adulthood and out of our "orbit." We want him to launch on his own, but he can never be so independent that he's in harm's way.

The uncomfortable truth about adults with disabilities is that they are still often overlooked, or shunned, because they aren't as "cute" as they were as children. Jeffrey has real worries about whether he will get a good job and about how people will treat him when he's on his own: he knows adults are expected to take on more responsibility, and he wants to show he can. At the same time, he's excited about being independent and living on his own.

I am confident this book will help make the life that Jeffrey and so many other young people with special needs dream of and deserve easier to achieve.

Judy Woodruff
Senior Correspondent and Co-Anchor
The PBS NewsHour

Foreword

National policy, legislation, and multiple federal programs recognize and support transition to inclusive community living for young people with disabilities and chronic conditions. For example, the Health Resources and Services Administration has for many years supported transition as a key element of a system of services for children and youth with disabilities and chronic health conditions. When in place, this system ensures that youth will partner with professionals at all levels of decision making; receive ongoing comprehensive, coordinated health care within the context of a medical home; receive early and continuous surveillance, screening, and intervention when needed; have adequate insurance to pay for needed services; have access to community services that are easy to locate and use; and receive services and supports necessary to make the transition to adult health care, work, and independence.

Despite national policy, legislation, and programs, too many young people today have spent their entire childhood receiving expert medical intervention and early intervention and special education in inclusive school environments only to reach young adulthood with few options for employment, comprehensive health care, and the support services needed for optimal participation in the communities where they choose to live. Whereas many models exist for preparing youth for transition, few have resulted in widespread, sustainable, and long-term transition outcomes.

Today, we have an unprecedented opportunity to ensure that young people with disabilities and chronic conditions can live and thrive in communities of their choice with the assurance that needed services and supports will be available. Signaling a renewed commitment to the rights of people with disabilities, the United States in 2009 joined more than 140 other countries in signing the United Nations' Convention on the Rights of Persons with Disabilities (United Nations Enable, n.d.), urging protection and equal benefits under the law for all citizens, rejecting discrimination in all forms, and promoting full participation and inclusion in society. As evidence of this renewed commitment here at home, the American Recovery and Reinvestment Act (ARRA) of 2009 (PL 111-5) provided billions of dollars in funding to improve programs benefiting young people with disabilities and chronic conditions, including Social Security Disability Insurance, services under the Individuals with Disabilities Education Improvement Act (IDEA) of 2004 (PL 108-446), Medicaid, and vocational rehabilitation services. In 2009, the first Special Assistant to the President for Disability Policy was appointed, ensuring a voice to advise on issues related to employment, housing, health care, and inclusive community living.

Acknowledging longstanding barriers to inclusive community living for people with disabilities and chronic conditions, the current administration has established principles to guide federal policy and program development to support a responsive system of services for people with disabilities. These principles include the following: 1) strengthening access to and improving the quality of health care, 2) promoting access to community living services, 3) protecting civil rights, 4) expanding educational opportunities, and 5) increasing access to employment. The renewed commitment to inclusive community living and these guiding principles provide an excellent context for addressing the specific issues, addressed in this book, that face young people with disabilities and chronic conditions as they make the transition to adult health care, postsecondary training and education, work, and independence.

Because comprehensive health reform is at the top of the current domestic policy agenda, we have an unprecedented opportunity to address persistent and long-standing issues facing young people with disabilities and chronic conditions. It is important to remember that youth with disabilities and chronic conditions can be otherwise healthy. Indeed, maintaining good health is a key factor in ensuring inclusive community living. Technological advances—such as the electronic health record—and quality improvement models—such as the medical home concept, with its emphasis on comprehensive and well-coordinated primary, acute, chronic, and subspecialty care—are well-suited to ensure the health care support needed to facilitate healthy community living for young people with chronic conditions and disabilities.

In a continuing effort to increase leadership toward promoting access to community living, all federal agencies have been charged with improving and coordinating existing programs and with developing new programs where none currently exist. All federal agencies are currently engaged in activities to enforce the Supreme Court's Olmstead decision (*Olmstead v. L.C.,* 1999) to break down barriers to community living for people with disabilities. Examples include the Money Follows the Person program, the Real Choice Systems Change grants supported by the Centers for Medicare & Medicaid Services, and the Healthy and Ready to Work program supported through the Health Resources and Services Administration.

Ensuring appropriate employment opportunities for youth with disabilities and chronic conditions is a persistent and ongoing issue. Increased flexibility in work hours and place—as well as technological advances in equipment, communication aids, and devices—has substantially changed and improved the work environment for all employees and provides an unprecedented opportunity to increase employment options for young people with disabilities and chronic conditions. Programs such as the Ticket to Work program sponsored by the Social Security Administration have been significantly improved, and both the Social Security Administration and the U.S. Department of Labor have implemented demonstration programs to improve employment opportunities for youth with disabilities and chronic conditions.

We know that transition is a process, not an event, and that it must begin early with high expectations, preparation for decision making, choices, and responsibility. With preparation, youth should be able to anticipate and expect the benefits of inclusive community living, good health, and satisfying work and relationships as adults. Only then can we ensure maximum return on the investments we have made in America's children and youth and ensure that our communities are designed to nurture and develop the potential of all citizens.

Bonnie Strickland, Ph.D.
Director
Division of Services for Children
with Special Health Care Needs
Health Resources and Services Administration
Maternal and Child Health Bureau

REFERENCES

American Recovery and Reinvestment Act (ARRA) of 2009, PL 111-5.

Individuals with Disabilities Education Improvement Act (IDEA) of 2004, PL 108-446, 20 U.S.C. §§ 1400 *et seq.*

Olmstead v. L.C., 527 U.S. 581 (1999).

United Nations Enable. (n.d.). *Convention on the Rights of Persons with Disabilities.* Retrieved January 29, 2010, from http://www.un.org/disabilities/default.asp?navid=13&pid=150

Preface

Transition to adulthood can be particularly challenging for youth with disabilities and special health care needs (SHCN). Successful transition incorporates several critical components, including education, employment, health care, and independence. Making transitions in these areas frequently involves seeking assistance from multiple service providers, navigating confusing service systems, and addressing physical and social environmental barriers. Available programs and services are rarely coordinated and respond to different legislative mandates. Eligibility criteria differ because definitions of *disability* or *special needs* often are contradictory, different levels of service may be available, and criteria for termination of service are inconsistent.

Increased national attention to the transition needs of youth with disabilities and special health care needs has resulted in significant progress in understanding the transition process and the factors that promote or impede it. However, the vision of a seamless transition that enables young adults with special health care needs and disabilities to assume responsibility for the effective management of their lives—with a base of health care, employment, transportation, education, and social supports—has yet to be realized. Despite calls for improving the process and outcomes of transition, little work has explored systematically the specific methods to ensure good outcomes in the multiple arenas of health, work, education, and community life. Unfortunately, much of the work on transition for youth with SHCN has come from the child health community, with much less work from (and connection with) the community of adults with disabilities and those who work with them. Current federal initiatives incorporate transition as a policy goal for youth with special needs and disabilities and provide a new impetus for creating a systematic approach to fostering successful transition. This impetus will transcend any specific federal administration. A comprehensive volume dedicated to the issues and solutions for this major life phase is needed.

The purpose of the book is to provide an integrative approach for helping adolescents with disabilities make the transition to adulthood. The conceptual approach for the book comes from several of the authors who are part of the Research Consortium on Children with Chronic Conditions who first suggested a noncategorical rather than a diagnostic approach to addressing the needs of this population. This cross-cutting approach—age, sector, diagnosis, disciplines, academic/implementer—allows a comprehensive perspective for making appropriate policy, program, and scientific decisions regarding transition. This is, indeed, a cutting edge approach to this set of issues and requires the student, scholar, researcher, or policy professional to move beyond the traditional comfort zone when thinking about transition. It also provides a foundation for moving toward a more pragmatic and realistic approach to addressing transition issues.

The Prologue is provided so that the reader of the volume has a synopsis of the issues being addressed through the eyes of the young people and families affected. Each subsequent topical chapter has at least two authors, one an expert in children and youth with disabilities, another an expert in adult disability. This approach integrates in each chapter the views of leading experts with expertise on both sides of the transition: the transition from childhood and the transition to adulthood. The authors are a balance of academics and implementers. We have also included consumers—young people making the transition and their parents—at each stage of the project. Scholarship is balanced with reality. The goal of this effort is to inform the development of governmental policy that allows young people with chronic health conditions and disabilities to find their way, along with young people in the general population, toward an autonomous and self-fulfilling life in a supportive community.

Prologue

Marissa is grinning from ear to ear as she processes down the aisle toward graduation from high school. She sees her mom smiling and waving through the tears of joy. "Mom seems to cry a lot as I grow up," she thinks to herself. She knows it's the sheer pride of a parent watching her child move toward adulthood. Marissa sees Bernard, a classmate, also graduating, and she remembers the tough times Bernard has had, having such a hard time learning and paying attention and getting along with his classmates. Bernard's parents are pretty well off, so they could afford some extra help outside school that made it possible for him to keep up and finally graduate. Marissa knows that she, too, had to work hard to get where she is today. She missed a lot of school due to operations to repair her back and to replace the shunt in her brain. Math was always a problem—and organizing her time and "stuff." But now, she is graduating. The truth is, however, that she's even more scared than she was before her operations. She's been living with a condition called spina bifida her whole life. She knows more about hospitals and doctors than she does about any school subject. Marissa reflects that her friend Angela, who is a couple of years older, is not graduating, and Marissa wishes she were here. Angela's dad was transferred and had to move a couple of years ago to another state. Angela's school didn't have the help she needed for her depression and so she dropped out. "What will she do?" Marissa thought.

Now the principal is welcoming everyone and talking about this being a commencement celebration, and how *commencement* means *beginning*, not an ending. Marissa senses that this next part of her life is going to be even more difficult than her life has been until now. She wonders about how Bernard is going to do. Marissa wants what every young person around her wants—to make her own decisions, get a job, move into her own place, have a relationship—that is, to live a full adult life. Transition is what her school counselor called it. She knows already some of the barriers that await her and Angela and Bernard and the many other young people with ongoing health conditions or disabilities who are moving through adolescence into young adulthood.

Marissa is almost 19 years old. Her mom has always had to work to support herself and her daughter after Marissa's dad left. He just could not handle the stress of a daughter with a physical disability. Marissa's mom always believed the old parenting adage, "Don't do for your children what they can do for themselves." Her mom seemed to know from the earliest days that Marissa would go through many transitions in her life and that each transition would set the foundation for the next phase of life. So Marissa had always been given the chance to do even difficult things for herself, despite some of her mom's friends and their relatives feeling that she should be helped because Marissa was "crippled." The hard work was paying off.

Bernard, on the other hand, had just the opposite problem as he grew up. His parents were told he was just "all boy" and would grow out of his inattention, poor social skills, and "being in his own world." He was not different from other kids, his parents' friends and family had said. He just needed more discipline. It was not until Bernard was in elementary school that teachers and the doctors finally agreed that Bernard was on the autism spectrum. Bernard's younger brother was also having similar problems and was getting assistance much sooner than Bernard. Bernard's parents wanted him to make his own decisions, but they often could not get Bernard to talk with them or make any decisions. They had the resources to get Bernard psychological help, and they went to family therapy to help learn how to get Bernard to respond. The help had really made a difference in how Bernard was now able to make decisions—difficult though it sometimes was.

Angela's mom died from cancer when Angela was 12. Angela, her dad, and her brother all struggled to adjust to her dying, but Angela had the most trouble. She became more and more sad, started feigning illness so she would not have to go to school, felt no energy, and decided she wanted to be with her mom. Angela's dad reached out for help and Angela went to counseling. Even with medication, she struggled throughout adolescence with poor grades, spotty school attendance, and no friends—except for Marissa, whom she had met in middle school. At least Angela's dad had insurance to pay for her therapy. Then Angela's dad had a chance to move to a better job but in a different state. Her dad was extremely torn about moving but felt it was best overall for the family to move. He did not realize that there would be fewer resources for Angela in the new state.

BARRIERS

Marissa and Angela and Bernard are in the approximately 20% of the population between the ages 14 and 28 and represent the approximately 10% of those young people who live with ongoing health conditions or disabilities, according to population health surveys (Centers for Disease Control and Prevention, 2006; Valluzzi, Grosse, & Newacheck, 2008). As of 2007, close to 2 million of these youth were ages 14–21. These adolescents have similar aspirations as their peers, and their parents have the same expectations for their offspring as do other parents. They are each different and have different needs, and varying supports will be required to assist them toward young adulthood. This group of young people lives not only with limitations associated with their conditions but also with the barriers that hinder their successful transition into adulthood. Barriers are faced by all adolescents as they work toward self-determination—making their own lives. Young people with disabilities face broader and deeper challenges to achieving this outcome. Some of Marissa's friends, and she doesn't have a lot of them, just assume that the limitations from her having spina bifida are her major liabilities.

Marissa and her family, however, know that people's attitudes are a major problem. Folks sometimes seem to think that if she is using a wheelchair she also cannot hear well, so they talk louder to her. Or they think her physical limitation also means she is not very smart. Expectations for what she can do are often low. Bernard has been described as having an autism spectrum disorder (ASD), and people in the community are hesitant to engage him in conversation, lest he say something or do something "strange." Neither Marissa nor Bernard nor Angela would easily be accepted in an apartment complex—or a dormitory.

Beyond community attitudes, however, there is a whole set of policies that undermines youth transition. Policies, programs, and services that were well intentioned when they were established often have requirements about who is eligible. Eligibility requirement differ across programs, thereby making it hard to coordinate the varied components leading to transition. For any young person to make the transition into young adulthood, requirements include housing, transportation, a source of income, an occupation such as school or work, opportunities to have friends, leisure activities, and participation in the community. These components are often difficult for all young people. College or the military are environments that provide most of those elements, so many in society forget the importance of these components for young people who may not fit the model most widely presented in the culture. Frankly, this group of young people highlights the needs of several major groups of youth vulnerable to transition problems—for example, young people who are living in poverty, who are homeless, or whose families are unstable. The United States has had difficulty coming to grips with the notion that society is more complex and transition for all adolescents is more difficult than in past times.

PROGRAMS

Federal agencies have developed numerous programs and services to help the transition. A Government Accountability Office (GAO) forum in 2007 concluded, however, that although there was some collaboration across services, there was no cohesive federal system to coordinate the multiple programs that exist. The programs to which Marissa and her friends might gain access cross a broad spectrum of needs, including job training, transportation, housing, postsecondary education, and health programs. Among the three of them, these young people have the opportunity, perhaps, to take advantage of numerous programs.

For example, there are various programs for employment. Programs are provided by Section 504 of the Rehabilitation Act of 1973 (PL 93-112), the Ticket to Work and Work Incentives Improvement Act of 1999 (PL 106-170), the Workforce Investment Act (WIA) of 1998 (PL 105-220), and the Occupational Safety and Health Act (OSHA) of 1970 (PL 91-596). In addition, the Office of Children with Special Health Care Needs in the Health Resources and Services Administration (HRSA) underwrites the Healthy and Ready to Work Program—a grant program to build capacity in states and communities to assist young people toward work (HRTW National Resource Center, n.d.).

Housing programs are offered through federal programs. The most important housing program overall is the Housing Choice Vouchers program, also commonly known as Section 8, which is locally controlled and often has a very long waiting list (U.S. Department of Housing and Urban Development, n.d.). For low-income people with disabilities, the Section 811 program is a tool for gaining access to affordable and accessible community housing with supportive services. In a recent study by the Center for Housing Policy (2006) funded by the John D. and Catherine T. MacArthur Foundation, a case was made that the burdens of housing and transportation should be considered together. The study, entitled *A Heavy Load: the Combined Housing and Transportation Burdens of Working Families,* reported that 57% of family incomes are spent on housing and transportation, 28% and 29%, respectively. Young people with disabilities are most likely to be in the low-income bracket families most affected with this disproportionate responsibility for two basic aspects of self-determination, or learning to take care of yourself.

HEALTH

The health care issues are also complicated. Marissa, Bernard, and Angela all had extensive medical experiences; Marissa's are due to spina bifida with accompanying hydrocephalus, Bernard's are associated with an ASD, and Angela's are due to recurring and severe depression. On the whole, each had found his or her way to appropriate services. These young people during childhood and adolescence would be considered children with special health care needs (CSHCN)—that is, "Children and youth who have or are at increased risk for chronic physical, developmental, behavioral, or emotional conditions and who also require health and related services of a type or amount beyond that required by children generally" (McPherson et al., 1998).

All individuals, particularly those with special health care needs, should have a stable health and medical setting for care. HRSA (n.d.) and the American Academy of Pediatrics (2008) jointly developed a concept called the medical home. The medical home concept encourages comprehensive, coordinated, and child-centered primary care services. This concept has also been endorsed by other medical societies. However, it is typically more challenging for young adults with special needs to find such a medical home as adults than as children. Plus, in Marissa's case, adult physicians are not usually trained or comfortable in providing services for young people with spina bifida. Autism, likewise, is a condition for which Bernard will have problems finding appropriate health care. There is often a chasm between pediatric and adult care, and adolescents with ongoing health conditions (no longer children with special health care needs) or disabilities are especially at risk for medical and related problems. This does not even touch the difficulty adolescents with chronic conditions have in gaining access to health and fitness activities. Marissa realizes that as she is getting older she is having more difficulty walking with her arm crutches. She knows she will soon be using a wheelchair most of the time, which will reduce her mobility, even though she will have more energy. She is working hard to eat healthily because she has seen friends and adults gain weight when they start using wheelchairs. Little health promotion emphasis is given by their health care professionals.

DEFINITIONS, ELIGIBILITY, AND CONSEQUENCES

Each medical, employment, housing, or transportation program focuses on a specific group by age or disability status—*disability status* may be defined differently according to the agency. Each of these programs may influence the job choices that a young person with an ongoing health condition or disability will make. Definitions of *health condition* or *disability* (for both adolescents and adults) or *children with special health care needs* (for adolescents alone) will determine a young person's ability to have access to a program. Definitions often require a medical diagnosis, such as cerebral palsy or autism. For other programs, the definition may emphasize the presence of functional problems, such as taking care of one's dressing or eating, or communication or mobility problems. Yet other services may focus on those young people who use medical services the most. Within these programs, there are often requirements that exclude young people if their parent(s) make more than a certain amount of money. For most programs, each state can set its own guidelines for who is eligible. Thus, when Angela moved to another state, she aged out of a program providing mental health services to her, and the state to which she moved had cut out funds for those services for adults.

The definitional issue has another more insidious dimension. For most young people, being like everyone else is a primary goal. Not being different is paramount. Yet to receive assistance, adolescents or young adults are required to apply and be found different from their peers. This labeling often more than counteracts any positive effects of services. Family tension develops as parents and young people, and often including extended family, struggle to balance identity with services. Many of these adolescents know about being stigmatized as different, and they hope to escape such designations as they enter this period of transition into young adulthood. For Bernard, this tension is the most pressing issue because his parents have the financial resources to help him toward transition but he is then forced to depend even more on his parents' largesse. He knows, however, that his interpersonal skills are not so great, and understands that the money will not buy friends or a steady job. He would like to get some support from other young people having similar relationship problems.

Bernard and his family want him to become more independent. Because Bernard's town has public transportation and Bernard lives pretty far from downtown but close to a bus stop, his parents thought it would be good for him to ride the bus to several meetings related to possible housing opportunities. Bernard had had three different meetings scheduled and needed to change buses twice to get to the housing office. He was late for each meeting due to bus pick-ups not being according to the printed schedule. Each time the housing officer scolded Bernard for being unmotivated and disorganized. Bernard knew he did not have great interpersonal skills, but he could tell time and had allowed enough time. He felt unfairly taken to task. Bernard and his parents were upset and felt that Bernard's opportunity to make a successful transition was being sorely tested from the very beginning.

Different from Bernard, Marissa realizes that she will have problems beyond just school or job or relationships. She hopes to go to junior college but knows that her math skills are pretty poor and her lack of organization gets her into trouble at school. It is hard to keep all of the assignments straight and the timelines clear. Deadlines keep slipping up on her. When she can keep things straight, she actually does average or above-average work. But she knows that there is no housing on campus and her town has poor public transportation. Actually, the buses stop a mile and a half from her home, outside the city limits. Using her arm crutches is just not possible for her with that distance. Her mom has to be at work at 7 A.M. and in the opposite direction. She just does not know if it's worth it. It might be easier to just stay at home and get her Supplemental Security Income payment.

The needs of these adolescents represent a small portion of the issues for young people with ongoing health conditions or disabilities trying to make the transition successfully toward self-determination. Many programs are available beyond those previously described, but there is almost no coordination or collaboration across programs or agencies. The most basic need to provide the level of support necessary for adolescents wanting to become more self-reliant is for the barrier across the age groups to be broken. Stability of programs across the 14- to 28-year age range would be the most fundamental change to be made. In addition, all of the programs are designed to assist; however, when difficulties arise, too often the blame for poor response to programs is placed at the feet of the young person or family, as the housing official did with Bernard.

U.S. society may be judged honorable for its attempts to help, but it is also judged ineffective given the poor outcomes for so many young people in this situation. Society has seen that these adolescents and young adults have needs but has not realized the extent of their vulnerability. The confluence of developmental period, expectations, and inconsistent and uncoordinated resources in the context of ongoing health conditions or disabilities should place this population in the forefront of sustained and cohesive efforts toward successful transition.

VALUES AND PRINCIPLES

The needs, even rights, of young people living with ongoing health conditions and disabilities are included in fundamental documents etched into law and policy at the national and international level. Along with other individuals living with disabilities, the United Nations has passed two resolutions, called Conventions, addressing the needs of these young people. In 1989, the United Nations General Assembly adopted the Convention on the Rights of the Child (CRC) (United

Nations Children's Fund, n.d.). The United States is one of two countries from the 191 in the United Nations that has yet to move beyond signing the Convention to ratifying it. Article 23 of the CRC focuses specifically on children and youth with disabilities, emphasizing that they should live in conditions that "ensure dignity, promote self-reliance and facilitate the child's active participation in the community." Assistance should be designed, the Article continues, to ensure effective access and receipt of education, training, health care, and preparation for employment. The second foundational document is the recently approved UN Convention on the Rights of Persons with Disabilities (CRPD) (United Nations Enable, n.d.). In 2006, the UN General Assembly responded to the observation that the potential of people with disabilities around the world is not being developed or used. This population continues to be marginalized by society across the life span. The content of the CRPD is based on the long-held notion by people with disabilities: "Nothing About Us Without Us." CRPD highlighted a change in attitudes and approach to people with disabilities. Rather than being viewed as objects of medical intervention and social protection, people with disabilities are being viewed as subjects with rights and capacities to make their own decisions and determine their own future. To gain access to reasonable work, the CRPD is clear that no gaps should exist between citizens with and without disabilities. For example, an individual may need access to public spaces, transportation, and accessible housing and work settings. CRPD indicates that different units need to be responsible for providing necessary opportunities and accommodations to people with disabilities. If one component of the network fails with these reasonable accommodations, people are unable to participate in the life of the society like everyone else. Marissa, Bernard, and Angela are recipients of this emphasis and international mandate.

Beyond these international Conventions, the United States has instituted laws that support transition: the Americans with Disabilities Act (ADA) of 1990 (PL 101-336), Section 504 of the Rehabilitation Act, and the Individuals with Disabilities Education Improvement Act (IDEA) of 2004 (PL 108-446). The ADA was amended in 2008 (PL 110-325) to clarify aspects of the original ADA addressing definitions of *physical or mental impairment, substantially limits,* and *major life activities.* Although these changes do not directly affect adolescents with disabilities in transition, the inclusion of concentration, thinking, and communicating as major life activities allows Bernard to be covered under the new ADA. Both Section 504 and IDEA address students, and both will now use similar definitions, expanding the criteria for inclusion for services and programs both at school and in the community.

DIRECTIONS

The situation for Marissa, Bernard, and Angela is both challenging and promising. Services and programs are available for some young people in certain locations in particular states or cities if the individuals meet eligibility requirements and have the physical, emotional, and cognitive resources to access these programs.

Overarching principles should drive a move to assist this group of adolescents approaching young adulthood. First, any support should be founded on developing young people's strengths, enabling them to grow toward self-determination. Because these youth have different needs, supports should be flexible and diverse. Of paramount importance is an emphasis on the universal nature of supports. That means that housing and worksites and community settings should be accessible, regardless of limitations. *Universal design* is the term that captures this principle, and this universality also helps the broader population. For example, curb cuts are used not only by individuals with mobility limitations such as Marissa but also by caregivers pushing strollers. Personal digital assistants (PDAs) are helpful not only for general use but also can be programmed to help individuals such as Bernard remember the steps to use when meeting a new person. Implicit in the concept of universality is inclusion at all levels of community activities for young people. Finally, universal health coverage would allow the continuation of appropriate medical and health services, supporting their assistive devices and technology and encouraging continuity of health care—expanding the medical home concept for children with special health care needs into adulthood. The final principle is that of interdependence. Just as there is interdependence between these young people and their families, friends, and communities as they work toward self-determination, governmental programs, services, and supports recognize the need for interdependence so that communication, cooperation, coordination, and collaboration are means to the end of successful transition.

Specific directions are needed in order for young people such as Marissa, Bernard, and Angela to become a part of the mainstream and maintain that status. First, supports should be implemented across the age span encompassing the transition years—generally conceived as 14–28 years of age. Second, a single point of entry for transition services would allow for substantially better coordination of supports. Third, a common definition of those young people who are eligible for supports should be implemented across programs and services, perhaps consistent with the new definition included in the ADA amendments of 2008. Finally, information and data regarding the process and outcomes during the transition years should be collected so that the effectiveness and efficiency of supports can be evaluated. With the fragmentation, gaps, and confusion around this area, the observation of Amartya Sen, the Nobel economist, is noteworthy, "We have to resist the massive neglect of the needs of disabled people through conceptual confounding. There is a need for clarity here as well as for commitment" (2004, p. 8).

Donald Lollar

REFERENCES

American Academy of Pediatrics. (2008). *Maternal and Child Health Bureau (MCHB) medical home grants.* Retrieved January 29, 2010, from http://www.medicalhomeinfo.org/grant/mchb.html

Americans with Disabilities Act (ADA) of 1990, PL 101-336, 42 U.S.C. §§ 12101 *et seq.*

Americans with Disabilities Act Amendment Act of 2008, PL 110-325.

Brault, M. (2008). Americans with disabilities: 2005. *Current Population Reports,* 70–117.

Center for Housing Policy. (2006). *A heavy load: The combined housing and transportation burdens of working families.* Retrieved January 29, 2010, from http://www.nhc.org/index/chp-research-publications

Centers for Disease Control and Prevention. (2006). *Disability and health state chartbook, 2006: Profiles of health for adults with disabilities.* Atlanta, GA: Author.

Government Accountability Office (2007). *Modernizing federal disability policy: Highlights of a forum.* Washington, DC: Author.

Health Resources and Services Administration, Maternal and Child Health Bureau. (n.d.). *Achieving and measuring success: A national agenda for children with special health care needs.* Retrieved January 29, 2010, from http://mchb.hrsa.gov/programs/specialneeds/measuresuccess.htm

HRTW National Resource Center. (n.d.). *About HRTW.* Retrieved January 29, 2010, from http://www.hrtw.org/about_us/index.html

Individuals with Disabilities Education Improvement Act (IDEA) of 2004, PL 108-446, 20 U.S.C. §§ 1400 et seq.

McPherson, M., Arango, P., Fox, H., Lauver, C., McManus, M., Newacheck, P., et al. (1998). A new definition of children with special health care needs. *Pediatrics,* 102 (1, Pt. 1), 137–140.

Occupational Safety and Health Act (OSHA) of 1970, PL 91-596, 29 U.S.C. §§ 651 *et seq.*

Rehabilitation Act of 1973, PL 93-112, 29 U.S.C. §§ 701 *et seq.*

Sen, A (2004). *Disability and justice.* Presentation at the Disability and Inclusive Development Conference, World Bank, Washington, DC.

Ticket to Work and Work Incentives Improvement Act (TWWIIA) of 1999, PL 106-170, 42 U.S.C. §§ 1305 *et seq.*

United Nations Children's Fund. (n.d.). *Convention on the Rights of the Child.* Retrieved January 29, 2010, from http://www.unicef.org/crc

United Nations Enable. (n.d.). *Convention on the Rights of Persons with Disabilities.* Retrieved January 29, 2010, from http://www.un.org/disabilities/default.asp?navid=13&pid=150

U.S. Department of Housing and Urban Development. (n.d.). *Housing Choice Voucher Program (Section 8).* Retrieved January 29, 2010, from http://www.hud.gov/progdesc/voucher.cfm

Valluzzi, J.L., Grosse, S.D., & Newacheck, P.W. (2008). *Unpublished tabulations, 2005 Medical Expenditure Survery data,* Atlanta, CA.

Workforce Investment Act (WIA) of 1998, PL 105-220, 29 U.S.C. §§ 2801 *et seq.*

Acknowledgments

The early impetus for this volume was provided by Jose Cordero, M.D., M.P.H., former Director, National Center on Birth Defects and Developmental Disabilities, and Merle McPherson, M.D., former Director, Office of Children with Special Health Care Needs, Maternal and Child Health Bureau (MCHB). These visionaries from the U.S. Centers for Disease Control and Prevention (CDC) and the Health Resources and Services Administration (HRSA), respectively, were supporters and provided the initial funding for the project through CDC's Disability and Health team and HRSA's Office of Children with Special Healthcare Needs. Without this backing, this initiative would not have gotten off the ground. Also, Jan Valluzzi provided impetus to the effort through her early work on state-based transition activities.

Bonnie Strickland, Ph.D., current Director of MCHB's Office of Children with Special Health Care Needs, has continued to support this effort and has even strengthened the resolve to highlight this major need among young people with chronic health conditions and disabilities. Through the Office's Healthy and Ready to Work program, parents of adolescents and young adults, along with young people in the targeted age group, were recruited to provide input into the process, including a meeting with the authors' group reviewing initial outlines of the chapters. This group included Fran Basche, Josie Badger, Julia Washenberger, and Brianne Schwantes. Patience White, M.D., also contributed to the initial authors' meeting. In addition, Josie Badger contacted a network of young adults with disabilities to review the chapters before final edits were made. This group's input was invaluable to the process of making real the lived experience of transition.

The Association of University Centers on Disability provided the structure for organizing the final meeting in Washington, D.C., whereas CDC's Disability and Health team held the initial meeting in Atlanta. Having authors meet two times face to face substantially increased the collaborative efforts of the group and provided a cohesion to the chapters that was noticed by the editors. Mary Sharkey provided additional editing expertise to the authors in order to give coherence to the volume.

The Research Consortium on Children with Chronic Conditions has provided leadership in the field of children with special health care needs and disabilities for the past 30 years. Individually, their contributions have been stellar. Collectively, they have built a field of research and policy on behalf of children and youth that is now stable and growing. Their contribution cannot be overestimated. Thank you, Laurie Bauman, Paul Newacheck, Debbie Klein Walker, Jim Perrin, and Ruth Stein.

*To the young people who are striving to find
their way toward satisfying and productive lives,
the parents who are struggling to support
their youth fully while working to let them pursue their own lives,
the professionals across disciplines and services
who work to facilitate opportunities for transition, and
the policy makers who will use this book to frame a new set of policies
that encourages full participation for this group of young people*

I

Foundations for Transition Policy

1

Transition Policies

Challenges and Services for Youth with Disabilities and Chronic Health Conditions

Deborah Klein Walker and George Jesien

The globalization of services and jobs in the past decade has highlighted the need for a well-educated workforce in the United States. No longer can we afford to exclude individuals with disabilities and chronic health conditions from productive jobs and well-integrated lives in the community. With globalization trends and aging demographics, the United States must ensure that every child today is prepared to be a member of a specialized workforce over his or her lifetime. By 2010 there will be fewer workers under 35 for every individual who turns 65, at which time many choose to receive Social Security benefits.

CHANGING DEMOGRAPHICS IN THE NATIONAL AND GLOBAL CONTEXT

According to the U.S. Census Bureau, there are close to 300 million people in this country, 26% of whom are 18 and younger, 61% are between 19 and 64 years of age, and 12% are 65 and older (Kaiser Family Foundation, 2008). The number of elders is expected to increase markedly in the near future with the aging of the "baby boom" generation. For example, it is estimated that the population age 65 or older and the population age 85 or older will increase by almost one half (48% and 43%, respectively) from 2005 to 2020 (AARP Public Policy Institute, 2006). As of 2006, about a third (31%) of people age 65 and older have a physical disability, and one out of ten individuals has a self-care disability (AARP Public Policy Institute, 2006). As expected, the incidence of chronic illnesses as well as physical and/or cognitive impairments increases with the aging population.

In addition to the growing numbers of aging people with disabilities in U.S. society, about 19% of adults report a disability due to physical, mental, or emotional problems (Kaiser Family Foundation, 2008). These disabilities can be attributable to chronic illness, intellectual or developmental disabilities, mental illness, injury, or other underlying conditions. Furthermore, the number and percentage of individuals with disabilities and/or chronic health conditions vary by the type of condition (e.g., cognitive impairment, physical impairment, sensory impairment), geography (e.g., region, state), and various demographic characteristics (e.g., education, race, gender, age) (Meyer & Zeller, 1999). For example, the percentage of adults with a disability reported on the Behavioral Risk Factor Surveillance System in 2005 ranged from 14% in the District of Columbia and Illinois to 27% in West Virginia (Kaiser Family Foundation, 2008). Also, analyses of the 1994 Disability Supplement of the National Institutes of Health survey revealed that most individuals with a disability from birth to age 64 are covered by private health insurance (55%); of the remainder, 15% are uninsured, 20% covered by Medicaid only, 5% by Medicare only, and 2% by Medicaid and Medicare (Meyer & Zeller, 1999). It is imperative that these individuals with disabilities and chronic conditions be given full access to employment and social and other services throughout their adult years to maximize their productivity and quality of life.

The terminology or descriptions of disability and chronic conditions also varies greatly across the life span (Perrin et al., 1993). For example, the term *children with special health care needs* (McPherson et al., 1998) is more frequently used than the term *disability* to discuss the various needs of the child and youth population. The National Survey of Children with Special Health Care Needs, conducted every 4 years in every state, documents the demographic characteristics of these children, the types of health and support services they and their families need, and their access to and satisfaction with the care they receive. The 2005–2006 survey found that 14% of children in the United States have a special health care need and 22% of households with children include at least one child with a special health care need. The prevalence of children with special health care needs ranged from 10% in California and Nevada to 18% in Delaware, Kentucky, and West Virginia (Maternal and Child Health Bureau [MCHB], 2007).

Because very few studies since the late 1980s used the same definition for chronic health conditions or disability across the life span, it is difficult to make comparisons in prevalence, access to health and other services, demographic characteristics, and/or coverage by health insurance and other public or private programs between the child and adolescent period and that of the young adult. This "critical transition" from adolescence to adulthood is a key time to ensure that the young adult with a disability or chronic health condition has access to employment, health services, and other social and community supports to ensure that the individual is fully included in his or her own community with full choice and control of his or her environment and options. This chapter and others in this volume refer to the term *disability and chronic health conditions* as a way of capturing the largest group of individuals during the transition period from childhood and adolescence to young adulthood.

WHY SUCCESSFUL TRANSITION IS IMPORTANT

The end result of the transition from adolescence is an emerging adult who takes increasing responsibility for his or her actions and their outcomes, is moving toward greater independence from parents and family members for decision making and guidance, and is poised to take his or her rightful place in society as a participating member of various social subgroups within his or her environment. Post-high-school learning choices abound, with college, technical schools, community colleges, and extended high school experiences among the alternatives. Work and career alternatives also need to be sought, weighed, and selected or applied for during the transition period. Moving from adolescence to adulthood is a pivotal stage of development, as it is a period of life reorientation that sets the stage for how the individual will exercise personal autonomy in work, play, continued learning, personal health care, social interaction, and community participation. It is a complex developmental stage influenced by a broad range of interconnected factors that either facilitate or complicate an adolescent's progress toward full adulthood. Children and adolescents with special health care needs and disabilities have had additional challenges in facing the complexities of moving toward adulthood due to a wide range of causes, some that the adolescent and family can control and others that are beyond their ability to influence. In each of the major components of the young adult's life—education, housing, employment, health care, financial stability and sufficiency, and social life—rapid changes take place for the general population of youth (Wehman, 2006). Chronic health conditions and disabilities pose additional hurdles as services and supports that were in place during the child's early development now either end or taper off. Finding and paying for adult health care providers, seeking educational opportunities without the benefit of extensive legal rights afforded through legislation, and entering the work force where competition is high and opportunities may be lacking all pose potential hurdles to successful transition to adulthood.

The degree of impairment and type of health condition or disability each pose their own specific requirements that need to be addressed. Unfortunately, in the United States, these needs are addressed by a range of different support systems with their own particular profile of eligibility requirements, points of access, procedural steps to traverse, and specific foci of attention. Each also has varying degrees of financial and human support available to the adolescent and his or her family. Each service system may also have a different conceptual view of chronic health conditions and disabilities ranging from a *medical model* perspective that may view health conditions or disabilities as "problems to be fixed" to a *social model* perspective that views disabilities as a natural part of the human condition. In the latter model, the degree of impairment is seen as an interaction between the individual and the environment and the degree to which that environment provides needed supports and services to facilitate functioning and participation (Siminski, 2003).

The overall and cumulative degree of complexity and array of differences among the different systems pose significant challenges in that they need to be understood, engaged, and navigated if they are going to meet the needs of the emerging adult. Adolescents and their families may have to form an entirely new set of relationships with a wide range of people and services including generic, specialty, and subspecialty health professionals; adult educators; employment services; mental health providers; and community services. Information will need to be shared, trust developed, and goals and directions selected without many of the familiar educational and health supports that the family has gotten to know and understand during their child's early development.

The degree to which the new relationships are developed and supports and services are put into place will in many respects determine the ease with which an adolescent makes the transition to the roles and responsibilities of adulthood. Lack of opportunity or not receiving needed supports and services will make each transition step and task more difficult. Lacking adequate health care, losing out on continuing education opportunities, and encountering obstacles to seeking and obtaining a career path can seriously set back an adolescent's development and thwart or seriously delay the move to responsible adulthood, with long-term consequences. Conversely, providing the needed guidance and support to traverse each of these systems in a coordinated and systematic manner can measurably increase the potential for a healthy, independent, productive, and fully participatory adulthood. During the transition period it is important to balance being supportive of the adolescent while encouraging autonomy/independence at the individual, service, and system levels.

STATUS OF TRANSITION TODAY: WHAT WE KNOW

In order to ensure an optimal transition from adolescence to the young adult period, there should be alignment of the basic legal and social frameworks for children and adults. As of 2010, this is difficult to accomplish. There are major inconsistencies and disconnects between a fairly comprehensive child and adolescent service system with a major legal mandate for education in the least restrictive setting and a paucity of services and legal mandates for young adults in a basically fragmented and inconsistent system of adult services. This system provides few protections and assurances for individuals with chronic conditions and disabilities.

This section provides a brief overview of the major pieces of legislation and resulting federal programs or services that affect the movement of youth with chronic health conditions and disabilities from adolescence to adulthood. Each is briefly described, as is its relationship to the transition process. These are presented according to the target population of the legislation or program: children and youth, young adults, or all age groups.

Children and Youth Program Options

The current major service systems for children and youth with chronic health conditions and disabilities are reviewed next.

Individuals with Disabilities Education Act (Part B) The Individuals with Disabilities Education Act (IDEA) of 1990 (PL 101-476), Section 300.29, addresses transition services as follows:

(a) Transition services means a coordinated set of activities for a student with a disability that
  (1) Is designed within an outcome-oriented process, that promotes movement from school to post-school activities, including post-secondary education, vocational training, integrated employment (including supported employment), continuing and adult education, adult services, independent living, or community participation;
  (2) Is based on the individual student's needs, taking into account the student's preferences and interests; and
  (3) Includes (i) Instruction; (ii) Related services; (iii) Community experiences; (iv) The development of employment and other post-school adult living objectives; and (v) If appropriate, acquisition of daily living skills and functional vocational evaluation.
(b) Transition services for students with disabilities may be special education, if provided as specially designed instruction, or related services, if required to assist a student with a disability to benefit from special education.

IDEA requires that transition planning begin at the earliest age appropriate, beginning at age 14 (or younger, if determined appropriate). Each child's individualized education program (IEP) must include a statement of the student's transition service needs that focuses on the student. Thus, beginning at age 14, the IEP team, in identifying annual goals and services for a student, must determine what instruction and educational experiences will help the student prepare for the transition from school to adult life. For example, if a student's transition goal is to secure a job, a transition service need might be enrolling in a career development class to explore career options and specific jobs related to that career. A statement of transition service needs should relate directly to the student's goals after high school and show how planned activities are linked to these goals. Beginning at age 16 (or younger, if determined appropriate), the IEP must also contain a statement of needed transition services for the student, including, if appropriate, a statement of interagency responsibilities. This includes coordinated activities with measurable outcomes that will move the student from school to postschool activities. The IEP plan must be updated annually and revised if expected progress is not being made. Appropriate transition activities can focus on preparation for postsecondary education experiences or employment preparation.

Title V of the Social Security Act   The Maternal and Child Health (MCH) Services Block Grant (Title V of the Social Security Act) has provided support to assure the health and well being of all mothers and children in all states since it was passed as part of the Social Security Act of 1935 (PL 74-271). When Title V was converted to a block grant as part of the Omnibus Budget Reconciliation Act (OBRA) of 1981 (PL 97-35), seven categorical programs serving children were consolidated; these programs were maternal and child health and services for children with special health needs, supplemental security income for children with disabilities, lead-based paint poisoning prevention programs, genetic disease programs, sudden infant death syndrome programs, hemophilia treatment centers, and adolescent pregnancy prevention grants. State Title V programs, administered in the state health agency, receive 85% of the Title V funds on a formula basis. States must provide a $3 match for every four federal dollars allocated, and at least 30% of the block grant funds must be used for children with special health care needs (CSHCN). States use the dollars for CSHCN for a variety of activities, including direct health care services; enabling services such as transportation, case management, respite care, and coordination with other health and social services; population-based services such as newborn screening, including hearing screening and follow-up; and infrastructure-building services such as needs assessment, finance planning, quality improvement, information systems, and parent leadership activities (MCHB, n.d.).

Medicaid Early and Periodic Screening, Diagnosis, and Treatment Component   Medicaid's early and periodic screening, diagnosis, and treatment (EPSDT) services are a preventive and comprehensive child health program for individuals under the age of 21 eligible for Medicaid services in their state. Medicaid, begun in 1965 as Title XIX of the Social Security Act, is the public health insurance program for poor children in every state. The OBRA of 1989 (PL 101-239) defined EPSDT to include periodic screening, vision, dental, and hearing services. Although the scope of coverage and eligibility criteria for Medicaid vary from state to state, Section 1905 (r)(5) of the Social Security Act requires "that any medically necessary health care service listed at Section 1905 (a) be provided to an EPSDT recipient even if the service is not available under the State's Medicaid plan to the rest of the Medicaid population" (Centers for Medicare & Medicaid Services, 2008). Medicaid state agencies are responsible for ensuring that the required health care services are available and accessible and that Medicaid recipients and their parents or guardians effectively use the resources.

Children's Health Insurance Program The State Children's Health Insurance Program (SCHIP) was funded in the Balanced Budget Act of 1997 (PL 105-33) as Title XXI of the Social Security Act to provide health insurance to children and youth not eligible for Medicaid or private insurance in their state. States can provide coverage through SCHIP via the state Medicaid program, a new stand-alone insurance program, or some combination of both. The stand-alone programs do not have to provide the EPSDT and other benefits of Medicaid coverage, leaving many important services for the CSHCN population uncovered. SCHIP was intended to cover children not eligible for Medicaid with incomes up to 200% of the federal poverty level, with the option to cover children of even higher income levels. When passed in 1997, Congress allocated $40 billion in federal funds for a 10-year period. Unlike Medicaid, SCHIP was funded as a capped block grant to states rather than as an individual entitlement. In 1997 SCHIP provided coverage for 6 million children.

The Children's Health Insurance Program Reauthorization Act (CHIPRA) of 2009 (PL 111-3) was signed into law in February 2009 to continue the SCHIP. The act increases state allotments for covering additional children, provides state options for premium assistance, requires new notice requirements related to coordinating public and private coverage in premium assistance programs, and allows state options to cover pregnant women and legal immigrant pregnant women and children.

Young Adult Program Options

The current major service systems for young adults with chronic conditions and disabilities are reviewed next.

Vocational Rehabilitation Transition services, as defined by the Rehabilitation Act of 1973 (PL 93-112), are a coordinated set of activities for students with disabilities to promote movement from school to postschool activities including postsecondary education, vocational training, inclusive employment (including supported employment), continuing and adult education, adult services, independent living, and community participation. A major purpose of transition services is the creation of a continuum of services that begin in school and result in successful postsecondary long-term employment outcomes based on the student's interests, needs, and abilities. Vocational rehabilitation (VR) transition services link students with disabilities, while still in school, with the VR program to create a continuum of services leading to long-term employment outcomes for eligible students.

Every state has a federally funded agency that administers VR, supported employment, and independent living services. State VR programs provide services that enable individuals with disabilities to pursue meaningful employment that corresponds with their abilities and interests. Although state VR is considered an adult service agency, VR counselors can join the transition team and attend IEP planning meetings before a student leaves high school. State VR agencies offer programs that can be of service to students with disabilities who may be leaving high school without employment skills, or who are already out of school and finding it difficult to find or keep a job without additional training.

Together, students and their counselors develop an individualized plan for employment (IPE) that identifies needed VR services. Family members can participate in this process—although youth who have reached their state's legal age of adulthood must give their written permission for parents to be involved. The services available through VR programs vary widely depending upon the state. They can include assessment, vocational evaluation, counseling, and guidance; referral to services from other agencies; vocational and other types of postsecondary education and training (including self-determination and self-advocacy training); interpreter and reader services; rehabilitation technology services and other job accommodations; placement in suitable employment; employer education on disability issues per the Americans with Disabilities Act (ADA) of 1990 (PL 101-336) and job accommodations; postemployment services; services to family members; and other goods or services necessary to achieve rehabilitation objectives identified in the IPE.

Healthy and Ready to Work Initiative A major goal of the Maternal and Child Health Bureau Division of Services for Children with Special Health Needs is to assure that all youth with special health care needs receive the services necessary to transition to all aspects of adulthood, including adult health care, employment, and independence. In 1996 the bureau initiated the Healthy and Ready to Work Initiative. The purpose of the initiative was to create demonstration projects to make health a part of transition planning for youth with special health needs and disabilities. From 1996 to 2001, nine demonstration grant projects were funded under the Health Resources and Services Administration Special Programs of Regional and National Significance. Since 2001, five Healthy and Ready to Work Phase II projects were funded as model state demonstration programs.

MCHB developed a 10-year action plan with six outcomes to create a comprehensive system of care for children with special health care needs. The sixth outcome states, "All youth with special health care needs will receive the services necessary to make appropriate transitions to all aspects of adult life, including adult health care, work and independence." The Healthy and Ready to Work projects were to develop models for improving adolescent transition by 1) providing information and support to youth and families in transition, 2) increasing the number of youth who have a medical home and a transition plan from pediatric to adult health care, 3) increasing the capacity of communities to support youth with special health care needs, 4) building family, youth, and provider skills related to necessary components of transition, and 5) connecting statewide organization around the area of transition.

Program Options for All Ages

The current program options for all ages are reviewed next.

Supplemental Security Income   Supplemental Security Income (SSI) is a federal income support program administered by the Social Security Administration that provides monthly cash assistance to people who have disabilities and limited income and resources. To be eligible for SSI benefits, both disability and financial criteria must be met. The disability must be a medically determined mental and/or physical condition that is expected to last for a year or longer. Financial criteria include earned income (wages) and resource assets (bank accounts and other fluid assets, but not home or automobile, if used for medical appointments or work). Earned income must be at or below the substantial gainful activity level that the Social Security Administration has established. At the time of application, resources must be under $2,000 and must never go over that amount while the applicant receives SSI. Upon reaching age 18, all factors of an SSI recipient's eligibility are reviewed, including a disability redetermination referred to as a continuing disability review. The Social Security Administration must redetermine the eligibility of individuals who were eligible for SSI based on disability in the month before the month in which they attained age 18 using the rules for determining initial eligibility for adults.

Americans with Disabilities Act of 1990   Signed into law on July 26, 1990, the ADA recognizes and protects the civil rights of people with disabilities and is modeled after earlier landmark laws prohibiting discrimination on the basis of race and gender. The ADA covers a wide range of disabilities, from physical conditions affecting mobility, stamina, sight, hearing, and speech to conditions such as emotional illness and learning disorders. The ADA addresses access to the workplace (Title I), state and local government services (Title II), and places of public accommodation and commercial facilities (Title III). It also requires telephone companies to provide telecommunications relay services for people who have hearing or speech impairments (Title IV) and miscellaneous instructions to federal agencies that enforce the law (Title V). Regulations issued under the different titles by various federal agencies set requirements and establish enforcement procedures.

Under Titles II and III of the ADA, accessibility guidelines are developed and maintained for buildings, facilities, and transit vehicles. The ADA accessibility guidelines serve as the basis of standards issued by the U.S Department of Justice and U.S. Department of Transportation to enforce the law. The building guidelines cover places of public accommodation, commercial facilities, and state and local government facilities. The vehicle guidelines address buses, vans, a variety of rail vehicles, trams, and other modes of public transportation.

Amendments to the ADA signed into law on September 25, 2008, clarify and reiterate who is covered by the law's civil rights protections. The ADA Amendments Act of 2008 (PL 110-325) revises the definition of *disability* to more broadly encompass impairments that substantially limit a major life activity. The amended language also states that mitigating measures, including assistive devices, auxiliary aids, accommodations, medical therapies, and supplies (other than eyeglasses and contact lenses) have no bearing in determining whether a disability qualifies under the law. Changes also clarify coverage of impairments that are episodic or in remission that substantially limit a major life activity when active, such as epilepsy or posttraumatic stress disorder. The amendments took effect January 1, 2009.

The ADA as amended is a powerful tool to provide access to structures, programs, and transportation at the same time that it prohibits employment discrimination on the basis of having a disability. Knowledge of the ADA and its provisions is an important element for the youth in transition and his or her family. As the adolescent leaves his or her secondary education setting, the rights and protections of IDEA come to an end and the young adult relies on the legal protections and provisions of the landmark ADA legislation.

New Freedom Initiative The New Freedom Initiative (Executive Order No. 13217, 2001) was announced by President George Bush on February 1, 2001, as part of a nationwide effort to remove barriers to community living for people with disabilities. The initiative called upon the federal government to assist states and local communities in implementing the *Olmstead v. L.C. and E.W.* (1999) Supreme Court Decision, which committed the United States to community-based alternatives for individuals with disabilities. The president directed six federal agencies, including the departments of Justice, Health and Human Services, Education, Labor, Housing and Urban Development, and the Social Security Administration to work together to improve policies and programs to swiftly implement community-based settings for individuals with disabilities. Congress has given substantial resources to the Centers for Medicare & Medicaid Services to implement systems change for individuals with chronic conditions and disabilities in order to promote consumer choice and control in community-based settings; these resources have funded a variety of state initiatives (e.g., Real Choices, Ticket to Work, Money Follows the Person) to promote independence, dignity, choice, and flexibility. The New Freedom Initiative addresses the barriers for full participation in the community in the following areas: employment, community inclusion housing, assistive technology, transportation, education, and health.

Medicaid Waivers to Promote Community Inclusion Medicaid has the authority to give states multiple waiver and demonstration options to allow flexibility in operating Medicaid programs. States have used three options to promote flexible community-based options for individuals with disabilities and chronic conditions across the life span: 1) Section 1115 Research and Demonstration Projects test policy innovations to further Medicaid objectives, 2) Section 1915 (b) Managed Care/Freedom of Choice Waivers allow states to implement managed care delivery systems or otherwise limit individual choice of provider, and 3) Section 1915 (c) Home and Community-Based Services Waivers waive Medicaid provisions in order to allow long-term care services to be delivered in community settings. Eligibility requirements and program components under the waivers vary by state as they provide alternatives to the provision of long-term services in institutional settings (Centers for Medicare & Medicaid Services, 2008). Even though transition is not mentioned specifically in the waivers and state plan amendments, they can be used by states to promote transition to community-based settings for young adults.

Section 8 Housing Choice Vouchers   The U.S. Department of Housing and Urban Development provides formula grants to local Public Housing Authorities (PHAs) who award rental subsidy vouchers to individuals who seek to rent privately owned housing. The vouchers are designed to serve families with the lowest income. Virtually all people with disabilities receiving SSI benefits are income-eligible. PHAs are able to establish preferences to meet the needs of people most at risk of homelessness. Because people with disabilities are at great risk, a local PHA can establish a preference in its Section 8 programs. Periodically since 1998, Congress has set aside allocations of vouchers for low-income families that have a family member with a disability. PHAs may apply for these vouchers on a competitive basis. Households with members who have disabilities may apply for these set-asides but are also eligible for other Section 8 vouchers including tenant-based vouchers, project-based vouchers, and home-ownership vouchers.

Though youth are not specifically targeted, they may benefit because they live in a household that qualifies or, if they are emancipated, they may qualify as a household of one. States determine the circumstances under which some minors are considered households of one (e.g., being a parent themselves or being of a certain age). A PHA may adopt priorities, including a priority for transition-age youth for allocation of Section 8 vouchers through its administrative plan, which must be developed with public participation and updated annually. However, long waiting lists are a significant problem as is a lack of funds to meet the current need for vouchers.

Section 504 of the Rehabilitation Act   Section 504 of the Rehabilitation Act of 1973 is a law that protects individuals with disabilities from discrimination based on their disability. As with all government policies, it includes a definition of a "qualified" individual. In Section 504, a person with a disability is defined as one who has a physical or mental impairment that substantially limits one or more major life activities, such as walking, seeing, self-care, working, or learning. In education, students may have disabilities that do not hinder their learning (and therefore do not qualify them for special education services), but their access to the process of education is impeded. Section 504 covers these young people so they can have access to learning. A major difference for the adolescent with a disability striving to transition into adulthood is that Section 504 follows the adolescent after he or she leaves the public schools. The education-oriented IEP stops when enrollment in school stops. A Section 504 plan takes into account the environment in which the person—whether child, adolescent, or adult—is engaged. For transition purposes, then, a college might write a Section 504 plan. In the area of employment, people can be eligible if, with reasonable accommodations (steps to accommodate the person's limitation), they can perform the basic functions of the job for which they have applied. In these cases, a plan would be written for the work setting.

CURRENT OBSTACLES TO SUCCESSFUL TRANSITIONS

As of 2010, there are major gaps in services and policies that hinder successful transitions from adolescence to adulthood for youth with disabilities and chronic health conditions. These are described next.

Seamless Movement from One Service System to Another

Some of the greatest gaps and difficulties facing adolescents and their families are encountered as they move from one service system to another. Examples include moving from secondary education to postsecondary, from pediatric to adult health care, from part-time work experiences to full-time employment, from local child services to adult systems of care and supports, and from child SSI to adult enrollment in SSI. Eligibility, legal frameworks, view of disability, array of services, and operational procedures all vary as the youth moves from child-based systems of services to adult services. Many express the frustration of having to learn new rules and terminology and having to make new contacts with little help or support in navigating the new service structures.

Collaboration Across Child Systems: Handing Off Programs

Although a good deal of federal and state investment has gone into building collaboration among child systems of care such as early intervention, school-based special education services, state programs for children with special health care needs, and school-to-work initiatives, these programs still have considerable work to do. The exchange of information and collaboration between health and education sectors still leaves a good deal of room for improvement. Schools often do not have sufficient information on a child's health conditions, medication, or treatments that a child may be undergoing. Similarly, health providers often do not have sufficient information on the impact of health conditions or treatments on daily school performance or behavior. Also, social and mental health services often operate with less than optimal information and communication with other systems of care.

Collaboration Across Child and Adult Service Systems

The challenges of information, communication, and collaboration are even greater between child and adult systems. Whereas many child-based services have a person who serves as a care coordinator (also often referred to as a case manager or navigator), many adult services lack this coordination function between the individual and their various service providers. Much greater effort is needed to build bridges of communication between sending and receiving programs across the adolescent-to-adult divide. Means for sharing information, mechanisms for ongoing communication, and encouragement for structural collaboration are needed.

Legal Structure that Covers the Transition Period

Reaching the age of majority can complicate the services for many individuals with disabilities and special health care needs. Whereas parents were in a primary decision-making role for the youth, once the child turns 18 and even more so after age 21, access to records, decisions about interventions or treatments, finances, and so forth become dependent on the young adult's decisions. Rights and responsibilities change dramatically as well as many of the legal protections afforded the individual. As one example, under IDEA the child is afforded, as a right, a free and appropriate education regardless of the type or severity of a disability. The young adult only has the legal protection of nondiscrimination for entry into postsecondary education but has no legal right to postsecondary educational opportunities. Much more information and preparation for the changing legal underpinnings are needed for both the youth in the transition process as well as his or her parents and caregivers.

Comprehensive Programs Other than Isolated Efforts that Point the Way

Whereas there is tendency for child programs to be more holistic in nature, adult programs seem to take on a more specific and singular focus. Services for employment, health, housing, and continuing education concentrate on their own specific area of concern. For youth who are making the transition into adulthood programs, creation of programs that promote healthy living to prevent secondary medical conditions while focusing on adult-oriented issues such as employment, continuing education, housing, and mental health would seem to at least merit further exploration and testing. Sufficient research has shown the important interrelationships among health, nutrition, physical activity, education, housing, and employment, thus meriting a much more concerted effort toward more comprehensive programs for adults with disabilities and special health care needs.

Financing Systems to Support Transition

Numerous questions too often arise regarding "who pays for what" as youth move from their adolescent programs to adult status. As individuals move from adolescence to adulthood they become ineligible for sources of funding that may have paid for a range of services and supports including special education, treatments and interventions, care coordination, and cash supplements to their families. Many of these programs end at either age 18 or 21 with no clear path for "handing off" the supports and services and their payment to other entities that will follow through into adulthood. Needed are bridges for funding the "handing off" period, or at least seamless systems where supports are continued from one provider or system until another takes over.

Crossing Traditional System Boundaries

One of the major challenges facing youth in the transition process is to piece together the necessary supports or services from the different sectors that affect their lives, including health care, education, employment, social services, housing, and transportation. There is no "one-stop" or "one door" entity that will relate these various sectors into an individualized system of support for individuals with disabilities as they move into adulthood. With varying requirements, eligibility criteria, and procedural steps that need to be taken, youth face a daunting task of working across systems. Much more work needs to be done on the interoperability of systems across sectors that affect the lives of youth making transitions (Podmostko, 2007).

These various sectors have their own organizational cultures and styles of operation. Each varies in how it may view the person with a disability or chronic health need. Most have their own data systems that do not interact with those of other agencies because of legal constraints, privacy issues, and systems software incompatibility.

Lack of a Life Span Approach

Too many child-serving systems seem to operate as if they did not fully understand that children grow into adolescents, who in turn grow and develop into adults with increasing needs for control, independence, and personal decision-making opportunities. Although provisions in IDEA exist for making transition plans as early as 14 years of age, other systems lack provisions and the capacity to plan for the needs of developing adolescents. Health care providers need to take on much earlier the task of instilling life-long health care and prevention behaviors and preparing youth to make health care decisions on their own. Similar work is needed to help the youth seek and obtain information and support in the areas of employment, finances, age-appropriate social services, and community supports.

Lack of Funds

Insufficient funding or absence of funding pose serious challenges to providing the needed services and supports for youth making transitions. Although a number of funding streams exist for youth during the transition years including the Workforce Investment Act of 1998 (PL 105-220), the Rehabilitation Act of 1973, Medicaid, mental health systems, and several work incentives under the Social Security Administration such as the Medicaid Buy-In Program and the Plan to Achieve Self-Support, there is a lack of coordination and ability to piece these funds together to meet the needs of individual youth. Often, expertise is needed in order to meld these different funding sources so that the specific needs can be met. Recent uses of both "blending" (i.e., combining funds into one stream) or "braiding" (i.e., using categorical funding toward unified objectives) funding streams to address the varied and complex needs of youth to provide more flexible and ultimately usable sources of funds may prove, at least in part, to ameliorate some of the challenges posed by the complex and fragmented funding system that we have today (Mooney & Luecking, 2006).

Lack of Accountability

Accountability is one of the most difficult hurdles facing organizations and their funders, as youth with disabilities and chronic health conditions move from one set of systems to another. Schools stop tracking their students as they leave high school, as do many child health systems and their providers. Outcomes are therefore difficult to identify for specific youth. New data records are formulated by receiving systems, resulting in an information gap between sending and receiving programs. Accountability becomes difficult to ascribe if outcome data cannot be linked to programs and supports provided earlier in the youth's life. Data systems that can bridge the different developmental stages are needed so that outcomes can be tracked and linked to antecedent supports to determine which had the greatest positive and negative influences. Tracking outcomes in education, employment, and health status will also provide valuable feedback to adolescent social service systems and providers in determining areas that need change or more emphasis to become more effective.

Lack of Sufficient Bipartisan Political Will

Ultimately, to change the current state of fragmentation and overly complex systems of care, policies will need to change. New laws and regulations will be needed to facilitate change and in some instances to mandate greater collaboration and interoperability among systems. In order to accomplish such changes, legislators will need to be educated, advocacy groups will need to coordinate their efforts, and youth and families will need to speak out and seek reform through advocacy and political pressure. It will be difficult to get the necessary attention, given all of the troublesome priorities that face legislators at national and state levels. But only concerted efforts on the part of constituencies and disability organizations will bring about the needed attention to the problems of youth in transition. Champions in Congress will need to be developed who will see this country's vulnerable youth as a high priority deserving of Congressional time and effort. Advocacy groups will need to provide a coordinated and consistent message to Congress about the policy remedies that are needed and to provide ongoing support and information as difficult decision points are addressed and new policies formulated.

CONCLUSION

In summary, the transition period from adolescence to adulthood for youth with disabilities and chronic health conditions is a critical time in which community-based supports must be put in place to ensure that the young adult can live, work, and play with maximum independence. Policies and services must be available to the youth and their families to ensure that the young adult can be productive, happy, and healthy. As described in this chapter, there are numerous policies to assist this process. Their use on behalf of young people, as of 2010, must be orchestrated by that very young person, his or her family, and sector-specific professionals. This book outlines the key challenges and issues addressed in each sector of society: health care, transportation, housing, education, employment, and community participation. It concludes with recommended directions to encourage successful transition.

REFERENCES

AARP Public Policy Institute. (2006). *Across the states: Profiles of long-term care and independent living.* Washington, DC: Author.

Americans with Disabilities Act (ADA) of 1990, PL 101-336, 42 U.S.C. §§ 12101 *et seq.*

Americans with Disabilities Act (ADA) Amendments Act of 2008, PL 110-325, 122 Stat. 3553, 42 U.S.C.

Balanced Budget Act of 1997, PL 105-33, 111 Stat. 251.

Centers for Medicare & Medicaid Services. (2008). *Medicaid state waiver program demonstration projects: General information.* Retrieved January 30, 2008, from http://www.cms .hhs .gov/MedicaidStWaivProgDemoPGI

Children's Health Insurance Program Reauthorization Act (CHIPRA) of 2009, PL 111-3, 42 U.S.C. 1305.

Individuals with Disabilities Education Act (IDEA) of 1990, PL 101-476, 20 U.S.C. §§ 1400 *et seq.*

Kaiser Family Foundation, State Health Facts. (2008). *Medicaid & CHIP.* Retrieved January 20, 2008, from http://www.statehealthfacts.org/comparecat.jsp?cat=4

Maternal and Child Health Bureau. (n.d.). *Understanding Title V of the Social Security Act.* Retrieved January 20, 2008, from http://mchb.hrsa.gov/about/understandingtitlev.pdf

Maternal and Child Health Bureau, Health Resources and Services Administration, U.S. Department of Health and Human Services. (2007). *The National Survey of Children with Special Health Care Needs chartbook 2005–2006.* Retrieved March 20, 2008, from http://mchb.hrsa.gov/cshcn05

McPherson, M., Arango, P., Fox, H., Lauver, C., McManus, M., Newacheck, P.W., Perrin, J.M., Shonkoff, J.P., & Strickland, B. (1998). A new definition of children with special health career needs. *Pediatrics, 102,* 137–140.

Meyer, J.A., & Zeller, P.J. (1999). *Profiles for disability: Employment and health coverage* [Report for the Kaiser Commission on Medicaid and the Uninsured]. Retrieved December 9, 2009, from http://www.kff.org/medicaid/2151-index.cfm

Mooney, M., & Luecking, R. (2006). *Blending lending and braiding funds and resources: The intermediary as facilitator.* Information Brief, Issue 18. Washington, DC: National Collaborative on Workforce and Disability.

New Freedom Initiative, Exec. Order No. 13217, 66 Fed. Reg. 33155 (Jun. 21, 2001).

Olmstead v. L.C. and E.W. Supreme Court Decision on June 22, 1999. Retrieved January 20, 2008, from http://www.accessiblesociety.org/topics/ada/olmsteadoverview.htm

Omnibus Budget Reconciliation Act (OBRA) of 1981, PL 97-35, 95 Stat. 357.

Omnibus Budget Reconciliation Act (OBRA) of 1989, PL 101-239, 42 U.S.C. §§ 1396 *et seq.*

Perrin, E.C., Newacheck, P., Pless, I.B., Drotar, D., Gortmaker, S.L., Leventhal, J., Perrin, J.M., Stein, R.E.K., Walker, D.K., & Weitzman, M. (1993). Issues involved in the definition and classification of chronic health conditions. *Pediatrics, 91,* 787–793.

Podmostko, M. (2007). *Tunnels and cliffs: A guide for workforce development practitioners and policymakers serving youth with mental health needs.* Washington, DC: National Collaborative on Workforce and Disability for Youth, Institute for Educational Leadership.

Rehabilitation Act of 1973, PL 93-112, 29 U.S.C. §§ 701 *et seq.*

Siminski, P. (2003). Patterns of disability and norms of participation through the life course: Empirical support for a social model of disability. *Disability & Society, 18,* 707–718.

Social Security Act of 1935, PL 74-271, 42 U.S.C. §§ 301 *et seq.*

Wehman, P. (2006). Transition: The bridge from youth to adulthood. In P. Wehman, *Life beyond the classroom: Transition strategies for young people with disabilities* (4th ed., pp. 3–40). Baltimore: Paul H. Brookes Publishing Co.

Workforce Investment Act (WIA) of 1998, PL 105-220, 29 U.S.C. §§ 2801 *et seq.*

2

Developmental Context

The Transition from Adolescence to Emerging Adulthood for Youth with Disabilities and Chronic Health Conditions

Grayson N. Holmbeck, Laurie J. Bauman, Bonnie S. Essner, Lauren M. Kelly, and Kathy Zebracki

Adolescence and emerging adulthood are critical periods in an individual's development of health-related behaviors (Williams, Holmbeck, & Greenley, 2002). Life-long patterns of positive health behaviors (e.g., diet, exercise), health risk behaviors (e.g., substance use, risky sexual behaviors), self-determination, and health-related self-advocacy are established and consolidated in adolescence and young adulthood. Even for chronic conditions that begin at birth or in early childhood, the manner in which affected individuals manage the adolescent and young adult transitions has important implications for later health outcomes (Williams et al., 2002).

"Change" is the defining construct for these developmental periods. Indeed, characteristics of disabilities and chronic health conditions change over time in individuals who are, at the same time, changing developmentally. Moreover, such change occurs within a larger environmental context that is also changing over time. In addition to these many ongoing changes, individuals with chronic

Completion of this chapter was supported by research grants from the National Institute of Child Health and Human Development (R01-HD048629) and the March of Dimes Birth Defects Foundation (12-FY04-47).

conditions also face any or all of the following multiple transitions: 1) the transition from pediatric-oriented medical care to adult-oriented care, 2) the transition from parent-controlled health care to self-care, which can include a lengthy period during which responsibilities for health care are shared between parent and child, 3) the transition from home to community, and 4) the transition from the school setting to the work setting (Hydrocephalus Association, 2003). Given the multitude of changes and transitions that individuals with chronic health conditions undergo during adolescence and emerging adulthood, it is critical that continuous and seamless health services be available to support them during these important developmental periods.

The purpose of this chapter is to provide an overview of the critical developmental milestones and psychosocial contexts of adolescence and emerging adulthood. Although the focus of the larger set of chapters is on the transition to adulthood for youth with disabilities and chronic health conditions, we chose to focus not only on the developmental events of emerging adulthood but also on the milestones of the adolescent developmental period. Indeed, adolescence is a transitional developmental period between childhood and adulthood that is characterized by more biological, psychological, and social role changes than any other stage of life except infancy (Feldman & Elliott, 1990). The ability of the individual to navigate the transition to adulthood is clearly dependent on the degree to which he or she has been successful in negotiating the important milestones of the adolescent developmental period (National Center for Youth with Disabilities, 1994).

Following an overview of typical development during the adolescent and emerging adulthood developmental periods, we discuss the potential interface between developmental issues and health outcomes in individuals with chronic conditions, including hypothetical case vignettes to illustrate our points. Finally, we conclude with recommendations for ways in which our knowledge of development can facilitate the development of policies that provide a seamless transition from adolescence to emerging adulthood in such youth with disabilities and chronic health conditions.

A BIOPSYCHOSOCIAL-CONTEXTUAL MODEL OF NORMATIVE ADOLESCENT DEVELOPMENT (AGES 10–18)

An organizing developmental framework for understanding adaptation and adjustment in typically developing adolescents is included in Figure 2.1 (see Hill, 1983, for an earlier version of this model). The model presented here is biopsychosocial in nature, insofar as it emphasizes the biological, psychological, and social changes of the adolescent developmental period. In addition to this focus on intraindividual development, we have also attempted to incorporate discoveries from studies of contextual effects during adolescence (e.g., Steinberg, 2002).

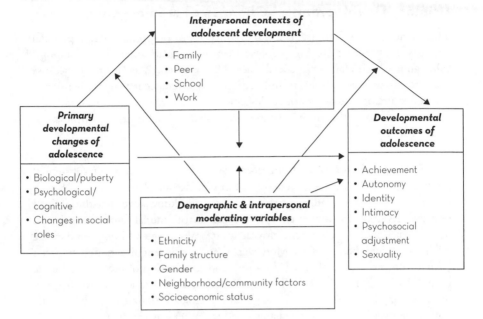

Figure 2.1. A framework for understanding adolescent development and adjustment. (From Holmbeck, G.N., & Shapera, W.E. [1999]. Research methods with adolescents. In P.C. Kendall, J.N. Butcher, & G.N. Holmbeck [Eds.], *Handbook of research methods in clinical psychology* [2nd ed., p. 638]. New York: Wiley; reprinted by permission.)

At the most general level, the framework presented in Figure 2.1 illustrates how the developmental changes of adolescence have an impact on the behaviors of significant others (e.g., parents, siblings, peers, teachers, nonfamily adults, employers) which, in turn, influence ways in which adolescents resolve the major issues of adolescence, namely, autonomy, sexuality, identity, and so forth.

For example, suppose that a young preadolescent girl begins to physically mature much earlier than her age mates. Such early maturity will likely affect her peer relationships, insofar as early maturing girls are more likely to date and spend time with older males than are girls who mature on time (Magnusson, Stattin, & Allen, 1985). Such changes in peer relations are, in turn, likely to influence an early maturing girl's level of sexual activity and her sexual identity. In this way, the behaviors of peers in response to the girl's early maturity could be said to mediate associations between pubertal timing and sexual outcomes (Holmbeck, 1997). Such mediational influences may also be moderated by demographic, intrapersonal, and interpersonal variables (see Figure 2.1; e.g., ethnicity, gender, socioeconomic status, family relations). For example, early pubertal maturity may lead to early sexual debut only when family members react to early pubertal development in certain ways (e.g., with increased chaperonage, restrictiveness, and supervision; Hill & Lynch, 1983).

Primary Developmental Changes of Adolescence

The framework in Figure 2.1 specifies three types of primary developmental changes that occur during adolescence: biological/pubertal, psychological/cognitive, and changes in social roles. They are viewed as "primary" because they are universal across culture and because they often occur temporally prior to the developmental outcomes of adolescence (i.e., changes in autonomy, identity, sexuality, and so forth). In this section, we provide a brief overview of these primary changes.

Biological/Pubertal Changes Adolescence is a time of substantial physical growth and change (Brooks-Gunn & Reiter, 1990; Tanner, 1962). Crucial to the understanding of this process is the knowledge that the peak of pubertal development occurs two years earlier in the modal female than in the modal male (e.g., the adolescent growth spurt peaks at age 12 in girls and at age 14 in boys; Steinberg, 2002). Moreover, there is substantial variation between individuals in the time of onset, duration, and termination of the pubertal cycle (Brooks-Gunn & Reiter, 1990). Thus, it is possible, for example, that two 14-year-old boys may be at very different stages of pubertal development, such that one boy has not yet begun pubertal changes and the other boy has experienced nearly all pubertal events. Research also suggests that both pubertal status (an individual's placement in the sequence of predictable pubertal changes) and pubertal timing (timing of changes relative to one's age peers) have an impact on the quality of family relationships and certain indicators of psychosocial adaptation and psychopathology (Holmbeck & Hill, 1991; Paikoff & Brooks-Gunn, 1991). With respect to pubertal timing, early maturing girls, for example, are at risk for a variety of adaptational difficulties, including depression, substance use, early sexual risk behaviors, eating problems and disorders, and family conflicts (American Psychological Association [APA], 2002). Early developing boys, on the other hand, are favored over later developing boys for involvement in athletic activities, dating, and social events, with late maturing boys being at risk for depression and school problems (APA, 2002).

Psychological/Cognitive Changes Piaget (1983) provided a comprehensive stage theory of cognitive development, which, until recently, has dominated this field of study. He identified adolescence as the period in which formal operational thinking emerges and when adult-level reasoning can take place. Adolescents who have achieved such thinking abilities are able to think more complexly, abstractly, and hypothetically and many are able to think realistically about the future. Moreover, they are able to employ metacognition, or the ability to think about one's own thoughts. Although there is general agreement that a shift in thinking occurs during the transition from childhood to adolescence, critics of the Piagetian approach have suggested alternatives (Moshman, 1998). Proponents of the information processing perspective, for example, maintain that there are significant advances in the following areas during adolescence: 1) processing capacity or efficiency (e.g., memory and organization of information), 2) knowledge base, and 3) cognitive self-regulation (Keating, 1990). As a precursor to the Piagetian and information processing perspectives, a third approach to cognitive development during adolescence is the contextualist perspective (Vygotsky, 1978). This perspective on cognitive development is unique because it emphasizes the role of the cognitive "environment" or context. Of interest here are the child's socially relevant cognitions such as the development of role-taking and empathy skills (Nelson & Crick, 1999).

Social Redefinition A variety of changes in the social status of children occur during adolescence (Steinberg, 2002). Although such social redefinition is universal, the specific changes vary greatly across different cultures. In some non-industrial societies, public rituals (i.e., rites of passage) take place soon after the onset of pubertal change. In Western industrialized societies, the transition is less clear, but analogous changes in social status do take place. Steinberg (2002) cites changes across four domains: interpersonal (e.g., changes in familial status), political (e.g., older adolescents are eligible to vote), economic (e.g., adolescents are allowed to work), and legal (e.g., older adolescents can be tried in adult court systems).

Interpersonal Contexts of Adolescence

Figure 2.1 specifies four interpersonal contexts, which will be reviewed in turn: 1) family, 2) peer, 3) school, and 4) work.

Family Context Adolescence is a time of transformation in family relationships (Holmbeck, 1996; Paikoff & Brooks-Gunn, 1991; Steinberg, 1990). Recent research involving large representative samples of adolescents (see Arnett, 1999) has not supported the extreme version of the early storm and stress perspective (Freud, 1958; Hall, 1904). Although serious parent–child relationship problems are not typical during early adolescence (Holmbeck, Paikoff, & Brooks-Gunn, 1995), a period of increased emotional distance in the parent–adolescent relationship appears at the peak of pubertal change (Holmbeck & Hill, 1991; Larson, Richards, Moneta, Holmbeck, & Duckett, 1996; Laursen, Coy, & Collins, 1998). Although there may be an increase in conflict and negative affect, most adolescents negotiate this period without severing ties with parents or developing serious disorders (Collins & Laursen, 1992). Any discontinuities in the parent–child relationship during the transition to adolescence tend to occur against a backdrop of relational continuity (Holmbeck, 1996). Moreover, some have argued that the conflicts that arise during the transition to adolescence may serve an adaptive role; indeed, increases in conflicts may indicate that adjustments are needed in parenting and the manner in which decisions are made in the family (Holmbeck, 1996). One of the major tasks for parents during this developmental period is to be responsive to adolescents' needs for increasing responsibility and decision-making power in the family while at the same time maintaining a high level of cohesiveness in the family environment and having clear developmental expectations (APA, 2002).

Peer Context One of the most robust predictors of adult difficulties (e.g., dropping out of school, criminality) is poor peer relationships during childhood and adolescence (Parker & Asher, 1987). Most now agree that child–child relationships are necessities and not luxuries and that these relationships have positive effects on cognitive, social-cognitive, linguistic, sex role, and moral development (APA, 2002; Berndt & Savin-Williams, 1993). Although controversial, some have even argued that peers have a more substantial impact on social development than do parents (Harris, 1998). Peer relationships during childhood and adolescence appear to evolve through a series of developmental stages (e.g., Brown, 1990; La Greca & Prinstein, 1999). Sullivan (1953), for example, provided a stage theory for the development of peer relationships where he described his notion of "chumship" and maintained that this (typically) same-sex friendship is a critical developmental accomplishment that serves as a basis for later close relationships. Peers tend to select as friends individuals like themselves (selection effects) and they tend to subsequently influence each other over time (socialization effects; Dodge & Pettit, 2003).

School Context Another context of adolescent development is the school environment. Scholars have maintained that we not only should be interested in the school's impact on cognition and achievement, but that we should also examine how the school is an important environment for the development of one's personality, values, and social relationships (Entwisle, 1990). Physical setting, limitations in resources, philosophies of education, teacher expectations, curriculum characteristics, and interactions between teacher and student have been found to be related to a variety of child and adolescent outcomes. Moreover, movement between schools (e.g. between an elementary school and a junior high school) can be viewed as a stressor, with multiple school transitions producing more deleterious effects (Simmons & Blyth, 1987).

Work Context The last context that we will consider is the work environment (see Greenberger & Steinberg, 1986). Although more than 80% of all high school students in this country work before they graduate (Steinberg, 2002) and many government agencies have recommended that adolescents work, little research has been done on the effects of such work on adolescent development and the adolescents' relationships with significant others. Based on the research done to date (see Steinberg, 2005), however, it seems clear that the work environment has both positive and negative effects on adolescent development. Although adolescent work tends to be associated with an increased sense of self-reliance, it is also associated with 1) cynical attitudes toward future work, 2) less time with families and peers, 3) less involvement in school, 4) a greater likelihood of drug abuse and delinquent acts, and 5) less time for self-exploration and identity development. Although the number of hours that an adolescent works is important to consider, the primary problem with many adolescent jobs seems to be their monotonous and stressful nature (APA, 2002).

Developmental Outcomes of Adolescence

As can be seen in Figure 2.1, the developmental changes of adolescence have an impact on the interpersonal contexts of adolescent development that, in turn, affect the developmental outcomes of adolescence.

Achievement For the first time in one's life, decisions made during one's adolescence can have serious consequences for one's future education, career, and choice of extracurricular activities (Henderson & Dweck, 1990). Some adolescents decide to drop out of school, whereas others complete their education and graduate from high school. Some decide to continue on to college or graduate school. For those who remain in school, it is during high school that most adolescents are, for the first time, given the opportunity to decide which classes they want to take. Such decisions present the adolescent with new opportunities, but also may limit the range of possible future educational options available to the adolescent.

Autonomy Autonomy is a multidimensional construct in the sense that there is more than one type of adolescent autonomy (Hill & Holmbeck, 1986; Steinberg, 1990). Emotional autonomy is the capacity to relinquish childlike dependencies on parents (Fuhrman & Holmbeck, 1995). Adolescents increasingly come to de-idealize their parents, to see them as "people" rather than simply as parenting figures, and to be less dependent on them for immediate emotional support. When adolescents are behaviorally autonomous, they have the capacity to make their own decisions and to be self-governing. Being behaviorally autonomous does not imply that one never relies on the help of others. Instead, adolescents become increasingly able to recognize those situations where they have the ability to make their own decisions versus those situations where they will need to consult with a parent or peer for advice.

Identity A major psychological task of adolescence is the development of an identity (Erikson, 1968; Harter, 1990). Adolescents develop an identity through role explorations and role commitments. One's identity is multidimensional and includes self-perceptions and commitments across a number of domains, including occupational, ethnic, academic, religious, interpersonal, sexual, and political commitments. Although the notion that all adolescents experience identity crises appears to be a myth, identity development is recognized as an important adolescent issue (Harter, 1990). Research in the area of identity development has isolated at least four identity statuses that are defined along two dimensions: commitment and exploration. These identity statuses are identity moratorium (exploration with no commitment), identity foreclosure (commitment with no exploration), identity diffusion (no commitment with no systematic exploration), and identity achievement (commitment after extensive exploration; Erikson, 1968; Harter, 1990). A given adolescent's status can change over time, reflecting increased maturation and development or, alternatively, regression to some less mature identity status. Perhaps most important, an adolescent's identity status can also vary depending on the domain under consideration (e.g., occupational versus religious).

Intimacy It is not until adolescence that one's friendships have the potential to become intimate (Savin-Williams & Berndt, 1990). An intimate relationship is characterized by trust, mutual self-disclosure, a sense of loyalty, and helpfulness. Intimate sharing between friends increases during adolescence, as does adolescents' intimate knowledge of their friends. All relationships become more emotionally charged during the adolescent period, and adolescents are more likely to engage in friendships with opposite-sex peers than are children. Some scholars have proposed that friendships change during the adolescent period because of accompanying social-cognitive changes (Savin-Williams & Berndt, 1990). That is, the capacity to exhibit empathy and take multiple perspectives in social encounters makes it more likely that friendships will become similarly more mature, complex, and intimate.

Sexuality Most children have mixed reactions to becoming a sexually mature adolescent. Parents also have conflicting reactions to such increasing maturity. Despite the high rates of sexual activity during adolescence (nearly 70% of adolescents have had sexual intercourse by age 18; Steinberg, 2002), we know very little about typical adolescent sexuality (whether heterosexual or homosexual), primarily due to the difficulty in conducting studies on this topic. There are a host of factors that are associated with the onset and maintenance of sexual behaviors. Pubertal changes of adolescence have both direct (hormonal) and indirect (social stimulus) effects on sexual behaviors and ethnic and religious differences in the onset of sexuality also exist. Finally, personality characteristics (e.g., the development of a sexual identity) and social factors (e.g., parent and peer influences) also serve as antecedents to the early onset of adolescent sexual behaviors.

Summary In summary, we have attempted to demonstrate how a developmentally oriented biopsychosocial model (see Figure 2.1) can be useful in highlighting potential linkages among many developmental changes for a given developmental period (in this case, adolescence). We now move to a discussion of typical development during emerging adulthood.

EMERGING ADULTHOOD AS A DISTINCT DEVELOPMENTAL PERIOD (AGES 18–30)

Historically, the adolescent developmental period has been viewed as a transitional period between childhood and adulthood. Recently, however, Arnett (2000) has argued that there is an additional developmental period that is distinct from adolescence and young adulthood, namely, emerging adulthood. Arnett (2000) maintains that this period typically occurs between the ages of 18 and 25 in industrialized countries and that individuals in this age range do not view themselves as adolescents or young adults. Indeed, when asked if they "see themselves as adults," more than half of individuals in this age range respond "in some respects yes, in some respects no" (Arnett, 2000). When they are asked what criteria would determine whether they "feel like an adult," issues such as marriage, educational attainment, career attainment, living on one's own, and becoming a parent were not always at the top of everyone's list (see Arnett, 2000, for a review). Instead, the following three criteria were listed most often: taking responsibility for one's self, making independent decisions, and becoming financially independent.

Arnett (2000) also argues that there is an additional way in which emerging adulthood is a distinct developmental period. Specifically, he argues that the identity explorations of the emerging adulthood period are quite different from such explorations during adolescence. Although identity explorations begin during the adolescent period (ages 10–18), such explorations in the areas of love, work, and worldviews become more serious and sophisticated and take on new meaning during emerging adulthood. Romantic relationships during adolescence are primarily recreational, whereas those during the emerging adulthood period tend to last longer and are more intimate. Similarly, work positions during adolescence are typically of a part-time nature and rarely have implications for one's future career. By contrast, positions during emerging adulthood are often directed toward gaining relevant career-related experiences (Arnett, 2000).

Interestingly, many risk behaviors also peak during emerging adulthood. For example, unprotected sex, most types of substance use, and reckless driving all peak in the early twenties. One explanation for these shifts in risk behavior during emerging adulthood focuses on the simultaneous shift in the degree of parental monitoring. During this developmental period, parental monitoring is decreasing in individuals who are still exploring different identities and who have also not yet committed to the adult roles of marriage and parenthood.

In sum, typical 18-year-old individuals who are moving into the stage of emerging adulthood bring with them a set of resolved and unresolved issues from adolescence across family and peer contexts and in the areas of identity development, achievement, autonomy, intimacy, and sexuality. In U.S. culture, the individual's status on these issues then interacts with the important developmental issues of emerging adulthood, namely, the abilities to become self-sufficient and establish a career and a family. These issues are no different and no less complex in individuals with disabilities and chronic health conditions. Indeed, such individuals experience the same developmental issues and concerns as typically developing adolescents and emerging adults, but they do so within the context of having a chronic health condition. As we will argue in the following sections, a seamless transition policy for the period between adolescence and emerging adulthood will only be possible if the normative developmental issues of adolescence and emerging adulthood are taken into account for each individual. We begin with a discussion of the interface between normative adolescent development and the presence of a disability or chronic health condition in individuals ages 10–18.

ADOLESCENT DEVELOPMENT, DISABILITIES, AND CHRONIC HEALTH CONDITIONS (AGES 10–18)

Adolescent Health Behavior

For individuals with disabilities and chronic health conditions, the period of adolescence is a significant time in the development and maintenance of health care behaviors. As noted earlier, many normative health-risk behaviors (e.g., smoking, substance use, unsafe sexual practices) and health-promotive behaviors (e.g., regular exercise, healthy eating, wearing a seatbelt) are initiated, established, or consolidated during this time. While limited experimentation with risky behaviors is considered normal during this developmental period, too much can compromise health trajectories for both typically developing adolescents and those with physical disabilities. Significant engagement in health-risk behaviors during this time may lead to the onset of new chronic health conditions or exacerbate preexisting conditions.

Research findings are inconsistent concerning the extent to which adolescents with chronic conditions engage in health-risk behaviors as compared to typically developing adolescents (Stam, Hartman, Deurloo, Groothoff, & Grootenhuis, 2006). Although some findings indicate that increased awareness of health dangers and parental involvement may discourage adolescents with chronic conditions from engaging in health-risk behaviors (Tyc, Hadley, & Crockett, 2001), others indicate that behaviors such as increased alcohol use may occur in these adolescents as a rebellion against restrictions of strict medical regimes or as a consequence of depression secondary to medical conditions (Erickson, Patterson, Wall, & Neumark-Sztainer, 2005). Likewise, establishing and maintaining health-promotive behaviors, such as regular exercise and healthy eating habits, is an issue that is salient for all adolescents but often has more immediate relevancy and direct consequences for adolescents with chronic health conditions. It is crucial to keep in mind that adolescents with disabilities not only face specific health risks associated with disability status (e.g., increased risk of infections), but they are also confronted with the same challenges to physical and psychological health maintenance as those of typically developing adolescents.

As children make the transition into adolescence, the responsibility for health care management typically shifts from primary caregivers to adolescents themselves. This shift occurs amid the dramatic changes in pubertal/biological, cognitive/psychological, and social role changes (as detailed previously), and the manner in which these changes are manifested ultimately has important implications for these adolescents' short- and long-term health. Because adolescents are just beginning to take on more health care independence, this is an opportune time to intervene to prevent health-risk behaviors, prevent behaviors that increase the likelihood of secondary complications of chronic health conditions, and promote positive health behaviors.

Interface Between Development and Chronic Conditions

The growth and development of adolescents with chronic physical disabilities are best conceptualized within the framework of the biopsychosocial model, described earlier in this chapter. This model provides a comprehensive overview for understanding adolescent development and adjustment, with the flexibility to take into account ways in which individual differences might influence developmental outcomes and adjustment in adolescents with chronic health conditions. Specifically, condition parameters such as visibility (i.e., the degree to which the chronic health condition is externally noticeable), cognitive involvement, mobility concerns, sensory limitations, and stigma associated with the condition, will determine how specific components of the model are manifested. In addition, the "primary change" aspects of the model (i.e., puberty, cognitive development, and so forth) could also include biological risks associated with the condition (e.g., neuropsychological risks). In keeping with this perspective, the following section describes ways in which the primary developmental changes of adolescence may be modified by the presence of chronic health conditions.

Primary Developmental Changes One way in which chronic physical conditions have an effect on the primary developmental changes in Figure 2.1 is through their impact on the timing of pubertal onset. For example, puberty often occurs early in adolescents with neural tube defects (e.g., spina bifida) as compared to peers with no physical disability (Blum, 1992). For adolescents with visible chronic health conditions, early pubertal development may exacerbate preexisting insecurities about physical appearance. Especially for females, the weight gain associated with puberty may put these adolescents at further risk for body dissatisfaction and mood disorders. Moreover, caregivers may assume advanced cognitive sophistication when they observe advanced pubertal development and, as a result, they may prematurely transfer responsibility for medical care tasks to adolescents.

Cynthia always felt different from her classmates. She relied on a wheelchair for mobility due to her diagnosis of spina bifida. At age 9, her feelings of social isolation increased as she began puberty earlier than most of her friends. Cynthia felt uncomfortable about her maturing body, until her fourth-grade teacher, Ms. Christenson, who noticed Cynthia's change in mood and behavior, conducted a class on sexual development highlighting the variability that occurs in development. Ms. Christenson helped Cynthia understand what was happening with her body and, as a result, Cynthia no longer felt embarrassed and instead felt more confident in her appearance.

Other chronic medical conditions, such as Crohn's disease or cystic fibrosis, often result in delayed pubertal onset (Blum, 1992). Late physical maturation may also be deleterious to adjustment for adolescents with disabilities who are reliant upon others for many areas of self-care. That is, a childish appearance may encourage caregivers to continue to provide a high degree of control and involvement in daily tasks and decision-making well after these adolescents have mastered the cognitive capacities to perform these activities independently, thus decreasing opportunities for autonomy development.

The quality and capacity for cognitive change during adolescence may also be affected by the presence of a chronic medical condition (Tarazi, Mahone, & Zabel, 2007). Central nervous system involvement is a primary or secondary feature of many conditions (e.g., traumatic brain injury, epilepsy, spina bifida) that may limit adolescents' potential to achieve autonomy in both medical self-care and normative activities of daily living. For adolescents with chronic health conditions and typical cognitive functioning (e.g., asthma, type 1 diabetes), the ability to foresee future implications of health behaviors can positively or negatively affect outcomes. Advancements in future orientation and problem-solving skills can be advantageous insofar as adolescents are able to use these newly developed skills to improve self-care and medical regimen adherence. However, declines in disease management have been found consistently across chronic health conditions in the adolescent health literature, suggesting that increased cognitive abilities do not necessarily facilitate improved illness management (Holmbeck, 2002). For example, adolescents with chronic conditions may choose to neglect medical adherence tasks when they are in social settings with peers because they wish to avoid drawing attention to themselves by performing such tasks.

Samantha, a 15-year-old female with type 1 diabetes, transferred to a new high school during her sophomore year. She desperately wanted to fit in with the "cool crowd" and thought that by becoming thinner she would be accepted by the group. Samantha began to deliberately change her insulin dose to achieve weight loss. Unfortunately, as a result of continuously shortchanging and skipping her insulin, she experienced diabetic ketoacidosis and required a brief hospitalization.

The final developmental change of adolescence, social role redefinition, refers to increased status within interpersonal relationships, as well as the experience of greater social responsibility, accountability, and rights in the political, economic, and legal arenas. Although adolescents are entitled to equal rights and privileges in these arenas according to law, physical disabilities may limit adolescents' ability to exercise these rights. For example, gaining access to a motor vehicle license, a significant privilege typically obtained during the adolescent years, may be unattainable for adolescents with motor or visual disabilities.

> Patrick, a 15-year-old male with Duchenne muscular dystrophy, and his father presented at a routine clinic appointment requesting a prescription for a power wheelchair. Patrick's current upper body strength allowed him to comfortably maneuver his wheelchair independently, which made his pediatric neurologist question the prescription request. Patrick's father replied that he may never have the opportunity to buy his son a car and that a power chair was the next best thing. Upon reflection, the physician provided the family with a prescription for the power chair.

Interpersonal Contexts As the initial socialization context, families play a critical role in one's adjustment to a chronic condition and the development of self-determination and self-advocacy. Research has consistently indicated that family environments high in support and cohesion and low in conflict are optimal for adolescents (Holmbeck, 1996). Parental adjustment indicators (e.g., parental psychological health, stress, coping) have also been shown to affect adolescent health and well-being both directly and indirectly (Friedman, Holmbeck, Jandasek, Zukerman, & Abad, 2004). More central to the discussion of health care transition outcomes, however, is the finding that specific parental behaviors around medical tasks have important implications for adolescents' development of autonomy in this area.

Parents are most often the chief medical caretakers of their children with chronic health conditions. As children make the transition to adolescence, however, there is typically a gradual shift in responsibility for medical tasks from parents to adolescents, accompanied by an intermediate phase when the responsibility for medical care is shared between parent and child. During this time of transition, a decline in adherence to the medical regimen is typically observed across chronic condition groups (Anderson, Brackett, Ho, & Laffel, 2000). Parents may help to protect against this typical decline by structuring the transfer of responsibility so that it is both gradual and is tailored to adolescents' individual levels of maturity and cognitive development. If complete transfer of medical care tasks takes place too early, when adolescents are not cognitively or psychologically prepared to take on these duties, a decline in medical adherence behavior may occur (Wysocki et al., 1996). Alternatively, when parents maintain excessive control over adolescent medical responsibilities, the adolescent's desire for autonomy may be undermined, resulting in dependency and low self-efficacy (Coyne & Anderson, 1988).

By maintaining collaboration around medical care throughout this developmental period, adolescents are able to gain a sense of self-efficacy and are more likely to have positive expectations for the future possibility of independence. It is essential that parents keep in mind that, for future independence, adolescents should strive (when possible and appropriate) to care for their own personal medical needs and navigate the daily challenges of transportation and chores, such as grocery shopping and food preparation, laundry, and bill-paying. Parental transferring of household chores and personal finance management to their offspring can go a long way toward the development of daily life skills and self-efficacy in the future.

> Emily, a 14-year-old female with spinal muscular atrophy, was actively involved in her medical care. Under her parents' supervision, she coordinated her medical appointments and appropriately monitored her medications. Since childhood, Emily's parents encouraged her to be involved in her personal and medical care. Together, Emily and her parents set age-appropriate goals to help Emily develop the skills needed to eventually live independently.

Although empirical research suggests that some affected adolescents' peer relations are similar to those of typically developing adolescents, some condition parameters have been associated with social difficulties (La Greca, 1990). Chronic health conditions or treatments that restrict physical activity or lifestyle may decrease adolescents' opportunities to participate in age-appropriate activities, resulting in social isolation. Adolescents who experience prolonged absences from school are sometimes perceived by classmates as socially withdrawn, which may also affect their opportunities to develop meaningful peer relationships (La Greca, 1990). Adolescents may also be more likely to struggle with friendship development if they have a chronic condition that is socially stigmatizing (e.g., HIV/AIDS) or affects physical appearance (e.g., cleft palate). Chronic physical conditions that involve central nervous system dysfunction (e.g., epilepsy, cerebral palsy, spina bifida) have been shown to affect significantly social competence and social cue recognition (Nassau & Drotar, 1997).

Although adolescents with chronic health conditions report peer relationships as a major source of distress (often more so than the medical care of the condition itself), peers can play a positive role in condition management. Whereas families appear to be the most significant source of instrumental support for medical adherence, friends of adolescents with chronic health conditions can provide emotional support that promotes psychological adjustment. Adolescents with chronic health conditions often experience increased emotional support from friends as they move into adolescence from childhood (Pendley et al., 2002). Thus, from a developmental perspective, programs that foster social support among peers may be especially beneficial for adolescents with chronic health conditions. Such programs could also take advantage of newer online technologies (e.g., MySpace, Facebook).

Transitions between elementary and middle/junior high school, and then again to high school can be a challenging time for all adolescents but especially for those with chronic health conditions. For those with mobility disabilities, the physical school environment can present practical challenges for moving between classes. Crowded hallways and inaccessible floor plans become more common as adolescents move through the academic system.

> Mark attended a small, private elementary school where he achieved good grades and was actively involved in extracurricular activates. During his first year at a large, public high school, his parents noted a change in Mark's mood and behavior. Mark appeared depressed and was frequently receiving detentions for being tardy to classes. Upon investigation, his parents learned that Mark, who required the use of ankle foot orthoses to treat deformities caused by spastic cerebral palsy, had difficulty navigating the large multi-level and populated school building. Mark indicated that he did not want to appear different from the other students and therefore did not request help when he experienced difficulty walking between classes. Together with his parents, Mark's school developed a plan that allowed Mark and a peer of his choosing to leave class 5 minutes earlier in order to safely travel between classes. His classmates viewed this as a treat and would often argue as to who could help Mark.

Past research suggests that the majority of teachers and school administrators feel that they do not have adequate knowledge of students' particular chronic health conditions. Adolescents, parents, and health care professionals must work collaboratively with school administrators and teachers to agree upon policies that meet the adolescents' needs. With time, adolescents should be encouraged to take the lead in communicating their needs and educating school personnel about their condition whenever appropriate.

As early as junior high, schools could be a primary source of vocational and life skills training for individuals with chronic conditions. Between the ages of 14 and 16, it would be beneficial if schools initiated transition planning for vocational training, integrated employment, and community participation (Luft & Koch, 1998). This early transition planning could also focus on mastery of general life skills that are likely to be useful for adolescents no matter what their career and vocational preferences. During middle to late adolescence, as students reach the end of secondary education, more specific skills pertaining to postsecondary jobs, school, or other training programs could be covered as well. Although adolescents with chronic health conditions who participate in vocational training are more likely to seek out, secure, and maintain paid employment following high school (Wagner & Blackorby, 1996), many barriers to prevocational training exist for these adolescents (e.g., inadequate transportation).

The medical community, another interpersonal context for adolescents with chronic health conditions, can also have a significant impact on patient self-efficacy, self-determination, and future health outcomes. Physicians, nurses, physical therapists, occupational therapists, mental health professionals, and other specialists are in a unique position to not only educate and advise adolescents and families on medical issues, but also lay the groundwork for future transitions to adult care through goal-setting and creating positive expectations for the future. During their patients' early adolescence, health care providers must begin to develop a collaborative plan for the gradual transfer of health care responsibilities from parents to adolescents. The health care team may be able to provide suggestions for appropriate timing and method of health care responsibility transfer for families who are anxious about the process. As youth experience the physical and cognitive changes of adolescence, medical providers could also begin to focus more attention on the adolescents themselves during medical visits, communicating directly and separately with them, unless adolescents prefer their parents to be present (Hallum, 1995). By encouraging adolescents to become more knowledgeable about their conditions and to take greater responsibility for preventing associated secondary conditions, medical providers promote self-efficacy and self-sufficiency and provide an opportunity for adolescents to practice autonomy skills while under the supervision and support of a familiar medical team.

> In addition to inquiring about the current status of their rheumatologic condition, Dr. Palmer routinely asks his pediatric patients about social, developmental, and emotional issues. He believes that presenting symptoms often have a combination of organic causes and psychosocial ones. Furthermore, Dr. Palmer routinely educates his patients and their families about the medical condition, encourages age-appropriate self-management, and discusses coping skills for common issues that may arise in the future.

EMERGING ADULTHOOD, DISABILITIES, AND CHRONIC HEALTH CONDITIONS (AGES 18–30)

Development in the areas of education, employment, marital status, parental status, and residential independence are all critical normative milestones of adult development (Wells, Sandefur, & Hogan, 2003) and may be particularly challenging for individuals with chronic conditions. Indeed, Wells et al. (2003) found that roughly 40% of men and women with disabilities were not successful in negotiating most of these milestones. Furthermore, youth with chronic conditions are often faced with unique barriers that make self-sufficiency very difficult to achieve (Weissberg-Benchell, Wolpert, & Anderson, 2007). Given that more than 90% of children with chronic health conditions are expected to live longer than 20 years (Blum, 1992), a critical issue facing youth, families, and health professionals is the need to define a successful transfer to adulthood for youth with chronic conditions and physical disabilities.

Defining a Successful Transition

A successful transition from childhood to adulthood is best conceptualized on an individual basis. There is considerable variability among medically healthy youth during the transition from childhood to adulthood; this variability is even more pronounced among individuals with a chronic health condition and/or a disability. Developmental psychopathologists acknowledge that early developmental maladjustment increases the probability that an individual will experience developmental difficulties later in life (Rutter, 1989). On the other hand, life-span transitions, such as the transition into adulthood, are key developmental periods for "strengthening emerging patterns of behavior and providing a means by which life trajectories may change direction" (Rutter, 1989). To capture the tremendous variability of pathways from childhood to adulthood, an integrative approach is necessary that accounts for genetic, biological, environmental, and psychosocial factors that serve as mediating and/or moderating influences on development.

Few longitudinal studies have examined the effects of chronic health conditions on the transition to adulthood and adult functioning, with the bulk of those that have been done tending to focus on less severe conditions (Bussing & Aro, 1996). In one study of a more severe condition, Anderson, Vogel, Betz, and Willis (2004) found that individuals with pediatric-onset spinal cord injury had educational achievement levels comparable with their peers, but they were less likely to be employed, to live independently, and to be satisfied with their lives. Factors associated with stable independent living for individuals with a spinal cord injury included physical independence, mobility, and having an occupation. Factors associated with stable employment included being white, being female, greater cognitive independence, and greater community participation (Anderson, Vogel, Willis, & Betz, 2006). Furthermore, Buran, Sawin, Brei, and Fastenau (2004) found that adolescents with meningomyelocele (spina bifida) report being hopeful about their future and that they hold generally positive beliefs and expectations about their ability to perform activities necessary to live independently. On the other hand, adolescents in this same study were not engaging in the full range of adolescent activities, including independent decision making, self-management, household responsibilities, and friendship activities.

> Sarah, an 18-year-old with spina bifida, was the youngest of four children. When she graduated from high school, she wanted to attend an out-of-state university, but was afraid to live independently. She acknowledged relying too much on her parents and siblings for help in managing her everyday activities and chronic condition. Consequently, Sarah decided to attend a local university and move into a transitional apartment complex designed to help individuals with chronic illness increase their skills in independence. After 2 years, Sarah felt comfortable with her ability to live on her own and transferred to the out-of-state university.

Social Development During Emerging Adulthood

Social support is a crucial factor for positive development among young adults (APA, 2002). In addition to providing an important source for emotional support, positive peer relationships facilitate adaptive disease adjustment and treatment management (La Greca, Bearman, & Moore, 2002). Moreover, some adolescents are resilient in the face of their chronic conditions and develop peer friendships and romantic relationships in adulthood similar to their medically healthy peers. For example, Bussing and Aro (1996) found that females with a chronic condition were more likely to be married or living with a steady partner in early adulthood, as compared to medically healthy peers. On the other hand, some individuals are more likely to experience rejection by their peers during adulthood than was the case in childhood (Stam et al., 2006). Although there is variability within chronic condition groups, several factors increase the probability that young adults with a chronic condition will experience increased peer rejection and maladaptive social skills in adulthood. First, young adults who have a condition in which their physical appearance is altered (e.g., obesity, craniofacial anomalies) are more likely to experience peer rejection than youth with a disorder that is not visually apparent (e.g., type 1 diabetes; Schuman & La Greca, 1999). Second, conditions with associated cognitive impairments may interfere with social understanding and social skills development (e.g., cerebral palsy, spina bifida). Third, severe physical disabilities may prevent the emerging adult from participating in activities with peers, leading to social isolation. Similarly, an emerging adult who does not attend college or find steady employment may experience a decrease in social contacts.

> Mike, a 20-year-old high school graduate with Becker muscular dystrophy, spent most of his day at home watching television. Most of his high school friends moved away to attend colleges in nearby cities and states. Despite his above-average intelligence, Mike did not pursue his college dreams for fear of being away from his family and having difficulties managing his health condition independently. On a routine medical visit, Mike learned of a social support group for young adults with muscular dystrophy. He decided to attend the group and made several new friends who eventually encouraged him to pursue his dream to attend college.

The Family Context During Emerging Adulthood

Because of the Health Insurance Portability and Accountability Act (HIPAA) of 1996 (PL 104-191) and privacy laws, parents of young adults with chronic conditions have less power to advocate for their young adult and keep track of their health care needs after the age of 18. Prior to this age, youth are best served if they can gradually develop the skills necessary to take on adult roles and responsibilities, particularly skills for self-advocacy, self-care, and the management of their condition. As youth move into adulthood, it is necessary for parents and young adults to work together toward developing a transition plan that accounts for the youths' cognitive, emotional, and physical abilities. Oftentimes, the parents' and young adult's goals for independent living, work, and health care differ. These disparate views of the transition to adult life should be discussed in a developmentally appropriate manner with the young adult.

Families should consider several important issues as they strive for a successful transition to adulthood. First, is the young adult able to discuss his or her condition with significant others? Past research suggests that many affected youth (57% in one study) are unable to explain their condition (Hydrocephalus Association, 2003). During emerging adulthood, parents can include their youth in discussions concerning their health care and encourage active participation of the young adult in medical decision-making and self-care tasks. Second, can the young adult articulate his or her medical and nonmedical needs? This question further highlights the necessity of emerging adults becoming educated about their condition, as well as about their health care options. It is also important for youth to know how to access information, including proactively negotiating the adult health care system. Third, does the young adult know how to access community resources and local agencies that provide additional services for young people outside of the hospital setting? Fourth, does the young person understand when he or she should and should not discuss his or her condition? The issue of appropriate versus inappropriate disclosure is most problematic for individuals with stigmatizing disorders. Individuals with a stigmatizing disorder may be more likely to be socially rejected after they disclose information about their condition. Finally, can the young adult advocate for him- or herself? Does he or she know when and with whom to discuss the need for help? When answering these types of questions, families must keep in mind the youth's level of cognitive functioning. In sum, all of these considerations are relevant for determining the youth's developmental readiness for transfer to an adult care clinic, including the timing and degree of care management.

Barriers During Emerging Adulthood

There are several barriers that could adversely affect the transition to adulthood among youth with disabilities or chronic health conditions. First, social development may be impeded by psychological maladjustment, including altered or poor self-esteem, social withdrawal, conflictual or poor parent–child relationships, social skills deficits, neuropsychological functioning that disrupts social skills, or exclusion from mainstream schooling. Second, chronic conditions may affect the rate at which young adults gain independence from their parents, enter committed relationships, and master the other milestones of emerging adulthood. The young person's academic education can be hampered by increased school absences, cognitive sequelea of the condition, or medications used in treatment. In addition, among young adults with chronic health conditions, there is an increased prevalence of psychological morbidity and clinical symptoms, particularly depressive symptoms (Lavigne & Faier-Routman, 1992). A successful transition into adulthood will be further confounded by the condition severity and the resources of one's parents. Finally, there is often a general lack of access to a normative adolescent experience insofar as youth with chronic conditions are less likely to have the same educational, social, recreational, and vocational experiences as typically developing adolescents.

Transition Programs During Emerging Adulthood

The probability of a successful transfer into adult health care is increased by prior successes in other developmental areas of life (Rutter, 1989). Failure to navigate successfully earlier developmental milestones in multiple areas of the emerging adult's life will likely complicate the transfer into adult health care. The purpose of a transition program is to increase the probability that an individual with a chronic health condition will make a successful transfer into adult care. Unfortunately, few transition programs exist for young people with chronic conditions and disabilities (LoCasale-Crouch & Johnson, 2005; Sawyer, Blair, & Bowes, 1997).

Several issues are important to consider when developing an individualized transition program. Youth with a chronic condition and their families establish long-term dependent relationships with their pediatric provider. Adult services have the expectation that youth should be self-reliant, but this is an unrealistic assumption for some adults who remain dependent for daily care. A well-conceived transition plan that decreases the dependency between the pediatrician and young person, by facilitating personal responsibility for decision-making, will strengthen the youth's relationship with an adult provider (see Chapter 4 in this book).

> Dr. Stevens, a pediatric pulmonologist and specialist in the treatment of cystic fibrosis, works closely with her team—which consists of pulmonologists, gastroenterologists, nurses, nutritionists, respiratory therapists, a social worker, and an exercise physiologist—to coordinate care and provide comprehensive treatment. She follows children from diagnosis until age 18, when she is required by hospital policy to transfer their care to an adult health care provider. To help patients and their families transition to adult care, Dr. Stevens encourages patients to schedule an intake appointment with the new provider(s) while still under her care. After the appointment, she holds a telephone conference call with the family and new provider(s) to discuss the patient's medical history, current treatment plan, and goals for the future.

An appropriate transition plan will attend not only to the medical needs of young people, but also to the broad spectrum of care that is necessary for a successful transfer to adult-oriented care, including physical, emotional, developmental, and social issues (Soanes & Timmons, 2004). Transition plans should address concerns typical of a developing adolescent, in addition to the individualized needs of youth with a chronic condition. Specific needs in young adults with a chronic health condition or disability that should be addressed in medical visits include the following: independence skills, personal counseling, age-appropriate information about disabilities, sex education, preparation for parenthood, genetic counseling, vocational awareness, alternatives to work, and leisure time use (Hallum, 1995). Clearly, most of these needs are related to the important developmental milestones of emerging adulthood (see earlier discussion).

CONCLUSIONS, FUTURE DIRECTIONS, AND POLICY CONSIDERATIONS

In this chapter, we have provided an overview of the normative developmental tasks of adolescence and emerging adulthood, emphasizing that the manner in which an individual negotiates the adolescent developmental period has clear implications for how the individual is likely to manage the emerging adulthood transition. Most important, it is critical to consider the manner in which these normative developmental periods are managed by individuals with disabilities and chronic health conditions and how developmental expectations may vary considerably across individuals with these conditions. Not only is the negotiation of developmental milestones more difficult for this population (Schultz & Liptak, 1998) but they also must confront certain types of transitions that are not faced by typically developing individuals (e.g., the transition to self-care from parent-provided care). Moreover, the transitions to education, employment, marriage, living on one's own, and parenthood and the degree to which they are attainable are more complicated for individuals with chronic conditions.

An important question remains: How do we provide a seamless transition to adulthood, across all relevant developmental and health-related domains, in individuals with chronic health conditions and disabilities? Drawing on the literature discussed above and recent recommendations by the Society for Adolescent Medicine (Rosen, Blum, Britto, Sawyer, & Siegel, 2003), we advance the following recommendations:

1. Youth with disabilities and chronic health conditions require individualized transition plans, tailored to the changing needs of the young person, his or her interpersonal contexts, and the preferences of the family. One word characterizes the transition process: change. The young person's health status and capacities may change over time, the person's family may change in composition and/or its ability or willingness to provide support, and any stressor—economic, occupational, medical, and personal—will place new demands on whatever transition plan is put into place. Transition planning needs to be tailored to the individual young person, evolving to accommodate maturation, flexible to respond to changes in informal and formal support systems, and long term, to cover at minimum the 10-year period from ages 14 to 24. It is

critical that continuous and seamless services be available to support youth throughout the transition period and that the need for services be reevaluated regularly to accommodate increasing or changing demands. We recommend that policies and programs be developed using the biopsychosocial model, which acknowledges the biological, psychological, and social changes of the adolescent developmental period.

2. Transition planning should include avoiding health risk behaviors, developing positive health behaviors, and managing the condition to achieve positive health outcomes. Life-long patterns of positive health behaviors, health risk behaviors, self-management, and health-related self-advocacy are established and consolidated in adolescence and young adulthood. The manner in which affected individuals manage the adolescent and young adult transitions has important implications for these health outcomes.

3. Each youth needs a centralized transition plan that targets the process of transition itself. Simply ensuring that domain-specific services (e.g., education, housing) are sensitive to transition issues is unlikely to be successful, as each domain will define transition differently, develop conflicting eligibility requirements, measure success too narrowly, and leave important gaps. Different kinds of transition need to be addressed in an integrated and centralized manner because they may not move in concert. It is preferable to have one "designated professional" who would take responsibility for the transition process in collaboration with the individual and family.

4. Transition planning policies should be based on research findings pertaining to those who have been successful during the transition to adulthood. We recommend that comprehensive measures of transition needs and milestones be developed, that periodic national surveys include measures of the adolescent transition, and that transition outcomes include autonomy, achievement, identity, intimacy, and sexuality, as well as the milestones of emerging adulthood.

5. Transition planners must be trained. The job of transition planning can be filled by professionals with different expertise, but they need specific preparation in three areas: a) knowledge of adolescent development and transition, so they can educate the young person and his or her family about the transition itself; b) knowledge of available services and their eligibility requirements, how to access them, and how to best fit the individual to the programs; and c) knowledge of family systems theory and how to work effectively with families. A transition planner will need to help parents and young people resolve conflicts over aspects of the transition process. Typically, the adolescent transition is characterized by young people pushing for increasing autonomy while parents maintain tighter control than the young person would prefer. When young people have a health condition or disability, this struggle is accompanied by heightened parental concern over health outcomes. In some instances, the opposite may occur, insofar as some young people with chronic

health conditions are fearful of independence and autonomy and their parents may need help in supporting their progress in these areas.

6. All adolescents need help during the transition to adulthood. If transition planning programs and skill building were made available to all youth, the transition to adulthood would be easier for youth with disabilities and chronic health conditions. As early as junior high, it would be beneficial if schools initiated transition planning for all youth, including vocational training, integrated employment, and community participation. Early transition planning could also focus on mastery of general life skills. During middle to late adolescence, as students reach the end of secondary education, more specific skills pertaining to postsecondary jobs, school, or other training programs could be covered as well.

7. Finally, there is a need for more intervention-based and developmentally oriented longitudinal research on the issue of making the transition to adulthood in individuals with chronic conditions. Randomized clinical trials would go a long way toward providing information about which programs work well. A multidimensional perspective would also need to be adopted with respect to outcome assessment. For example, we would need to evaluate transition programs with respect to how well they help youth manage and successfully negotiate the various developmental tasks of adolescence and emerging adulthood. At an even more complex level of analysis, future research on making transitions could answer important questions about why and for whom certain interventions and prevention programs work. It is only in this way that we will come to provide a seamless transition for youth affected by disabilities and chronic health conditions.

REFERENCES

American Psychological Association. (2002). *Developing adolescents: A reference for professionals.* Washington, DC: Author.

Anderson, B.J., Brackett, J., Ho, J., & Laffel, L.M.B. (2000). An intervention to promote family teamwork in diabetes management tasks: Relationships among parental involvement, adherence to blood glucose monitoring, and glycemic control in young adolescents with type 1 diabetes. In D. Drotar (Ed.), *Promoting adherence to medical treatment in chronic childhood illness: Concepts, methods, and interventions* (pp. 347–365). Mahwah, NJ: Lawrence Erlbaum Associates.

Anderson, C.J., Vogel, L.C., Betz, R.R., & Willis, K.M. (2004). Overview of adult outcomes in pediatric-onset spinal cord injuries: Implications for transition to adulthood. *Journal of Spinal Cord Medicine, 27,* 98–106.

Anderson, C.J., Vogel, L.C., Willis, K.M., & Betz, R.R. (2006). Stability of transition to adulthood among individuals with pediatric-onset spinal cord injury. *Journal of Spinal Cord Medicine, 29,* 46–56.

Arnett, J.J. (1999). Adolescent storm and stress, reconsidered. *American Psychologist, 54,* 317–326.

Arnett, J.J. (2000). Emerging adulthood: A theory of development from the late teens through the twenties. *American Psychologist, 55,* 469–480.

Berndt, T.J., & Savin-Williams, R.C. (1993). Peer relations and friendships. In P.H. Tolan, & B.J. Cohler (Eds.), *Handbook of clinical research and practice with adolescents* (pp. 203–220). New York: Wiley.

Blum, R. (1992). Chronic illness and disability in adolescence. *Journal of Adolescent Health, 13,* 364–368.

Brooks-Gunn, J., & Reiter, E.O. (1990). The role of pubertal processes. In S.S. Feldman & G.R. Elliott (Eds.), *At the threshold: The developing adolescent* (pp. 16–53). Cambridge, MA: Harvard University Press.

Brown, B.B. (1990). Peer groups and peer cultures. In S.S. Feldman, & G.R. Elliott (Eds.), *At the threshold: The developing adolescent* (pp. 171–196). Cambridge, MA: Harvard University Press.

Buran, C.F., Sawin, K.J., Brei, T., & Fastenau, P.S. (2004). Adolescents with myelomeningocele: Activities, beliefs, expectations, and perceptions. *Developmental Medicine and Child Neurology, 46,* 244–252.

Bussing, R., & Aro, H. (1996). Youth with chronic conditions and their transition to adulthood: Findings from a Finnish cohort study. *Archives of Pediatrics and Adolescent Medicine, 150,* 181–186.

Collins, W.A., & Laursen, B. (1992). Conflict and relationships during adolescence. In C.U. Shantz & W.W. Hartup (Eds.), *Conflict in child and adolescent development* (pp. 216–241). New York: Cambridge University Press.

Coyne, J.C., & Anderson, B.J. (1988). The "psychosomatic family" reconsidered: Diabetes in context. *Journal of Marital and Family Therapy, 14,* 113–123.

Dodge, K.A., & Pettit, G.S. (2003). A biopsychosocial model of the development of chronic conduct problems in adolescence. *Developmental Psychology, 39,* 349–371.

Entwisle, D.R. (1990). Schools and the adolescent. In S.S. Feldman & G.R. Elliott (Eds.), *At the threshold: The developing adolescent* (pp. 197–224). Cambridge, MA: Harvard University Press.

Erickson, J.D., Patterson, J.M., Wall, M., & Neumark-Sztainer, D. (2005). Risk behaviors and emotional well-being in youth with chronic health conditions. *Children's Health Care, 34,* 181–192.

Erikson, E. (1968). *Identity: Youth and crisis.* New York: Norton.

Feldman, S.S., & Elliott, G.R. (Eds.). (1990). *At the threshold: The developing adolescent.* Cambridge, MA: Harvard University Press.

Freud, A. (1958). Adolescence. *Psychoanalytic Study of the Child, 13,* 231–258.

Friedman, D., Holmbeck, G.N., Jandasek, B., Zukerman, J., & Abad, M. (2004). Parent functioning in families of preadolescents with spina bifida: Longitudinal implications for child adjustment. *Journal of Family Psychology, 18,* 609–619.

Fuhrman, T., & Holmbeck, G.N. (1995). A contextual-moderator analysis of emotional autonomy and adjustment in adolescence. *Child Development, 66,* 793–811.

Greenberger, E., & Steinberg, L. (1986). *When teenagers work: The psychological and social costs of adolescent employment.* New York: Basic.

Hall, G.S. (1904). *Adolescence: Its psychology and its relations to psychology, anthropology, sex, crime, religion, and education: Vols. 1–2.* New York: Appleton-Century Crofts.

Hallum, A. (1995). Disability and the transition to adulthood: Issues for the disabled child, the family, and the pediatrician. *Current Problems in Pediatrics, 25,* 12–50.

Harris, J.R. (1998). *The nurture assumption: Why children turn out the way they do.* New York: Free Press.

Harter, S. (1990). Self and identity development. In S.S. Feldman & G.R. Elliott (Eds.), *At the threshold: The developing adolescent* (pp. 352–387). Cambridge, MA: Harvard University Press.

Health Insurance Portability and Accountability Act (HIPAA) of 1996, PL 104-191, 42 U.S.C. §§ 201 *et seq.*

Henderson, V.L., & Dweck, C.S. (1990). Motivation and achievement. In S.S. Feldman & G.R. Elliott (Eds.), *At the threshold: The developing adolescent* (pp. 308–329). Cambridge, MA: Harvard University Press.

Hill, J.P. (1983). Early adolescence: A framework. *Journal of Early Adolescence, 3,* 1–21.

Hill, J.P., & Holmbeck, G.N. (1986). Attachment and autonomy during adolescence. In G.J. Whitehurst (Ed.), *Annals of child development* (Vol. 3, pp. 145–189). Greenwich, CT: JAI Press.

Hill, J.P., & Lynch, M.E. (1983). The intensification of gender-related role expectations during early adolescence. In J. Brooks-Gunn & A.C. Petersen (Eds.), *Girls at puberty: Biological and psychosocial perspectives.* New York: Plenum.

Holmbeck, G.N. (1996). A model of family relational transformations during the transition to adolescence: Parent-adolescent conflict and adaptation. In J.A. Graber, J. Brooks-Gunn, & A.C. Petersen (Eds.), *Transitions through adolescence: Interpersonal domains and context* (pp.167–199). Mahwah, NJ: Lawrence Erlbaum Associates.

Holmbeck, G.N. (1997). Toward terminological, conceptual, and statistical clarity in the study of mediators and moderators: Examples from the child-clinical and pediatric psychology literatures. *Journal of Consulting and Clinical Psychology, 65,* 599–610.

Holmbeck, G.N. (2002). A developmental perspective on adolescent health and illness: An introduction to the special issues. *Journal of Pediatric Psychology, 27,* 409–416.

Holmbeck, G.N., & Hill, J.P. (1991). Conflictive engagement, positive affect, and menarche in families with seventh-grade girls. *Child Development, 62,* 1030–1048.

Holmbeck, G.N., Paikoff, R.L., Brooks-Gunn, J. (1995). Parenting adolescents. In M. Bornstein (Ed.), *Handbook of parenting* (Vol. 1, pp. 91–118). Mahwah, NJ: Erlbaum.

Holmbeck, G.N., & Shapera, W.E. (1999). Research methods with adolescents. In P.C. Kendall, J.N. Butcher, & G.N. Holmbeck (Eds.), *Handbook of research methods in clinical psychology* (2nd ed., pp. 634–661). New York: Wiley.

Hydrocephalus Association. (2003). *Health-care transition guide for teens and young adults with hydrocephalus.* San Francisco: Author.

Keating, D.P. (1990). Adolescent thinking. In S.S. Feldman & G.R. Elliott (Eds.), *At the threshold: The developing adolescent* (pp. 54–89). Cambridge, MA: Harvard University Press.

La Greca, A.M. (1990). Social consequences of pediatric conditions: Fertile area for future investigation and intervention. *Journal of Pediatric Psychology, 15,* 285–307.

La Greca, A.M., Bearman, K.J., & Moore, H. (2002). Peer relations of youth with pediatric conditions and health risks: Promoting social support and healthy lifestyles. *Developmental and Behavioral Pediatrics, 23,* 271–280.

La Greca, A.M., & Prinstein, M.J. (1999). Peer group. In W.K. Silverman & T.H. Ollendick (Eds.), *Developmental issues in the clinical treatment of children* (pp. 171–198). Boston, MA: Allyn and Bacon.

Larson, R.W., Richards, M.H., Moneta, G., Holmbeck, G., & Duckett, E. (1996). Changes in adolescents' daily interactions with their families from ages 10 to 18: Disengagement and transformation. *Developmental Psychology, 32,* 744–754.

Laursen, B., Coy, K.C., & Collins, W.A. (1998). Reconsidering changes in parent-child conflict across adolescence: A meta-analysis. *Child Development, 69,* 817–832.

Lavigne, J.V., & Faier-Routman, J. (1992). Psychological adjustment to pediatric physical disorders: A meta-analytic review. *Journal of Pediatric Psychology, 17,* 133–157.

LoCasale-Crouch, L., & Johnson, B. (2005). Transition from pediatric to adult medical care. *Advances in Chronic Kidney Disease, 12,* 412–417.

Luft, P., & Koch, L.C. (1998). Transition of adolescents with chronic illness: Overlooked needs and rehabilitation considerations. *Journal of Vocational Rehabilitation, 10,* 205–217.

Magnusson, D., Stattin, H., & Allen, V.L. (1985). A longitudinal study of some adjustment processes from mid-adolescence to adulthood. *Journal of Youth and Adolescence, 14,* 267–283.

Moshman, D. (1998). Cognitive development beyond childhood. In D. Kuhn & R.S. Siegler (Eds.), *Handbook of child psychology: Cognition, perception, and language* (Vol. 2, pp. 957–978). New York: Wiley.

Nassau, J.H., & Drotar, D. (1997). Social competence among children with central nervous system-related chronic health conditions: A review. *Journal of Pediatric Psychology, 22,* 771–793.

National Center for Youth with Disabilities. (1994, Fall). Moving on: Transition from pediatric to adult health care. *Connections: The Newsletter of the National Center for Youth with Disabilities, 5,* 1–5.

Nelson, D.A., & Crick, N.R. (1999). Rose-colored glasses: Examining the social information-processing of prosocial young adolescents. *Journal of Early Adolescence, 19,* 17–38.

Paikoff, R.L., & Brooks-Gunn, J. (1991). Do parent-child relationships change during puberty? *Psychological Bulletin, 110,* 47–66.

Parker, J.G., & Asher, S.R. (1987). Peer relations and later personal adjustment: Are low-accepted children at risk? *Psychological Bulletin, 102,* 357–389.

Pendley, J.S., Kasmen, L.J., Miller, D.L., Donze, J., Swenson, C., & Reeves, G. (2002). Peer and family support in children and adolescents with type 1 diabetes. *Journal of Pediatric Psychology, 27,* 429–438.

Piaget, J. (1983). Piaget's theory. In P.H. Mussen (Series Ed.), W. Kessen (Vol. Ed.), *Handbook of child psychology: Vol 1. History, theory, and methods* (pp. 103–128). New York: Wiley.

Rosen, D.S., Blum, R.W., Britto, M., Sawyer, S.M., & Siegel, D.M. (2003). Transition to adult health care for adolescents and young adults with chronic conditions. *Journal of Adolescent Health, 33,* 309–311.

Rutter, M. (1989). Pathways from childhood to adult life. *Journal of Child Psychology and Psychiatry, 30,* 23–51.

Savin-Williams, R.C., & Berndt, T.J. (1990). Friendship and peer relations. In S.S. Feldman & G.R. Elliott (Eds.), *At the threshold: The developing adolescent* (pp. 277–307). Cambridge, MA: Harvard University Press.

Sawyer, S.M., Blair, S., & Bowes, G. (1997). Chronic illness in adolescents: Transfer or transition to adult services? *Journal of Pediatric Child Health, 33,* 88–90.

Schultz, A.W., & Liptak, G.S. (1998). Helping adolescents who have disabilities negotiate transitions to adulthood. *Issues in Comprehensive Pediatric Nursing, 21,* 187–201.

Schuman, W.B., & La Greca, A.M. (1999). Social correlates of chronic illness. In R.T. Brown (Ed.), *Cognitive aspects of chronic illness in children* (pp. 289–311). New York: Guilford Press.

Simmons, R.G., & Blyth, D.A. (1987). *Moving into adolescence: The impact of pubertal change and school context.* New York: Aldine De Gruyter.

Soanes, C., & Timmons, S. (2004). Improving transition: A qualitative study examining the attitudes of young people with chronic illness transferring to adult care. *Journal of Child Health Care, 8,* 102–112.

Stam, H., Hartman, E.E., Deurloo, J.A., Groothoff, J., & Grootenhuis, M.A. (2006). Young adult patients with a history of pediatric disease: Impact on course of life and transition into adulthood. *Journal of Adolescent Health, 39,* 4–13.

Steinberg, L. (1990). Interdependence in the family: Autonomy, conflict, and harmony in the parent-adolescent relationship. In S.S. Feldman, & G.L. Elliott (Eds.), *At the threshold: The developing adolescent* (pp. 255–276). Cambridge, MA: Harvard University Press.

Steinberg, L. (2002). Clinical adolescent psychology: What is, and what it needs to be. *Journal of Consulting and Clinical Psychology, 70*(1) 124–128.

Steinberg, L. (2005). *Adolescence* (7th ed.). Boston, MA: McGraw-Hill.

Sullivan, H.S. (1953). *The interpersonal theory of psychiatry.* New York: Norton.

Tanner, J. (1962). *Growth at adolescence* (2nd ed.). Springfield, IL: Charles C. Thomas.

Tarazi, R.A., Mahone, E.M., & Zabel, T.A. (2007). Self-care independence in children with neurological disorders: An interactional model of adaptive demands and executive dysfunction. *Rehabilitation Psychology, 52,* 196–205.

Tyc, V.L., Hadley, W., & Crockett, G. (2001). Brief report: Predictors of intentions to use tobacco among adolescent survivors of cancer. *Journal of Pediatric Psychology, 26,* 117–121.

Vygotsky, L. (1978). *Mind in society: The development of higher psychological processes.* Cambridge, MA: Harvard University Press.

Wagner, M.M., & Blackorby, J. (1996). Transition from high school to work or college: How special education students fare. *Special Education for Students with Disabilities, 6,* 103–119.

Weissberg-Benchell, J., Wolpert, H., & Anderson, B.J. (2007). Transitioning from pediatric to adult care: A new approach to the post-adolescent young person with type 1 diabetes. *Diabetes Care, 30,* 2441–2446.

Wells, T., Sandefur, G.D., & Hogan, D.P. (2003). What happens after the high school years among young persons with disabilities? *Social Forces, 82,* 803–832.

Williams, P.G., Holmbeck, G.N., & Greenley, R.N. (2002). Adolescent health psychology. *Journal of Consulting and Clinical Psychology, 70,* 828–842.

Wysocki, T., Taylor, A., Hough, B.S., Linscheid, T.R., Yeates, K.O., & Naglieri, J.A. (1996). Deviation from developmentally appropriate self-care autonomy. *Diabetes Care, 19,* 119–125.

3

Measuring Success

Data on Adolescents and Young Adults in the United States with Special Health Care Needs or Disabilities

Scott D. Grosse, Janet L. Valluzzi, and Paul W. Newacheck

A clear understanding of the characteristics of adolescents and young adults with disabilities or special health care needs (SHCN) is essential to monitor and promote successful transition to adulthood, including transitions to work, new residential settings, and adult health care. Substantial information exists regarding subgroups of individuals based on different definitions of disability or special needs, but each data set is limited in the information it provides. Valid, reliable data are essential to develop and measure clinical and public health evidence and outcomes regarding transitions to adult roles and tasks.

This chapter describes available data sets and summarizes what is known, including estimates of the numbers of youth with disabilities and SHCN that may be involved in the transition process and their receipt of services that address transition needs. Included are relevant national- and state-level survey data sets that are overseen by the U.S. Department of Health and Human Services, the U.S. Department of Commerce, the U.S. Department of Education, and the Social Security Administration (SSA). The chapter is intended to inform research

The lead author's contribution to this chapter was written in his capacity as a U.S. Government employee and, as such, this chapter shall remain in the public domain. The views expressed in this chapter are solely those of the authors and are not to be construed as official or reflecting the view or policy of the U.S. Government.

We gratefully acknowledge helpful comments from Brian Armour, Matthew Brault, Vince Campbell, Pam Costa, Gloria Krahn, Mitch Loeb, Don Lollar, Patricia Pastor, and Mark Swanson.

and policy audiences of the availability, strengths, and limitations of different sources of information on the target population for this volume—adolescents and young adults ages 14–28 years with disabilities or special needs.

With the exception of an analysis of data from one survey, the 2005 Medical Expenditure Panel Survey–Household Component, which was conducted specifically for this chapter, all data come from published analyses, reports, or online tabulations. As a result, there is no consistency in the age intervals for which prevalence estimates are reported. Few data sets include both adolescents and young adults in their sampling frames; consequently, many estimates are limited to either children and adolescents or adults.

We faced several challenges in identifying relevant data sets. Historically, little attention has been given to the collection of data on youth with disabilities and SHCN during the period stretching from adolescence into adulthood. There has been a lack of coordination of efforts with respect to issues such as consistency of definitions, measurement of constructs across age ranges, and differences between broader survey and specific programmatic definitions that track use of social service resources. Few surveys ask the same disability-related questions for both children and adults. There is a paucity of longitudinal data suitable for describing and studying the transition process, and most available data sets are cross-sectional. Adolescents and adults represent distinct populations in cross-sectional data sets. Longitudinal surveys that track the same individuals beginning in adolescence into adulthood often refer to the respondents as youth. The term *youth* is indeed less age-delimited and hence more appropriate for addressing the transition status bridging adolescence and adulthood.

In reviewing available data sources that might be used to describe the characteristics of youth with disabilities or special needs undergoing transitions, we reviewed the literature and consulted experts to identify national surveys with information on disability or special needs among adolescents or young adults, with the target age range of 14–28 years. For each survey we reviewed available data from both published and unpublished sources.

Most data sets emphasize one domain (e.g., health, education) with less attention to other domains, particularly environmental factors (e.g., housing, transportation). This is because the purpose of each data set differs. The purpose influences the conceptualization, definition, and measurement of disability and special needs; the sampling frame; and data collection methods, each of which can affect the resulting prevalence estimates. Survey research has identified differences in reported prevalence rates of disability due to the type of survey administration. In particular, one study in Washington State found that surveys that use random-digit telephone dialing, which have lower response rates than the Census 2000 Supplementary Survey (U.S. Census Bureau, n.d.), appeared to significantly overrepresent adults with disabilities (Kinne & Topolski, 2005). Consequently, it should come as no surprise that different data sets are associated with marked differences in estimates of prevalence.

DEFINITIONS

Children or adolescents with SHCN, referred to collectively as CSHCN, are defined by the federal Maternal and Child Health Bureau (MCHB) as children who have or are at increased risk for a chronic physical, developmental, behavioral, or emotional condition and who require health care-related services of a type or amount beyond that required by children generally (McPherson et al., 1998). In the first empirical operationalization of this concept, Newacheck and colleagues (1998) distinguished two groups of children as having SHCN: 1) children who had above-average use of physician services, therapists, or prescription medications because of a chronic condition; used special equipment for mobility, hearing, vision, or other needs (chiefly breathing equipment); or received special education or early intervention services; and 2) children with developmental delays, learning disabilities, vision or hearing impairments, or other functional limitations and disabilities who were not identified as using services at an elevated level. Thus, the SHCN concept broadly encompasses children or adolescents with any type of disability or chronic health condition with increased service use or need, regardless of functional or activity limitation.

A subsequent operational CSHCN screener administered to parents was developed and adopted in national surveys. The CSHCN screener (Bethell et al., 2002) consists of a series of question-sequences for each of five health domains: 1) need or use of medicines prescribed by a doctor; 2) need or use of more medical care, mental health, or education services than is usual for most children; 3) limitations in, or being prevented from, doing things most children can do; 4) need or use of special therapy such as physical, occupational, or speech therapy; and 5) need or use of treatment or counseling for emotional, developmental, or behavioral problems. Children with positive responses to at least one of the five health domains, along with an underlying medical, behavioral, or other health condition that has lasted or is expected to last at least 12 months, were identified as having an SHCN.

Definitions of disability are more diverse. The medical model of disability uses categorical definitions based on medical diagnoses and impairments, such as autism or cerebral palsy (Drum, 2009). The functional model of disability likewise focuses on the individual but addresses reported functional, activity, and social participation limitations that are attributed to chronic health problems or impairments (Drum, 2009). Social models of disability use functional measures of disability, but instead of focusing on the individual, these models place emphasis on social and environmental barriers in attitudes, construction, or policy as limiting participation by people with disability (Drum, 2009). Disability is sometimes also defined on the basis of eligibility for participation in service programs, such as special education or disability benefits.

According to the Americans with Disabilities Act (ADA) of 1990 (PL 101-336), a person with a disability is one who has a physical or mental impairment that substantially limits one or more major life activities, who has a history or record of such impairment, or who is perceived by others as having such impairment. Major life activities are defined in the legislation and case law as anything that people do routinely: walking, sitting, stooping, reaching, eating, seeing, hearing, speaking, breathing, learning, and working (Smith, 2001).

The current internationally accepted standard for conceptualizing disability is the *International Classification of Functioning, Disability and Health (ICF)*, adopted by the World Health Organization (WHO, 2001). In the ICF, disability relates to functional or structural impairments, limitations in personal activities, and restrictions on social participation within the context of environmental factors. The ICF views disability as a continuum rather than as a dichotomy. Although injuries, illnesses, and developmental problems can be associated with activity limitation and limitation in social participation, within that framework one cannot equate specific medical diagnoses or health conditions with disability (Grosse, Lollar, Campbell, & Chamie, 2009), regardless of the level of use of health, developmental, or educational services. Consequently, the SHCN concept does not fit neatly within the ICF framework.

Although all adolescents addressed in this volume fit under the SHCN umbrella, different subsets will meet various definitions of disability. As noted by Newacheck et al. (1998), the majority of children with SHCN are not reported to have functional or activity limitations. For instance, although most adolescents with asthma fit the SHCN definition, most children with mild asthma do not have a disability by conventional criteria, although they might have a disability according to the ADA definition of impairment in breathing as a major life activity. Also, because of its high prevalence, asthma is one of the leading causes of disability in children as defined by activity limitations (Newacheck & Halfon, 2000). Children with speech problems who qualify for special education services may not be classified as having a functional or activity limitation disability but meet the ADA definition of disability.

Case definitions depend in part on the age group. The CSHCN definition developed by the MCHB (McPherson et al., 1998) and operationalized by the CSHCN screener (Bethell et al., 2002) only applies to children younger than 18 years of age for whom parents serve as the respondent. One approach to broaden the applicable age range is to devise an algorithm based on survey or administrative data to classify individuals as having elevated use of health care services as a result of an underlying condition (e.g., Newacheck et al., 1998). Special education statistics are restricted to individuals ages 3–21 years. Finally, data on the frequency of activity limitations are also age-dependent, because norms for activities vary as individuals make the transition from childhood into adulthood. Consequently, it is difficult to ascertain comparable information across age groups.

DATA SETS AND ESTIMATES

Data sets and estimates for the prevalence of children and adolescents with SHCN, of overall disability, and of service-specific disability are reviewed next.

Special Health Care Needs

The first data set used to estimate the prevalence of children and adolescents with SHCN was the National Health Interview Survey on Disability (NHIS-D), which was collected by Centers for Disease Control and Prevention (CDC)'s National Center for Health Statistics (NCHS) during 1994–1995 (Table 3.1). Newacheck et al. (1998) reported that 12% of children younger than 18 years of age had a chronic physical, developmental, behavioral, or emotional condition and required health, developmental, or educational services of a type or amount beyond that required by children generally. An additional 6% had a disability or impairment without elevated service use, for a total SHCN prevalence of 18%. The prevalence of SHCN was 21% among adolescents ages 11–14 and 15–17 years.

A series of national surveys of families of children and adolescents with SHCN have been conducted since 2001 by CDC with sponsorship from MCHB. The surveys have used the State and Local Area Integrated Telephone Survey (SLAITS) mechanism with respondents sampled through random-digit telephone dialing. Surveys using the SLAITS mechanism provide estimates at the state level as well as the national level. The National Survey of Children with Special Health Care Needs (NS-CSHCN) was conducted in 2001 and 2005–2006, and the National Survey of Children's Health (NSCH) in 2003 and 2007. Each survey incorporated the CSHCN screener.

The NS-CSHCN surveys collected data on 38,866 children from birth through 17 years of age with SHCN in 2001 and 40,723 children with

Table 3.1. Prevalence estimates of adolescents with special health care needs

Survey	NHIS-D[a]	NS-CSHCN[b]	NSCH[c]	MEPS[d]
Definition of disability	Chronic physical, developmental, behavioral, or emotional condition that required health, developmental, or educational services of a type or amount beyond that required by children generally	CSHCN screener	CSHCN screener	CSHCN screener
Year(s)	1994–1995	2001	2003	2001–2004
Ages (in years)	11–14 and 15–17	12–17	12–17	12–17
Estimate	21.0%–21.5%	15.8%	21.4%	23.9%–24.6%

[a]Newacheck et al. (1998).
[b]Bethell, Read, Blumberg, and Newacheck (2008).
[c]Bethell, Read, Blumberg, and Newacheck (2008).
[d]Bethell, Read, Blumberg, and Newacheck (2008).

Key: NHIS-D, National Health Interview Survey on Disability; NS-CSHCN, National Survey of Children with Special Health Care Needs; NSCH, National Survey of Children's Health; MEPS, Medical Expenditure Panel Survey; CSHCN, children with special health care needs.

SHCN in 2005–2006, and the NSCH collected data on 102,353 children in 2003. Bethell, Read, Blumberg, and Newacheck (2008) reported that in the 2001 NS-CSHCN, the prevalence of SHCN was 15.8% at 12–17 years and in the 2003 NSCH the prevalence in the same age group was 21.4%. Bethell et al. (2008) note that although the two surveys asked the same questions, differences in how they were administered might have led to fewer children being identified with SHCN in the NS-CSHCN, as discussed in detail later in the chapter.

The NS-CSHCN and NSCH included questions about functional and/or activity limitations:

1. In the past 12 months, how often has the child's medical, behavioral, or other health conditions or emotional, developmental, or behavioral problems affected his or her ability to do things other children his or her age do? (response options: never, sometimes, usually, or always)
2. Does the child's condition affect his or her ability to do things a great deal, some, or very little?

The second question was asked only if the response to the first question was sometimes, usually, or always. In both surveys, 21% of children or adolescents with SHCN were reported to have a functional limitation according to the responses to the second question (Bethell et al., 2008). Multiplying this percentage by the respective prevalence estimates of SHCN yields an overall prevalence of function limitation in the two surveys of 2.7% and 3.7%, respectively. However, it is unlikely that all children with functional limitations were identified through the CSHCN screener, because more than one question would be needed to do so reliably.

A separate analysis of 2001 NS-CSHCN data reported that 40% of children or adolescents with SHCN had no functional limitations, 37% had very little or some limitations, and 23% had relatively severe limitations (Nageswaran, Silver, & Stein, 2008). Use of early intervention or special education services was reported for 13%, 25%, and 53% of children in the three respective functional limitations severity categories.

Another survey using the CSHCN screener is the Medical Expenditure Panel Survey—Household Component (MEPS-HC), co-sponsored by the U.S. Agency for Healthcare Research and Quality and CDC and linked to the National Health Interview Survey (NHIS; see following section). In 2000, the CSHCN screener was included in a parent-administered questionnaire; since 2001, it has been included in the Child Health and Preventive Care section of the MEPS-HC, which has resulted in more consistent administration. An analysis of MEPS-HC data from 2001, 2002, 2003, and 2004 showed stable prevalence of SHCN both overall, 18.8%-19.3%, and among adolescents ages 12–17 years, 23.9%-24.6% (Bethell et al., 2008). Logistic regressions of data from the 2001 NS-CSHCN, 2003 NSCH, and 2004 MEPS-HC consistently show the adjusted odds ratios for presence of a SHCN to be approximately 1.5 for family income below the poverty level, 0.7 for females, 0.8 for Hispanics, and 0.3–0.5 for use of Spanish language in the interview (Bethell et al.).

An analysis of data from the 2000 MEPS-HC examined the degree of overlap between SHCN and special education among children ages 5–17 years (Sices, Harman, & Kelleher, 2007). Overall, 4.3% of children were reported to receive special education services and 15.2% to have SHCN, with 2.6% of children dually classified as both having SHCN and receiving special education.

Overall Disability

A number of national surveys collect information on children, adolescents, or adults with various types of disabilities defined on the basis of functional or activity limitations. This section reviews those surveys, grouped according to the federal department or agency responsible for data collection. Tables 3.2 and 3.3 summarize prevalence estimates by age group, with estimates for children and adolescents summarized in Table 3.2 and for adolescents and young adults in Table 3.3.

Table 3.2. Prevalence estimates of children or adolescents with disabilities

Survey	NHIS-D[a]	NHIS-D[b]	NHIS[c]	MEPS[d]
Definition of disability	Activity limitations due to a chronic condition	Four types of disabilities described by an activity limitation	Activity or functional limitations; self-care; communication; mobility; learning; or attention or ADD/ADHD	Use of early intervention or special education and activity limitations
Year(s)	1992–1994	1994	1998–2004	1999–2000
Ages (in years)	Birth–17	5–17	5–17	Birth–17
Estimate	Birth–17: 6.5% 12–17: 8.4%	9.0% disability 12.3% functional limitations	18% (1998–2003) 20% (2004)	Birth–17: 7.3% 12–17: 7.5%

[a]Newacheck and Halfon (1998).
[b]Hogan, Msall, Rogers, and Avery (1997).
[c]Child Trends Databank (n.d.).
[d]Newacheck, Inkelas, and Kim (2004).
Key: NHIS-D, National Health Interview Survey on Disability; NHIS, National Health Interview Survey; MEPS, Medical Expenditure Panel Survey; ADD/ADHD, attention-deficit disorder/attention-deficit/hyperactivity disorder.

Table 3.3. Prevalence estimates of adolescents and young adults with disabilities

Survey	MEPS[a]	ACS[b]	SIPP[c]	SIPP[d]	Add Health[e]
Definition of disability	Any limitation	Four types of disability identified for participants age ≥ 5 years: sensory disability, physical disability, mental disability, self-care disability Two additional types of disability for participants age ≥ 15 years: go-outside-the-home disability and employment disability	"Severe" disability—unable to perform an activity or needed help to perform an activity; or report of a condition that limited the ability to work around the house or made it difficult to remain employed; or used a wheelchair, a cane, crutches, or a walker. "Non-severe" disability—reported learning disability or mental or emotional condition that did not seriously interfere with everyday activities	Report of learning or mental impairments, limit in functional activities, limitation in ability to work, limitation in activities of daily living or instrumental activities of daily living, or use of assistive devices	Physical disability, functional limitations, and personal care assistance needed
Year	2005	2003	2005	2001	1996
Ages (in years) or grades; estimate	14–18; 5.0% 19–23; 10.5% 24–28; 12.6%	15–17; 6.3% any disability 18–24; 6.5% any disability	15–24; 5.4% non-severe disability 15–24; 5.0% severe disability	16–25; 11.4% met "some" criteria for disability	Grades 7–12; 6.0%

[a]Valluzzi, Grosse, Newacheck, unpublished data.
[b]Weathers (2005).
[c]Brault (2008)
[d]Callahan and Cooper (2007).
[e]Cheng and Udry (2002).

Key: MEPS, Medical Expenditure Panel Survey; ACS; American Community Survey; SIPP, Survey of Income and Program Participation; Add Health, National Longitudinal Study of Adolescent Health.

U.S. Department of Health and Human Services Surveys The U.S. Department of Health and Human Services sponsors three ongoing household surveys to collect information on disability using nationally representative samples of the civilian, noninstitutionalized population, as well as two national surveys using state-based samples. First, each year since 1957, CDC has conducted the NHIS, which includes multiple questions about functional limitations, activity limitations, and impairments. Second, the Agency for Healthcare Research and Quality and CDC cosponsor the MEPS, which has been conducted by the Agency for Healthcare Research and Quality since 1996 using a subset of the NHIS sample from the preceding year. Third, the National Health and Nutrition Examination Survey (NHANES), conducted continuously by CDC since 1999, collects information on functional and activity limitations from a relatively small sample of individuals; NHANES participants also undergo physical examinations and the collection of biological specimens.

The core NHIS instrument, redesigned in 1997, consists of three modules: a brief family module to collect limited information on each family member and adult and child modules that are completed for one randomly selected adult and child per household. The family module contains a series of questions about household members 3 years or older relating to self-care limitations—both personal care items included as activities of daily living (ADLs) and independent living items included as instrumental activities of daily living (IADLs)—due to a physical, mental, or emotional problem. Respondents are asked about play limitations for children younger than 5 years of age, use of special education or early intervention services for children younger than 18 years of age, and work disability for individuals ages 18 years or older. Finally, the family module includes questions on walking without special equipment, problems with remembering, and limitations due to a physical, mental, or emotional problem. For each individual who is reported to have an activity limitation, the questionnaire asks what condition or conditions cause the limitations.

Currie and Lin (2007) analyzed pooled data on children from the 2001–2005 waves of the NHIS family core module. They calculated that among adolescents ages 13–17 years, 7.8% of those in households with incomes above the poverty level and 14.1% of those in households with incomes below the federal poverty level (18.8% of all children were reported to live in poverty) had one or more activity limitations. Roughly 10 times as many children were reported to have trouble hearing or seeing as were reported with activity limitations for which hearing or vision problems were the cause.

NCHS has created two disability scales for adults using NHIS data, one reflecting "complex activity limitation" and the other, "basic actions difficulty" (Altman & Bernstein, 2008). Complex activity refers to the ability to conduct tasks necessary for the performance of social roles, including work, leisure, and household maintenance. This category has three subtypes: self-care limitation (ADLs or IADLs), social limitation, and work limitation. Social limitation is defined through three NHIS questions:

By yourself, and without using any special equipment, how difficult is it for you to

- Go out to things like shopping, movies, or sporting events?
- Participate in social activities such as visiting friends, attending clubs and meetings, or going to parties?
- Do things to relax at home or for leisure (reading, watching TV, sewing, listening to music)?

Basic actions, according to NCHS, refer to limitations in movement, sensory, emotional, and cognitive functioning without the use of assistive devices. During 2001–2005, nearly 30% of U.S. adults included in the NHIS sample reported difficulty with one or more basic actions, mostly movement or sensory functioning (Altman & Bernstein, 2008). These questions do not specify duration of limitations. For self-care and cognitive disability, NCHS required that a condition causing the limitation be present for at least 3 months. Most disability surveys require a condition causing a limitation to be present for at least 12 months for the individual to be classified as having a disability.

Altman and Bernstein (2008) reported prevalence of limitations or disability for adults ages 18–44 years using the pooled 2001–2005 NHIS sample. Overall, 18.2% of individuals in this age group were reported to have some type of disability, with 16.7% reporting basic actions difficulties and 6.8% reporting complex activity limitations. The most common basic actions difficulties in the 18–44 age group were movement limitations, reported by 10.3%, and difficulty seeing or hearing without assistive devices, reported by 6.8%. Relatively few younger adults reported cognitive difficulties (1.2%) or self-care limitations (1.4%). The most common complex activity limitation was work disability, reported by 5.4% of respondents.

Beginning in 1997, the NHIS child core module incorporated 13 questions on activity or functional limitations, including 6 questions on self-care, 2 on communication, 2 on mobility, and 3 on learning or attention (Wells & Hogan, 2003). These data are collected from a parent or other household respondent for children and adolescents ages 5–17 years. A reduced set of 6 questions identified 99.7% of all children identified by the complete set of 13 questions (Wells & Hogan, 2003). The percentage of children ages 5–17 years who have one or more limitations according to these six questions was reported to be stable at 17%–18% from 1998 through 2003; it rose to 20% in 2004 (Child Trends Databank, n.d.).

An unpublished analysis of disability prevalence for 24,324 children ages 5–17 years in the 2004–2006 NHIS compared two different operational definitions of disability (Pastor & Reuben, 2007). The study found that the prevalence of limitations for children ages 12–17 years was 19.0% using the Child Trends Databank definition that is based on a communication, mobility, learning, or attention limitation and 9.0% using an operational definition from the Federal Interagency Forum on Child and Family Statistics (2008) that is based on use of special education, difficulty remembering, need for help with personal care, difficulty walking, or any other limitation. For all children, Pastor and Reuben reported that the Interagency Forum definition was dominated by use of special education, which alone identified 78% of children with disabilities. The Child Trends definition was dominated by attention-deficit/hyperactivity disorder (ADHD) and learning disabilities; using that definition, 68% of children had ADHD or a learning disability reported with no activity limitation mentioned.

Because of the redesign, data from the NHIS, including the NHIS-D, before and after 1997 are not directly comparable. Newacheck and Halfon (1998) analyzed data for roughly 100,000 children pooled from the 1992, 1993, and 1994 NHIS samples and reported that based on the questions about activity limitations due to a chronic condition, 6.5% of all children experienced disability. Among adolescents ages 12–17 years, the prevalence of disability was 8.4%. These figures compare with SHCN prevalence of 18% and 21%, respectively (Newacheck et al., 1998), implying that about 40% of the adolescents with SHCN had a disability. However, the pre-1997 NHIS questions did not ask questions about children's limitations in ability to walk or run and thereby slightly understate child disability (Wells & Hogan, 2003).

The NHIS-D consisted of two phases of data collection. Phase I, or the NHIS Disability Supplement, was asked of all individuals in the 1994 and 1995 NHIS samples, a total of more than 200,000 people. It included some questions that were asked only of adults (e.g., IADLs, functional limitations); others that were asked of participants of all ages (including vision, hearing, and mobility aids; ADLs; and perceived disability); and others asked only for children (including special health care needs and use of special education). Phase II of the NHIS-D, or the Disability Follow-Back Survey, collected additional information for individuals found to have a disability in either Phase I or the NHIS core, including medically diagnosed problems or conditions and the use of medical facilities, medications, and special diets and equipment.

An analysis of 1994 NHIS-D data for 21,415 children and adolescents ages 5–17 years used multiple measures of disabilities (Hogan, Msall, Rogers, & Avery, 1997). Disability as measured by limitations in school and other activities was reported for 9.0%. Additional questions indicated that 12.3% of children and adolescents had some type of functional limitation, of which 10.6% of children had a limitation in their learning ability, 5.5% had a limitation in communication, 1.3% had a limitation in mobility, and 0.9% had a limitation in self-care. Eight percent of children and adolescents had one or more "serious" functional limitations. Hogan and colleagues also reported that 3.5% of children were considered by their parents or others to have a disability.

A subsequent analysis by Msall et al. (2003) of data for 41,300 children and adolescents from the pooled 1994 and 1995 NHIS-D samples reported that 15%–18% of children with chronic medical conditions, including asthma, had severe disability, compared with 4.7% of those with no reported medical condition or use of medical services. Chronic medical conditions had a stronger association with school disability. Of those with a medical impairment, 20.1% used special education services and 4.7% were unable to attend school (asthma was the leading cause of attendance difficulties); of those without a reported medical condition, 2.4% received special education services, and 0.3% were unable to attend school. Overall, 4.1% of school-age children were reported to receive special education services and 0.7% were unable to attend school.

The MEPS-HC collects information from individuals ages 17 years and older (or from proxy respondents if unavailable) and from parents of children younger than 17 years. Respondents are a subset of individuals included in the NHIS core sample from the previous year. Thus, the 2005–2006 MEPS-HC sample was derived from the 2004 NHIS, and linked files are available (Agency for Healthcare Research and Quality, 2008). To measure disability, a constructed any limitation (ANYLIM) variable in the MEPS-HC file indicates whether a survey participant has a limitation in IADLs, ADLs, life role activities such as school or work, walking, seeing, or hearing. Prevalence of disability, as measured by the ANYLIM variable, increased with age in the 2005 MEPS-HC within the target age range: 14–18 years old, 5.0%; 19–23 years old, 10.5%; 24–28 years old, 12.6%. The increase in reported prevalence of disability at the 18-year cutoff may reflect a jump in reported activity limitations due to the rapidly paced and amplified demands placed on individuals as they enter young adulthood and a change from parental report to self-report.

An analysis of 1999–2000 MEPS-HC data for 13,792 children ages birth through 17 years combined information on activity limitations and early intervention or special education to classify children as having a disability (Newacheck, Inkelas, & Kim, 2004). The prevalence of disability using this definition was 7.3% overall and 7.5% at 12–17 years. Prevalence was higher among white non-Hispanic respondents, those in families with income less than 200% of the federal poverty level, and males. Prevalence of disability was higher among those with health insurance (7.4%) than among the uninsured (5.5%). This finding may reflect a higher likelihood that children with chronic health problems are enrolled in public insurance, but the analysis did not distinguish between public and private insurance status.

NHANES collects data from about 5,000 individuals of all ages each year, and participants also undergo clinical and laboratory examinations. Individuals are asked about the degree of difficulty, if any, experienced in each of 16 areas of function or ADLs (Cook et al., 2006). Regrettably, no report of NHANES data on disability among youth was identified.

CDC and state health departments conduct two state-based surveys of the civilian, noninstitutionalized population using random-digit telephone dialing: the Behavioral Risk Factor Surveillance System (BRFSS) and the National Youth Risk Behavior Surveillance System (YRBS). The BRFSS collects information each year from roughly 350,000 adults ages 18 years and older selected randomly from sampled households. The BRFSS contains two disability questions:

1. Are you limited in any way in any activities because of physical, mental, or emotional problems?

2.   Do you now have any health problem that requires you to use special equipment, such as a cane, a wheelchair, a special bed, or a special telephone?

Individuals who respond positively to either question are classified as having a disability (CDC, 2008).

In addition, an optional BRFSS Disability Supplement has been collected in certain states in different years. For example, the Disability Supplement collected in the state of Washington in 2001 included two additional census questions on mental and self-care disability, and the 2003 supplement included all six disability questions included in the 2000 census (Kinne & Topolski, 2005). A comparison of data showed that the prevalence of census-defined disability among adults ages 18 years and older in Washington was 18.2% in the 2000 census and 29.3% in the 2003 BRFSS Disability Supplement, which had a 48% response rate. It appears that people with disabilities are considerably more likely to respond to the BRFSS, which therefore yields a higher prevalence estimate for a given definition of disability (Kinne & Topolski, 2005).

The YRBS is a national school-based sample of high school (grades 9–12) students. Every other year, approximately 15,000 students are surveyed. This survey has a three-stage cluster sample, the third stage of which consists of randomly selecting one or two intact classes of a required subject (e.g., English or social studies) from grades 9–12 at each chosen school (Westat, 2006). The YRBS core module includes two questions related to disability: 1) "Do you have any long-term emotional problems or learning disabilities?" and 2) "Do you have any physical disabilities or long-term health problems?" Neither question distinguishes youth with a disability from those with health issues. In the 2005 YRBS, 10.3% of 13,917 students responded affirmatively to the second question (Everett Jones & Lollar, 2008).

U.S. Census Bureau Surveys   The U.S. Census Bureau collects disability information through the American Community Survey (ACS), which has taken the place of the decennial population census long-form survey, the Survey of Income and Program Participation (SIPP), the Current Population Survey (CPS), as well as the American Time Use Survey, which is administered to a subset of the CPS sample. The ACS from 2000 to 2007 asked certain questions for all noninstitutionalized Americans ages 5 years and older, and other questions were asked only for adults ages 16 years and older (Stern & Brault, 2005; Waldrop & Stern, 2003). Beginning in 2006, the ACS has also included people living in group quarters (Brault, 2008).

A redesign of the ACS in 2003 makes disability statistics difficult to compare directly with previous estimates in part because of changes in skip patterns (Stern & Brault, 2005). From 2003 through 2007, the ACS collected data on four types of disability for people ages 5 years and older:

• Sensory Disability—Conditions that include blindness, deafness, or a severe vision or hearing impairment.

- Physical Disability—Conditions that substantially limit one or more basic physical activities such as walking, climbing stairs, reaching, lifting, or carrying.
- Mental Disability—Difficulty learning, remembering, or concentrating because of a physical, mental, or emotional condition lasting 6 months or more.
- Self-Care Disability—Difficulty dressing, bathing, or getting around inside the home because of a physical, mental, or emotional condition lasting 6 months or more.

Information on two other types of disability was collected for adolescents ages 15 years and older (Weathers, 2005), although this information was made publicly available only for those ages 16 and older (M. Brault, personal communication, May 12, 2009):

- Go-Outside-Home Disability—Difficulty going outside the home alone to shop or visit a doctor's office because of a physical, mental, or emotional condition lasting 6 months or more.
- Employment Disability—Difficulty working at a job or business because of a physical, mental, or emotional condition lasting 6 months or more.

An analysis of 2003 ACS data by age group reported that the prevalence of any type of disability was stable between the 15–17 and 18–24 age groups: 6.3% and 6.5%, respectively (Weathers, 2005). By type of disability, prevalence rates for the two age groups were 2.0% and 2.8% for employment disability and 1.3% and 1.5% for go-outside-home disability. Comparing the 5–17 and 18–24 age groups, the prevalence was 0.8% and 0.7% for self-care disability, 5.1% and 3.7% for mental disability, 1.2% and 2.1% for physical disability, and 1.1% and 1.4% for sensory disability (Weathers, 2005). An analysis of ACS 2007 public use data found that the prevalence of disability in the 16–20 age group was 6.8% overall, with prevalence of 0.7% for self-care disability, 4.6% for mental disability, 1.6% for physical disability, 1.3% for sensory disability, 2.4% for employment disability, and 1.6% for go-outside-home disability (Erickson & Lee, 2008). These data indicate low sensitivity of prevalence estimates to the exact ages included.

In 2008, the ACS underwent yet another redesign of disability survey questions (Brault, 2008). The employment disability question was dropped and the sensory disability question was split into separate questions on hearing and vision limitations, which were asked of all household residents regardless of age. The following questions were asked in the 2008 ACS, the third, fourth and fifth of which were asked of individuals ages 5 and older and the last of which was asked of individuals ages 15 and over (M. Brault, personal communication, May 26, 2008):

- Is this person deaf or does he or she have serious difficulty hearing?
- Is this person blind or does he or she have serious difficulty seeing even when wearing glasses?
- Because of a physical, mental, or emotional condition, does this person have serious difficulty concentrating, remembering, or making decisions?
- Does this person have serious difficulty walking or climbing stairs?

- Does this person have difficulty dressing or bathing?
- Because of a physical, mental, or emotional condition, does this person have difficulty doing errands alone, such as visiting a doctor's office or shopping?

Although the number of disability questions remained the same, only two questions yielded prevalence estimates similar to the 2006 ACS Content Test (Brault, 2008). One of these two is the last question, which yielded similar responses to the previous go-outside-home disability question.

The SIPP attempts to collect information directly from each individual ages 15 years and older in sampled households. The SIPP, conducted since 1996, is a continuous series of national panels with a multistage, stratified random sample. The duration of the 2004 panel was 2.5 years, during which a series of eight interviews were conducted by computer-aided personal interviewing for a sample of 46,500 households. The SIPP includes disability and health questions, along with detailed data on employment, earnings, assets, and receipt of public benefits or services. The 2001 panel included an Adult Disability Topical Module with 49 questions on health and functional limitations for respondents ages 15 years and older.

The SIPP includes 7 disability items for children ages 6–14 years and 11 items for adolescents and adults ages 15 years and older (Brault, 2008). The latter include three pairs of items on functional activities, ADLs, and IADLs that distinguish "difficulties" from tasks participants were "unable to perform or needed help to perform." For instance, individuals who report a learning disability or a mental or emotional condition that does not seriously interfere with everyday activities are classified as having "non-severe" disability, whereas those who report mental retardation or developmental disability or a mental or emotional condition that seriously interferes with everyday activities are classified as having severe disability. Anyone who reports a condition that limits the ability to work around the house or makes it difficult to remain employed or who uses a wheelchair, a cane, crutches, or a walker is classified as having severe disability (Brault, 2008). In 2005, an estimated 5.4% of individuals ages 15–24 years had a non-severe disability, and 5.0% had a severe disability.

An analysis of disability in the 2001 SIPP included 5,170 subjects ages 16–25 years at the first interview who had complete data (Callahan & Cooper, 2007). Overall, 11.4% met one or more criteria for disability, of whom 58% met multiple criteria. The highest prevalence rates were for learning or mental disabilities (5.5%), functional limitations (5.1%), and work disability (4.2%). The prevalence of disability did not vary appreciably by age group within this age range but was markedly higher among those with lower income levels and among non-Hispanic blacks.

Because the SIPP is a panel survey, it is possible to assess the test-retest reliability of disability measures. Unfortunately, measures are often answered differently in different waves. For example, a majority of people who reported at one time being unable to see the words in a newspaper reported a year or two later that they had no visual impairments (McNeil, 2001). The Disability Statistics Center (n.d.) found in an analysis of the 1996 SIPP panel that 40% of children reported as having special education services in one wave were later reported as never having used special education services.

Until 2008, the CPS only collected information on work disability, defined as being limited in ability to work or being unable to work. In June 2008, questions were added to the CPS to identify people with a disability in the civilian, noninstitutionalized population ages 16 years and older. The collection of these data is sponsored by the U.S. Department of Labor's Office of Disability Employment Policy. Publication of CPS disability data began in February 2009 (Bureau of Labor Statistics, n.d.). The six questions used to identify people with a disability in the new CPS are the same as those included in the 2008 ACS redesign (described previously) and do not include employment disability. The number of adults ages 16 years and older with disabilities in the February 2009 CPS was estimated to be 26.7 million, about half as many as previously reported using other data sources and definitions.

U.S. Department of Labor Surveys   Two National Longitudinal Survey of Youth (NLSY) have been sponsored by the Bureau of Labor Statistics, U.S. Department of Labor. The first, the NLSY79, conducted by Ohio State University, collected data for 12,686 people ages 14–21 years in 1979. Interviews were conducted with NLSY79 participants annually through 1994 and biennially since then. The NLSY79 collects information on health-related work limitations and the receipt of disability-related federal benefits for adult respondents. Since 1986, the offspring of all female NLSY79 respondents have been included in biennial Children and Young Adult Surveys, funded by the National Institute for Child Health and Human Development. The 2002 survey collected data on 3,229 children ages 14 and younger and 4,238 young adults ages 15 years and older, including more than 1,700 who were 21 years or older. The only disability-related questions asked of respondents 15 years or older are whether their health limits work or school activities (Bureau of Labor Statistics, 2006).

A second NLSY survey, the NLSY97, enrolled 8,984 youth who were 12–16 years old at the end of 1996 and who have been followed up annually. Information was collected from parents on four domains of activity limitations of their adolescent: learning or emotional disability, sensory limitations, physical disability, and chronic illness associated with disability. Parents were also asked about use of special education services. For each measure, respondents were asked about the presence of the condition both in the present and in the past and whether their children were currently limited a lot, a little, or not at all. An analysis of cross-sectional data from 1997 reported that of 2,780 youth ages 12–14 years living in two-parent families, 10.2% were "limited a little" and 2.1% were "limited a lot"; the equivalent percentages for 1,110 youth living in single-mother families were 14.0% and 4.1% (Hogan, Shandra, & Msall, 2007).

Other Surveys The National Longitudinal Study of Adolescent Health (Add Health) is a longitudinal study conducted by the Carolina Population Center at the University of North Carolina with a sample of 20,745 U.S. adolescents who were in grades 7–12 during the 1994–1995 school year. The Add Health cohort was followed into adulthood with 15,197 young adults roughly 18–26 years old interviewed during 2001–2002. In Wave 1, respondents were asked about physical disability:

> Do you: (a) have difficulty using your limbs because of a permanent physical condition; (b) use a cane, crutches, a walker, medically prescribed shoes, a wheelchair, or a scooter to get around; (c) use a brace; (d) use an artificial limb?

Based on responses to these questions, participants were asked the specifics of their disabilities, functional limitations, and personal-care assistance. In Wave 1, 6.0% had some level of physical disability or sensory impairment (Cheng & Udry, 2002).

Also in Wave 1 of Add Health, parents (available for 84.6% of the youth sample) were asked whether the child had a learning disability, including difficulties with attention, dyslexia, reading, spelling, writing, or math. Parents were also asked if the child had received special education services. Among 16,340 adolescents with parent-reported data, 1,603 were reported to have a learning disability and to have received special education services, for a prevalence of 9.8% (Svetaz, Ireland, & Blum, 2000). Students with learning disabilities were significantly more likely to be male (by 2 to 1), African American or Hispanic, and to live in a single-parent family.

Finally, the Panel Study on Income Dynamics (PSID) is a longitudinal cohort study followed since 1967. The PSID collects data from adults on health-related limitations in the amount or type of work and the receipt of disability-related benefits. Since 2003, the PSID has collected data from respondents ages 18 years or older on limitations in ADLs and IADLs and whether a doctor has ever told them that they had 1) emotional, nervous, or psychiatric problems; 2) permanent loss of memory or loss of mental ability; or 3) a learning disorder (Burkhauser, Weathers, and Schroeder, 2006). Data from the 2003 PSID for 449 adults ages 18–24 years indicate that 14.9% had some type of mental health, cognitive, or learning problems. Work disability was reported by 11.4% of respondents in this age group, IADL disability by 4.2%, and ADL or self-care disability by 1.6%.

Since 1997, a PSID Child Development Supplement has collected information on physical health, activity limitations, emotional well-being, intellectual achievement, and social relationships for a sample of 3,500 children from birth through 12 years old in 1997. In 2005 and 2007, a Transition to Adulthood module was administered to those individuals who had reached 18 years of age and were no longer enrolled in high school.

Service-Specific Disability

Two major disability programs are special education services and SSA disability benefits. Surveys of beneficiaries of these programs provide important information on the characteristics of adolescents and young adults with SHCN or disabilities.

U.S. Department of Education Surveys The U.S. Department of Education and its partners have conducted two national longitudinal surveys in which parents were asked about special education services received by their children. First, the National Educational Longitudinal Study of 1988 (NELS:88), conducted by the National Center for Education Statistics, included a stratified random sample of 24,599 students and had follow-ups through 1994 and in 2000. Respondents were approximately 26 years old in 2000. The NELS:88 data show relatively little overlap among measures of disability and special education services (Rossi, Herting, & Wolman, 1997). Approximately 12% of 1,602 8th-graders identified by parents as having a disability had ever been in special education, and among 368 students who had received special education services, 50% were classified by their parents as having a disability, impairment, or health problem. Second, the National Center for Education Statistics is currently conducting the Education Longitudinal Study of 2002 to monitor the transition of young people from 10th grade through to postsecondary education or the world of work. It follows a nationally representative cohort of high school sophomores, who were re-interviewed in 2004 and 2006.

Two national longitudinal surveys have identified adolescents receiving special education services and tracked them through the early transition to adulthood. First, the National Longitudinal Transition Study (NLTS) followed more than 8,000 youth ages 13–21 years enrolled in special education within secondary schools during 1985–1986 for 3 to 5 years after they left school. Outcomes include school completion, postsecondary education, employment, earnings, and involvement with the criminal justice system. A subsequent 10-year study, NLTS2, started with a national sample of more than 11,000 youth ages 13–16 years in December 2000 who were receiving special education services in grade 7 or above. Comparing the NLTS and NLTS2 cohorts, the most dramatic shift was a rise in the percentage of respondents who did not use English as their primary language at home: 3.3% in 1987 and 14.2% in 2001. The comparable shift in the general U.S. population ages 15–19 years during the same time was from 3.5% to 5.0%. Postsecondary school outcomes for the NLTS and NLTS2 cohorts showed a 17-percentage-point increase in high school completion, 70% in 2003, and a doubling in the percentage with postsecondary schooling, to 32%, mostly in 2-year colleges (Wagner, Newman, Cameto, & Levine, 2005). Employment outcomes did not differ between the 1987 and 2003 surveys.

Wells, Sandefur, and Hogan (2003) analyzed NELS and NLTS data. They noted that the two samples differed in multiple ways, including the exclusion from the NELS sample of students who could not complete the written questionnaire. For the NELS, they compared 1,570 respondents who reported a disability (NELS-D) and 10,920 who did not, and for NLTS 5,297 respondents who had all been in special education. The NLTS sample had much lower attainments than the NELS sample. For example, 22% of females in the NLTS sample reported ever attending postsecondary school compared with 48% of the NELS-D sample and 68% of the NELS sample that did not report a disability. The percentages reporting independent living were 32%, 59%, and 53%, respectively. The patterns for males were similar.

Another survey, the Special Education Elementary Longitudinal Study, provides information on the transition from childhood to adolescence for roughly 13,000 special education students who were ages 6–13 years in 2000 and 12–18 years when the study ended in 2006 (U.S. Office of Special Education Programs, n.d.). Data collected in 2000 showed that fewer Hispanics received special education services (14%) compared with all students (17%), and children living in poverty constituted 24% of those enrolled in special education compared with 17% of all students (Wagner & Blackorby, 2004). The most common functional limitations were in mobility (20%), vision (20%), and hearing (8%). Parental agreement with school classifications was 65% for children classified as having a learning disability and 30% for those classified as having mental retardation.

Social Security Administration Data Data on individuals receiving disability benefits are available from the SSA, which administers the Social Security Disability Insurance (SSDI) program and the Supplemental Security Income (SSI) disability program. In 2003, these programs paid cash benefits to nearly 11.2 million people with disabilities. More than 90% of these individuals were adults, including all enrolled in SSDI.

Data on SSI beneficiaries, both adolescents and young adults, are available from SSA data and the 2001–2002 National Survey of SSI Children and Families, which includes those receiving SSI at the end of 2000 or who previously received or applied for SSI payments and were not institutionalized. A mental disability was reported by 56% of children ages 6–12 years and 59% of adolescents ages 13–17 years. About 76% of children reported receiving special education services within the past 12 months, compared with 51% of adolescents, although 60% of adolescents reported having an individual education plan (Rupp et al., 2005–2006). Approximately 2% of U.S. adolescents received SSI payments during 2007 (SSA, 2008).

DISCUSSION

The prevalence of disability or special needs among Americans varies depending on the age group studied and the definition and data source employed. Many data sources are restricted to children and adolescents, including all data about SHCN, which are restricted to the birth to 17-year-old age range for these surveys and do not extend across the continuum of age ranges encompassed by the transition process. Four national data sources identify both adolescents and adults with disabilities using the same identifying questions: the MEPS-HC (all ages), the SIPP and ACS (15 years and older), and the CPS since 2008 (16 years and older). The state-specific prevalences of disability or SHCN among youth might be associated with differences in criteria for eligibility for programs such as special education services.

The prevalence of disability or special needs among adolescents varies from roughly 24% for SHCN to 2% for SSI disability. Typical estimates of overall disability for adolescents are in the range of 6%–10%, with the singular exception of the Child Trends definition using post-1997 NHIS data, for which the prevalence is close to 20% (Child Trends Databank, n.d.; Pastor & Reuben, 2007). A number of researchers include either use of assistive devices or impairments as indicating disability even though individuals using assistive devices do not necessarily report activity limitations or consider themselves to have a disability. The prevalence of education-related disability among adolescents is higher, 10%–15%. The reported prevalence of work-related disability among adolescents and young adults ranges from 3% to 11%, but this is a problematic concept for these age groups. It is interesting to note that the ACS and CPS in 2008 stopped attempting to measure employment disability, reportedly because of difficulties some respondents had in understanding the question (Brault, 2008).

The majority of youth classified under one measure are not typically classified under another measure. Data reviewed in this chapter reveal that most youth with education-related disability (i.e., learning disability or receipt of special education services) do not meet commonly used criteria for functional disability or elevated medical needs and vice versa, although they meet both the ICF and ADA definitions of activity limitations and disability. The greatest overlap is found for severe disabilities. For example, roughly three quarters of youth receiving SSI benefits also receive special education services. Investigators must specify which population is of interest for a given analysis and choose data sets and measures accordingly.

The demographic characteristics of youth with disabilities also differ by type of measure. Using measures of SHCN or disability as reported by parents or youth, Hispanic youth appear to have a lower prevalence than youth in other racial and ethnic groups. This difference is most marked among individuals living in households where Spanish is the primary language of communication (Bethell, Read, Blumberg & Newacheck, 2008). Conversely, children living in Spanish-speaking households are overrepresented among youth with education-related disability according to one source (Wagner, Newman, Cameto & Levine, 2005) but not another (Wagner & Blackorby, 2004). An important research need is an improved understanding of how individuals in Spanish-speaking households define disability and special needs.

Cross-sectional survey data are potentially useful for descriptive purposes, but most surveys cover either only children and adolescents or only adults. Surveys with disability questions asked about both adolescents and adults are the ACS, NHIS, SIPP, and MEPS-HC. The MEPS-HC yields estimates of disability prevalence that differ between adolescents and adults, whereas the ACS provides similar estimates of the prevalence of disability and impairments for adolescents (15 years and older) and young adults. The ACS has the advantages of a larger sample size and the ability to provide state and sub-state estimates, but it lacks data on health status. The U.S. Government Accountability Office (2008) has noted that, although data on individuals with disabilities are collected on a national level, these data do not share consistent definitions of disability and as a result cannot be easily compiled to create a comprehensive picture of the status of individuals with disabilities.

The construct validity of survey questions on activity limitation is likely to differ between children and adults because of differences in constructs of play, school, work, and housework and of transition in expectations regarding roles and tasks. An implication is that individuals with the same level of impairment may report a disability in one age group, but not in another. Differences in reported limitations across age groups may reflect changes in body function or structure, activities and participation, or the environment. Access to school health or health-related services, such as physical, occupational, or speech therapy, that assist in sustaining health, function, and educational readiness may be lost or fragmented upon leaving the secondary education system (Zuckerbrod, 2008). For example, a young adult with a mobility limitation who lacks access to public transportation may report having a higher level of activity limitation than a similar young adult who has such access. Consequently, we are limited in the ability to use cross-sectional data to make inferences about the dynamic process of how individuals move between age groups.

To describe patterns of transition to adulthood, it is essential that longitudinal cohort studies be used that identify youth with special needs or disabilities and follow them into adulthood, preferably for the full 14 to 28 years of age range targeted in this volume. The most promising of such longitudinal data sets are the NLSY97, Add Health, and the Education Longitudinal Study of 2002. The Transition to Adulthood module of the PSID may also prove useful, although it is not clear whether the number of youth with disabilities will prove sufficiently large for stratified statistical analyses. Given the large numbers of adolescents with disabilities making the transition to adulthood each year, consideration should also be given to development of a survey designed specifically to track their well-being and functional status.

Few survey questions address environmental barriers, such as lack of accessible transportation, lack of accessible housing, attitudinal barriers, or system-level barriers. Few survey questions address deficiencies in supports, such as access to assistive technology or personal assistance services to life roles that are essential to effective transition. In accordance with the recommendations of the 2007 Institute of Medicine report *The Future of Disability in America* (2007), the ICF should be used as a framework for further survey and program evaluation development. Also, the quality and compatibility of federal interagency data collection and data analysis should be coordinated and monitored by a federal, interagency group such as the Federal Interagency Forum on Aging Related Statistics (2007). The U.S. Government Accountability Office (2008) has called for the creation of an interagency entity that would coordinate federal disability programs as well as data collection efforts.

Transition to adulthood is a dynamic, multidimensional process that takes place over an extended period of time. Future research should examine the growing diversity of the target population and its relationship to factors such as reporting of activity limitations, access to health care, education, and employment. Standardized definitions of disability are needed, as are longitudinal cohort studies that collect information on each dimension of transition as well as measures of family and community context. In the absence of better data, it is difficult to draw inferences about the transition process for youth with disabilities or special needs.

REFERENCES

Agency for Healthcare Research and Quality. (2008). *MEPS HC-106: MEPS Panel 10* [Longitudinal Data File]. Retrieved April 24, 2009, from http://www.meps.ahrq.gov/mepsweb/data_stats/download_data/pufs/h106/h106doc.pdf

Altman, B., & Bernstein, A. (2008). *Disability and health in the United States, 2001–2005.* Hyattsville, MD: National Center for Health Statistics. Retrieved February 17, 2009, from http://www.cdc.gov/nchs/data/misc/disability2001–2005.pdf

Americans with Disabilities Act (ADA) of 1990, PL 101-336, 42 U.S.C. §§ 12101 *et seq.*

Bethell, C.D., Read, D., Blumberg, S.J., & Newacheck, P.W. (2008). What is the prevalence of children with special health care needs? Toward an understanding of variations in findings and methods across three national surveys. *Maternal and Child Health Journal, 12,* 1–14.

Bethell, C.D., Read, D., Stein, R.E., Blumberg, S.J., Wells, N., & Newacheck, P.W. (2002). Identifying children with special health care needs: Development and evaluation of a short screening instrument. *Ambulatory Pediatrics, 2,* 38–48.

Brault, M. (2008). *Americans with disabilities: 2005,* Current Population Reports, P70-117, U.S. Census Bureau, Washington, DC. Retrieved April 4, 2009, from http://www.census.gov/prod/2008pubs/p70-117.pdf

Bureau of Labor Statistics. (2006). Children of the NLSY79. In *NLS Handbook, 2005.* Retrieved May 17, 2009, from http://www.bls.gov/nls/handbook/2005/nlshc4.pdf

Bureau of Labor Statistics. (n.d.). *Labor force statistics from the Current Population Survey.* Retrieved May 8, 2009, from http://www.bls.gov/cps/cpsdisability.htm

Burkhauser, R., Weathers, R., II, & Schroeder, M. (2006). *A guide to disability statistics from the Panel Study of Income Dynamics.* Ithaca, NY: Rehabilitation Research and Training Center on Disability Demographics and Statistics, Cornell University. Retrieved February 14, 2009, from http://digitalcommons.ilr.cornell.edu/cgi/viewcontent.cgi?article=1207&context=edicollect

Callahan, S.T., & Cooper, W.O. (2007). Continuity of health insurance coverage among young adults with disabilities. *Pediatrics, 119,* 1175–1180.

Centers for Disease Control and Prevention (CDC). (2008). Racial/ethnic disparities in self-rated health status among adults with and without disabilities—United States, 2004–2006. *MMWR Morbidity and Mortality Weekly Report, 57,* 1069–1073.

Cheng, M.M., & Udry, J.R. (2002). Sexual behaviors of physically disabled adolescents in the United States. *Journal of Adolescent Health, 31,* 48–58.

Child Trends Databank. (n.d.). *Children with limitations.* Retrieved April 4, 2009, from http://www.childtrendsdatabank.org/indicators/44ChildLimitations.cfm

Cook, C.E., Richardson, J.K., Pietrobon, R., Braga, L., Silva, H.M., & Turner, D. (2006). Validation of the NHANES ADL scale in a sample of patients with report of cervical pain: Factor analysis, item response theory analysis, and line item validity. *Disability and Rehabilitation, 28,* 929–935.

Currie, J., & Lin, W. (2007). Chipping away at health: More on the relationship between income and child health. *Health Affairs, 26,* 331–344.

Disability Statistics Center. (n.d.). *Survey of Income and Program Participation (SIPP)*. Retrieved May 11, 2009, from http://dsc.ucsf.edu/main.php?name=sipp

Drum, C.E. (2009). Models and approaches to disability. In C.E. Drum, G.L. Krahn, & H. Bersani, Jr. (Eds.), *Disability and public health* (pp. 27–44). Washington, DC: American Public Health Association and American Association of Intellectual and Developmental Disabilities.

Erickson, W., & Lee, C. (2008). *2007 disability status report: United States.* Ithaca, NY: Cornell University Rehabilitation Research and Training Center on Disability Demographics and Statistics. Retrieved May 12, 2009, from http://digitalcommons .ilr.cornell.edu/cgi/viewcontent.cgi?article=1256&context=edicollect

Everett Jones, S., & Lollar, D.J. (2008). Relationship between physical disabilities or long-term health problems and health risk behaviors or conditions among US high school students. *Journal of School Health, 78,* 252–257.

Federal Interagency Forum on Aging Related Statistics. (2007). *History of the forum.* Retrieved February 20, 2008, from http://www.agingstats.gov/Agingstatsdotnet/ Main_Site/About/About_Forum.aspx

Federal Interagency Forum on Child and Family Statistics. (2008). *America's children: Key national indicators of well-being, 2008.* Washington, DC: U.S. Government Printing Office. Retrieved May 19, 2009, from http://childstats.gov

Grosse, S.D., Lollar, D.J., Campbell, V.A., & Chamie, M. (2009). Disability and disability-adjusted life years: Not the same. *Public Health Reports, 124,* 197–202.

Hogan, D.P., Msall, M.E., Rogers, M.L., & Avery, R.C. (1997). Improved disability population estimates of functional limitation among American children aged 5–17. *Maternal and Child Health Journal, 1,* 203–216.

Hogan, D.P., Shandra, C.L., & Msall, M.E. (2007). Family developmental risk factors among adolescents with disabilities and children of parents with disabilities. *Journal of Adolescence, 30,* 1001–1019.

Institute of Medicine. (2007). *The future of disability in America.* Washington, DC: The National Academies Press.

Kinne, S., & Topolski, T.D. (2005). Inclusion of people with disabilities in telephone health surveillance surveys. *American Journal of Public Health, 95,* 512–517.

McNeil, J. (2001). *Americans with disabilities. Current population reports: Household studies, no. 1997.* Retrieved April 24, 2009, from http://www.census.gov/prod/ 2001pubs/p70-73.pdf

McPherson, M., Arango, P., Fox, H., Lauver, C., McManus, M., Newacheck, P.W., Perrin, J.M., Shonkoff, J.P., & Strickland, B. (1998). A new definition of children with special health care needs. *Pediatrics, 102,* 137–140.

Msall, M.E., Avery, R.C., Tremont, M.R., Lima, J.C., Rogers, M.L., & Hogan, D.P. (2003). Functional disability and school activity limitations in 41,300 school-age children: Relationship to medical impairments. *Pediatrics, 111,* 548–553.

Nageswaran, S., Silver, E.J., & Stein, R.E. (2008). Association of functional limitation with health care needs and experiences of children with special health care needs. *Pediatrics, 121,* 994–1001.

Newacheck, P.W., & Halfon, N. (1998). Prevalence and impact of disabling chronic conditions in childhood. *American Journal of Public Health, 88,* 610–617.

Newacheck, P.W., & Halfon, N. (2000). Prevalence, impact, and trends in childhood disability due to asthma. *Archives of Pediatrics and Adolescent Medicine, 154,* 287–293.

Newacheck, P.W., Inkelas, M., & Kim, S.E. (2004). Health services use and health care expenditures for children with disabilities. *Pediatrics, 114,* 79–85.

Newacheck, P.W., Strickland, B., Shonkoff, J.P., Perrin, J.M., McPherson, M., McManus, M., Lauver, C., Fox, H., & Arango, P. (1998). An epidemiologic profile of children with special health care needs. *Pediatrics, 102,* 117–123.

Pastor, P.N., & Reuben, C.A. (2007). *Counting disabled youth: A comparison of two survey measures.* Poster session presented at the annual meeting of the American Public Health Association, Washington, DC.

Rossi, R., Herting, J., & Wolman, J. (1997). *Profiles of students with disabilities as identified in NELS:88.* Washington, DC: U.S. Department of Education, National Center for Education Statistics.

Rupp, K., Davies, P.S., Newcomb, C., Iams, H., Becker, C., Mulpuru, S., Ressler, S., Romig, K., & Miller, B. (2005–2006). A profile of children with disabilities receiving SSI: Highlights from the National Survey of SSI Children and Families. *Social Security Bulletin, 66,* 21–48.

Sices, L., Harman, J.S., & Kelleher, K.J. (2007). Health-care use and expenditures for children in special education with special health-care needs: Is dual classification a marker for high use? *Public Health Reports, 122,* 531–540.

Smith, T.E.C. (2001). *Section 504, the ADA, and public schools.* Retrieved May 7, 2009, from http://www.ldonline.org/article/Section_504,_the_ADA,_and_Public_Schools

Social Security Administration. (2008). *SSI annual statistical report, 2007.* Retrieved February 12, 2009, from http://www.ssa.gov/policy/docs/statcomps/ssi_asr/

Stern, S., & Brault, M. (2005). *Disability data from the American Community Survey: A brief examination of the effects of a question redesign in 2003.* U.S. Census Bureau, Housing and Household Economic Statistics Division. Retrieved February 14, 2009, from http://www.census.gov/hhes/www/disability/ACS_disability.pdf

Svetaz, M.V., Ireland, M., & Blum, R. (2000). Adolescents with learning disabilities: Risk and protective factors associated with emotional well-being: Findings from the National Longitudinal Study of Adolescent Health. *Journal of Adolescent Health, 27,* 340–348.

U.S. Census Bureau. (n.d.). *2000 supplementary survey.* Retrieved November 30, 2009, from http://factfinder.census.gov/servlet/DatasetMainPageServlet?_program=ACS

U.S. Government Accountability Office. (2008). *Federal disability programs: Coordination could facilitate better data collection to assess the status of people with disabilities. GAO-08–872T, a testimony before the House Subcommittee on Information Policy, Census, and National Archives, Committee on Oversight and Government Reform.* Retrieved April 29, 2009, from http://www.gao.gov/new.items/ d08872t.pdf

U.S. Office of Special Education Programs. (n.d.). *SEELS home and news.* Retrieved May 16, 2009, from http://www.seels.net/grindex.html

Valluzzi, J.L., Grosse, S.D., Newacheck, P.W. (2008). *Unpublished tabulations, 2005 Medical Expenditure Panel Survey data,* Atlanta, GA.

Wagner, M., & Blackorby, J. (2004). *Overview of findings from wave 1 of the Special Education Elementary Longitudinal Study (SEELS).* Menlo Park, CA: SRI International. Retrieved May 16, 2009, from http://www.seels.net/designdocs/seels_wave1_9-23–04.pdf

Wagner, M., Newman, L., Cameto, R., & Levine, P. (2005). *Changes over time in the early postschool outcomes of youth with disabilities. A report of findings from the National Longitudinal Transition Study (NLTS) and the National Longitudinal Transition Study-2 (NLTS2).* Menlo Park, CA: SRI International. Retrieved February 14, 2009, from www.nlts2.org/reports/2005_06/nlts2_report_2005_06_complete.pdf

Waldrop, J., & Stern, S.M. (2003). Disability status: 2000. *Census 2000 brief.* Retrieved May 8, 2009, from http://www.census.gov/prod/2003pubs/c2kbr-17.pdf

Weathers, R. (2005). *A guide to disability statistics from the American Community Survey.* Ithaca, NY: Rehabilitation Research and Training Center on Disability Demographics and Statistics, Cornell University. Retrieved February 14, 2009, from http://digitalcommons.ilr.cornell.edu/cgi/viewcontent.cgi?article=1123&context=edicollect

Wells, T., & Hogan, D. (2003). Developing concise measures of childhood activity limitations. *Maternal and Child Health Journal, 7,* 115–126.

Wells, T., Sandefur, G.D., & Hogan, D.P. (2003). What happens after the high school years among young persons with disabilities? *Social Forces, 82,* 803–832.

Westat. (2006). *Data on health and well-being of American Indians, Alaska Natives, and other Native Americans Data Catalog.* Retrieved May 20, 2009, from http://aspe.hhs.gov/hsp/06/Catalog-AI-AN-NA/YRBSS.htm

World Health Organization. (2001). *International classification of functioning, disability and health.* Geneva: Author. Retrieved February 20, 2009, from http://www.who.int/classifications/icf/en/

Zuckerbrod, N. (2008, March 31). Life after special ed has challenges [Electronic version]. *Washington Post.* Retrieved April 1, 2008, from http://www.washingtonpost.com/wp-dyn/content/article/2008/03/31/AR2008033101064.html

II

Basic Needs for Transition Success

4

Health Care

Access and Medical Support for Youth and Young Adults with Chronic Health Conditions and Disabilities

Ruth E.K. Stein, James M. Perrin, and Lisa I. Iezzoni

Opinions about the U.S. health care system fall into two distinct camps. On the one hand, observers recognize that breathtaking technological advances now save the lives of many people who, even just a decade ago, would have died. On the other hand are concerns—articulated by both health policy experts and the public—about lack of financial access to care, difficulties finding basic primary care, health care quality and safety problems, soaring costs, and lower health and well-being of Americans compared with populations in many other nations worldwide. In its seminal report *Crossing the Quality Chasm*, the Institute of Medicine Committee on Quality of Health Care in America (2001, p. 2) noted this irony:

> At no time in the history of medicine has the growth in knowledge and technology been so profound. . . .Genomics and other new technologies on the horizon offer the promise of further increasing longevity, improving health and functioning, and alleviating pain and suffering. Advances in rehabilitation, cell restoration, and prosthetic devices hold potential for improving the health and functioning of many with disabilities. . . .
>
> As medical science and technology have advanced at a rapid pace, however, the health care delivery system has floundered in its ability to provide consistently high-quality care to all Americans.

Children and youth with chronic health conditions and disabilities fall squarely in the midst of this dueling duality. Many are alive today precisely because of stunning scientific achievements that have translated into effective treatments. Sophisticated care, such as treatments for children with congenital heart defects or cystic fibrosis, provide comprehensive, coordinated, life-saving services, often regardless of extraordinary costs. Consequently, these children are passing through adolescence and into young adulthood at unprecedented rates, which is where they can run headlong into the darker realities of U.S. health care. Certainly, during their early years, many children with chronic health conditions and disabilities confront significant challenges to obtaining the care they need. For these children, as well as many youth with chronic health conditions who have received care in specialized pediatric settings, the passage into the adult health care world can prove rocky.

Maintaining continuous and effective health care services as they make the transition to adulthood is essential to maximize the functioning and quality of life of young people with chronic health conditions and disabilities. As noted in other chapters, this is a time when young people face transitions in many dimensions of their lives. Feeling as physically and emotionally healthy as possible fosters such diverse life transitions, giving young people strong foundations for later adult years. Minimizing, to the extent possible, the functional impairments and long-term clinical sequelae of underlying health conditions could also maximize the likelihood of individuals living into later years.

As noted below, trying to achieve a successful transition with good continuity of health care services can demand considerable investments in time, energy, and dollars, diverting these resources away from other aspects of integration into adult life. Youth with common single conditions, such as asthma, may face the same basic difficulties finding care as do many older adults. But young people with the greatest health care needs, such as individuals with life-threatening conditions or those who need technological or intensive service support for survival, often confront enormous barriers to finding care for their adult years. In the worst case scenarios, failure to negotiate the health care transition can threaten the health and even survival of individuals with unstable serious health conditions.

In the sections that follow, we provide an overview of prototypical differences in the organization of adolescent and adult health services, expectations about decision making, mechanisms of insurance and financing of services, and practicalities of finding care and issues in the available quality of care.

OVERVIEW OF ADOLESCENT AND ADULT HEALTH CARE SERVICES

Infants and children typically receive care in their own particular subsystem of the broader U.S. health care delivery system. (Although we use the shorthand convention of referring to the U.S. health care delivery system, we recognize—as do many others—that the United States does not truly have a system of care. Instead, at best, there is a fragmented patchwork of health care delivery settings, coexisting geographically but rarely integrated into true, seamless delivery systems.) Adult and child care does overlap in selected settings, such as family medicine practices and physicians jointly trained in pediatrics and internal medicine. For the most part, however, pediatric and adult care systems exist side by side within health care institutions and communities. According to the 2005–2006 National Survey of Children with Special Health Care Needs, almost two thirds of children with ongoing conditions and disabilities who receive care obtain at least part of that care from pediatricians or pediatric subspecialists. Older adolescents and young adults who do not continue with a family practitioner over the course of these years can fall betwixt and between—no longer pediatric, but perhaps not quite adult, according to typical assumptions of these respective care settings (Table 4.1).

Table 4.1. Differences between adolescent and adult health care systems

	Adolescent	Young Adult
System characteristics	Paternalistic	Based on autonomy of individuals
	Oriented to medical home	Tends to manage conditions in subspecialty model/"disease management" model
	Often subspecialists are consultants	
	Divided between usual and emergency	Can be unclear who is primary clinician
Medical decision making: Legally responsible party	Parent	Patient (no parental rights unless guardianship is assigned by court)
Consent	Parental consent with patient assent	Patient consent with determination of guardian for those unable to consent on their own
Insurance	Title V	Medicaid
	Medicaid	High rates of uninsurance
	SCHIP	Private—usually via employment or student status
	Private—usually through family policy	
Providers	Grew up with and often can speak in shorthand to patients	At outset unfamiliar with patient's history; can have little knowledge of condition
	Longitudinal	New
	Familiar with medical history and usual pattern of illness or condition	Inherit complex situation
Caregiving unit partnership	Health care professionals	Health care professionals
	Parents	Primarily the patient
	Patient	Confidentiality concerns limit involvement of family without patients' explicit permission
Views about adherence	Parental obligation	Personal choice
	In extreme situations, failure is considered a form of neglect and parents can be criminally liable	

Perhaps because of this, along with various other reasons (e.g., specific health care needs, individual preferences), the majority of older adolescents and young adults use far fewer health care services than young children or middle-age and older adults. As a group, older adolescents and young adults are among the least likely to have insurance or a usual source of care (Institute of Medicine Committee on Disability in America, 2007, p. 116). Healthy teenagers and young adults typically may obtain limited health services such as physical examinations for school enrollment, athletic team participation, or employment; episodic care at university or college health centers; reproductive health services, frequently at free clinics; and emergency services at urgent care centers or emergency rooms. Depending on personal preferences when they become sexually active and contemplate having children or preventing unintended pregnancies, young women may enter health care services through the reproductive health care portal (e.g., obstetricians, gynecologists). No comparable entry conduit exists for young men.

Thus, no organized health care transition process exists for older adolescents who do not have chronic health conditions or disabilities as they move to their adult years. No system or scaffolding of health care is therefore available upon which to build transition services for youth with ongoing conditions and disabilities. In addition, adolescents with ongoing health conditions may lack many of those opportunities mentioned above that other adolescents use as substitutes for an orderly transition of care, such as employment, higher education, or team sports. Even if they have these opportunities, health care needs are obviously more complicated for young adults with ongoing health conditions or disabilities than for other youth.

Regardless of individuals' ages, health care services play varying roles for people with different types of chronic health conditions and disabilities. Conditions that are fixed or constant, such as congenital blindness, deafness, or certain instances of cerebral palsy or intellectual disabilities, may not require explicit medical interventions. (These conditions nonetheless can affect the need for communication and other accommodations in health care, as well as many other aspects of daily life.) In contrast, other disabling conditions require that basic bodily needs be continually monitored and managed. For instance, young people with cystic fibrosis require frequent monitoring of pulmonary and pancreatic function and daily treatments to improve or maintain that functioning. Conditions such as asthma and sickle cell anemia may present as specific diseases requiring episodic acute management; over time they may become profoundly disabling (e.g., cause chronic physical impairments, physiologic changes) (Newacheck & Halfon, 2000). Sometimes, patients' behaviors can affect their clinical course. Conditions such as overweight and obesity may not be interpreted initially as causes for medical attention, but over time they too can both become profoundly disabling (e.g., impair mobility) and contribute to significant medical conditions (e.g., diabetes, cardiovascular disease) that are themselves disabling and require careful clinical oversight (Baker, Olsen, & Sorensen, 2007).

In a sense, therefore, all young people making the transition into adulthood with an ongoing health condition or disability must construct or create their own individualized care system. They typically need routine primary care, including standard preventive, screening, and wellness services that are supported by scientific evidence (e.g., as determined by the U.S. Preventive Services Task Force) but inconsistently obtained by young adults regardless of disability. Beyond that, each individual must assess the range of condition-specific, specialized services that he or she will need and determine how to access those services in the adult health care delivery system. As described later in this chapter, this can require mastery of issues relating to health insurance eligibility and benefits packages, understanding and navigating complex local service networks with specialists and subspecialists, negotiating access and establishing relationships with new health care professionals who are unfamiliar—at the outset—with the particulars of the individual's medical history.

One of the greatest challenges is finding a primary care physician willing and able to coordinate care across specialty and subspecialty silos. In adult health care, specialists and subspecialists frequently fail to communicate effectively and do not put patients at the center of decision making (Institute of Medicine Committee on the Consequences of Uninsurance, 2001). This fragmentation and lack of coordination causes significant risks to patients' safety and well-being, regardless of the nature of the health condition. The declining availability of primary care services for adults caused considerable political consternation as the Obama administration and Congress wrestled with constructing plans for fundamental health care reform in early 2009. With many internal medicine physicians leaving the field or closing their practices and fewer medical school graduates entering primary care, it is unclear that the future physician work force is sufficient to provide coordinated primary and preventive care to an aging U.S. population.

This daunting prospect in adult settings contrasts poorly with the coordinated and concentrated systems in which some young children with ongoing health needs have obtained care, perhaps even since birth. Of course, the utopian vision of perfectly coordinated care centered on the best interests and preferences of young children with chronic health conditions and their parents often proves elusive, especially for disadvantaged children. But—with more or less success— many child health care professionals aspire to provide a medical home. Therefore, adolescents with chronic health conditions and disabilities frequently have grown up with and have intimate familiarity with their childhood clinicians and health care delivery systems, including both primary care and subspecialty settings. These health care professionals will often have started providing care when the youngster was small, working closely with parents and the growing youth.

By the time these young people are ready to make the transition, most will have an established medical home where they interact with a point person who knows their medical history in great detail, as well as their personality, family members, and home and community supports. Optimally, clinicians will transfer selected aspects of care and management decisions to their young patient, increasing the youth's involvement as his or her capacity for independent decision making grows and matures. Given this level of intimacy and continuity in their relationships, patients, clinicians, and families often find themselves able to communicate in shorthand about complex health care questions and needs. Severing such long-standing ties is wrenching, on a personal as well as medical level, especially because—by definition—the new care team will have little first-hand knowledge of the patient's clinical or personal history. Achieving close relationships with their pediatric care clinician(s) was a work of many years, perhaps a lifetime, and it is unrealistic to expect that new clinicians can immediately step in and fully take their place, regardless of the adult physician's medical and interpersonal skills. These changes are particularly difficult when youth face extreme health challenges (Peter, Forke, Ginsburg, & Schwarz, 2009).

Given the developmental and decision-making capacity of children versus young adults, modes of interactions and expectations between clinicians and their patients evolve and alter fundamentally as young people grow and mature physically, cognitively, and emotionally. Child-oriented health care professionals tend to adopt paternalistic attitudes, expecting their young patients to comply with recommended therapies and their parents to oversee and ensure this adherence. State law often supports this position, with failure to seek and obtain needed treatment viewed as medical neglect in many states and thereby constituting a form of child maltreatment. In these states, failure to receive essential therapy is a reportable offense and can lead to removal of child custody.

In contrast, clinicians caring for adults assume their patients have full decision-making authority for their care. From this perspective, adults who choose not to adhere to prescribed therapies are autonomous individuals exercising their right to free choice, presumably after clinicians have informed them fully of the pros and cons of various treatment options. This assumption may prove problematic for some adolescents in transition to early adulthood, especially if they lack the cognitive and emotional maturity to assume this full responsibility or to understand completely the implications of failing to comply with necessary treatments. Furthermore, inadequate health literacy is widely documented among adults generally and clearly compromises people's abilities to make fully informed medical decisions. Suboptimal health literacy may be especially prevalent among youth making the transition into young adulthood.

Finally, as children age into early adulthood, specific medical aspects of their care—such as dosages and methods of administration of medications, approaches for monitoring clinical markers of conditions, and methods for performing certain procedures—may change. Fundamental biological and anatomical changes as young bodies grow and mature can cause such shifts. But when they coincide with a disjuncture of the care system (i.e., as the patient moves from the pediatric to adult care system), patients may become confused and alarmed. Without sufficient planning and preparing the older adolescent for these changes, these transitions can prove traumatic and perhaps compromise clinical outcomes, as well as cause stress and anxiety. The ideal health care transitions would ensure seamless, high-quality, comprehensive, community-based, patient-centered health care that would allow informed patients to move smoothly from a pediatric to an adult-oriented care system.

HEALTH CARE DECISION MAKING

As suggested above, changes in health care decision-making authority and expectations mark a fundamental difference between pediatric and adult health care settings. While this holds consequences for the patient, equally important are the potentially abrupt shifts in parental roles, which in certain instances can also prove traumatic or disruptive without careful transition planning. In most states, prior to the adolescent's 18th birthday, medical treatment requires parental consent, except in very specific circumstances. An adolescent's assent is recommended but not required. On the adolescent's 18th birthday, legal responsibility for consent shifts to the adolescent. Under privacy provisions of the federal Health Insurance Portability and Accountability Act (HIPAA) of 1996 (PL 104-191), health care professionals cannot discuss health information with their patient's parent or guardian unless the adolescent specifically grants permission. Strict adherence to HIPAA provisions might result in parents and guardians suddenly losing access to information about a youth's health and health care that they had long viewed as their right and responsibility. Depending on interpersonal dynamics (e.g., among the patient and parents) and capabilities of the young adult, managing this transition in decision-making authority, information sharing, and responsibility requires careful planning.

When a young adult is clearly not fully competent to make independent health care decisions, there must be a designation of a guardian who can act on his or her behalf. Unless the individual is competent to designate someone and voluntarily agrees to do so, it may fall to the court to declare a guardian, following proper applications to local legal authorities—another process that requires preparation. Parents may petition the court to become their child's guardian. Complexities arise in those gray zones such as when the young adult is not sufficiently mature and self-confident to assume full responsibility for medical decision making but is not obviously incompetent to do so. These young adults may elect to include their parent in medical decision making and sign a HIPAA waiver to give them access to their medical information; however, no legal requirement or mechanism stipulates that they do so. Thus, parents may find themselves in charge of their child's medical care one day and excluded the next.

These issues are especially difficult when the young adult has a mild cognitive impairment and/or is emotionally immature. Special problems can arise when young adults are intermittently competent and incompetent because of fluctuations in their underlying medical conditions or mental health. In such circumstances, accurately determining what is in the young adult's best interest can present difficulties and challenge relationships among patients, parents (or guardians), and the health care team. A survey of internists about their concerns in taking on young adults with long-standing health issues identified lack of family involvement as an important barrier to clinicians' comfort with the situation (Peter, Forke, Ginsburg, & Schwarz, 2009).

Virtually all youth making the transition to adulthood will confront questions relating to sexuality and reproductive choices. People with disabilities of all kinds have long experienced societal discomfort with—and sometimes outright rejection of—the possibility of their having intimate relationships or becoming parents. According to data from the 1994 National Health Interview Survey Disability Supplement combined with the Healthy People 2000 Supplement, only 14.7% of women of child-bearing age with major lower extremity mobility difficulties were asked about contraception by their physicians during a recent routine check-up, compared with 39.8% among all women (Iezzoni & O'Day, 2006, p. 110). Similarly, physicians do not discuss reproductive health issues with adolescents with chronic health conditions as often as with their healthy age-mates (Coupey and Wager, 1987). Physicians may erroneously believe that women with disabilities are not sexually active and therefore not at risk of unintended pregnancy (Sipski, Alexander, & Sherman, 2005). In the past surgical sterilization was performed to prevent young men and women with physical and intellectual disabilities from ever conceiving children, and this practice continues in some settings. Depending on the individual situation, this may or may not be appropriate. Nonetheless, the history of forced sterilizations (and present-day instances of this practice) raises serious ethical and moral questions. Many decisions about sterilization occur outside medical precincts (e.g., in the courts or other legal venues), but physicians and other health care professionals obviously must participate in performing any surgery. Issues of informed consent, who makes decisions, and how decisions are made are not simple and can cause conflict and distrust among people with disabilities, family members, legal guardians, and clinicians involved with the case.

HEALTH INSURANCE

Most people must pay to get health care in the United States. Typically, people get public or private health insurance to help cover these costs: insurance pools the risks and resources of a large group of people so that each is protected from financially disruptive medical expenses resulting from an illness, accident, or disability (Institute of Medicine Committee on the Consequences of Uninsurance, 2001, p. 20). Uninsured people—15.3% (45.7 million) of Americans in 2007 (DeNavas-Walt, Proctor, & Smith, 2008)— must pay out of-pocket, find free care, or do without. Young adults are the fastest growing segment of the population that lacks health insurance, and this poses a problem in terms of paying for needed health care services (Table 4.2). As described below, various public health insurance programs provide health insurance specifically for children with disabilities, while other children receive coverage under their parents' policies. The question for youth with disabilities who are making the transition to adulthood is whether they will lose the

Table 4.2. Health insurance coverage by selected age groups: 2005

Health insurance coverage type	Entire population[a]	Selected age groups[a]				
		Birth to 13	14 to 18	19 to 28	29 to 35
Overall						
Insured	249,020 (84.7)	50,585 (89.7)	18,590 (86.4)	27,884 (69.2)	21,495 (77.5)
Uninsured	44,815 (15.3)	5,805 (10.3)	2,930 (13.6)	12,396 (30.8)	6,257 (22.5)
Specific insurance types						
Any private insurance	201,167 (68.5)	36,480 (64.7)	14,921 (69.3)	23,888 (59.3)	19,067 (68.7)
Private insurance through employer	176,924 (60.2)	34,263 (60.8)	13,080 (60.8)	20,221 (50.2)	17,915 (64.6)
Any public insurance	80,213 (27.3)	17,769 (31.5)	4,893 (22.7)	5,453 (13.5)	3,242 (11.7)
Medicare	40,177 (13.7)	422 (0.7)	141 (0.7)	330 (0.8)	453 (1.6)
Medicaid	38,104 (13.0)	16,062 (28.5)	4,269 (19.8)	4,141 (10.3)	2,318 (8.4)
Military care	11,166 (3.8)	1,761 (3.1)	621 (2.9)	1,195 (3.0)	716 (2.6)

Source: U.S. Census Bureau (2006).
[a]In thousands (percentage).

coverage they had as children and face the considerable risks of lacking health insurance in America.

Although the majority of Americans believe that uninsured individuals get necessary medical services, they often do not. When people are uninsured or underinsured they report high rates of delays in seeking and getting needed services. If they have chronic conditions, their chronic conditions are often neglected or poorly treated, worsening disease and disability (Institute of Medicine Committee on the Consequences of Uninsurance, 2001, p. 22). Lacking insurance for only 1–4 years can decrease overall health and, over the long term, heighten risks of premature death (Institute of Medicine Committee on the Consequences of Uninsurance, 2002a, p. 4). Having health insurance only intermittently is also associated with poor health (Olson, Tang, & Newacheck, 2005). The negative consequences of being uninsured extend beyond individuals, because the health of one member of the family can affect the health of the other members and of the unit as a whole (Institute of Medicine Committee on the Consequences of Uninsurance, 2002b, p. 8). Lacking insurance coverage can also cause considerable emotional stress, further eroding family members' physical and mental health. Children's health and well-being is especially threatened when adult family members' health worsens because of absent health insurance. Children's ill health affects parental health and well-being (Silver, Westbrook, & Stein, 1998, Thyen, Kuhlthau, & Perrin, 1999).

Being uninsured primarily affects children and working-age adults, because nearly all elderly people have Medicare. As shown in Table 4.2, individuals age 19 to 28 have the highest rate of uninsurance of all age groups: 30.8% compared with 15.3% for all Americans (see also Adams, Newacheck, Park, Brindis, & Irwin, 2007). For nonelderly people, the source of health insurance varies across age groups. Most working-age adults under age 65 still receive voluntary, employer-based, private health insurance. However, rates of employer-based health insurance started falling in the 1970s. About 80% of uninsured people belong to families with at least one wage earner, and roughly 60% of uninsured individuals are employed (Institute of Medicine Committee on the Consequences of Uninsurance, 2001, p. 60). Most uninsured wage earners have low-paying jobs with limited benefits.

No statistics exist that directly quantify health insurance coverage among youth with chronic health conditions and disabilities making the transition into adulthood. Limited insurance data on youth with disabilities, but not on the broader category of those with ongoing conditions, are summarized in Chapter 3. As suggested by Table 4.2, those making transitions into adulthood are moving into the age group with the highest uninsurance rate. As described later in this chapter, however, certain public and private health insurance programs might serve at least for some time as their safety net (e.g., Medicaid linked to Supplemental Security Income [SSI], extended coverage under a parent's private policy). For working-age adults with disabilities in general, the employment picture is often bleak; individuals may have access only to low-wage or part-time jobs that seldom include health insurance benefits. The Americans with Disabilities Act (ADA) of 1990 (PL 101-336) does not specifically address employment-based health insurance, although it prohibits employers from discriminating against employees in terms, conditions, and privileges of employment (Section 102[a]). Such terms presumably encompass health insurance, among other benefits. HIPAA restricts the ability of group health insurance plans to limit coverage for preexisting conditions for more than 12 months. However, federal law permits insurers to charge one employer more than another on the basis of the claims experience or health status of their employees (Institute of Medicine Committee on Disability in America, 2007). This may contribute to persistent discriminatory attitudes of employers about hiring individuals with disabilities (Moss & Burris, 2007).

Even people with chronic health conditions and disabilities who have health insurance may not get items or services they need. High costs cause substantial barriers to care, as shown by a survey (late 2002 to early 2003) of working-age people with disabilities, 95% of whom had health insurance (Hanson, Neuman, Dutwin, & Kasper, 2003). Respondents cited prescription drugs and dental care as the major problems (reported by 32% and 29% of the sample, respectively); 36% said they skipped medication doses, split pills, or went without filling a prescription altogether to save money (Hanson et al.). In addition, 21% of those who used equipment to manage their disabilities said they had serious difficulties paying for the equipment. No surveys have specifically queried youth with chronic health conditions and disabilities to find out whether they face comparable barriers, but one might reasonably expect that they do.

Public Health Insurance Programs

Various public programs specifically cover children, thus reducing their levels of uninsurance. Medicaid and the State Children's Health Insurance Program (SCHIP) insure large numbers of children and youth with chronic health conditions and disabilities. Although children can obtain Medicaid through various eligibility criteria, key qualifying factors for children and youth with chronic health conditions and disabilities include Temporary Assistance for Needy Families, the means-tested program resulting from 1990s welfare reform, and participation or eligibility through Social Security's Supplemental Security Income (SSI) program. SSI, a program to provide income support for individuals with severe health-related disabilities, is strictly means-tested for adults (SSI clinical requirements and other eligibility criteria also differ for children compared with adults). For children, SSI means-testing income requirements are based on family income, although they vary from state to state for Medicaid eligibility. Social Security's disability requirements for SSI limit eligibility to people with severe disabilities. Many children and adults with substantial disability will not meet SSI requirements. Most children who qualify medically for SSI gain access to Medicaid coverage even when higher family income and other demographic characteristics might otherwise exclude them from Medicaid eligibility and SSI income benefits (Perrin & Stein, 1991). Congress designed SCHIP to insure children in households with incomes above Medicaid eligibility limits, with stipulations that uninsured children identified through SCHIP outreach initiatives but eligible for Medicaid should be enrolled in Medicaid. Despite some expectations that children insured by SCHIP would have fairly low rates of chronic disease, studies indicate relatively high prevalence of ongoing conditions in this population (Macon, Miller, Gaboda, Simpson, & Cantor, 2007; Stein, Shenkman, Wegener, & Silver, 2003; Yu, Dick, & Szilagyi, 2006).

Regular eligibility ends at age 21 for Medicaid and at age 18 for SCHIP. Reauthorization of SCHIP (now simply called the Children's Health Insurance Program or CHIP) in February 2009 did not change the main age eligibility limitations for the program. Nonetheless, Section 1115 waivers allow states to experiment with some flexibility in implementation of both Medicaid and CHIP programs (Kaiser Family Foundation, 2009, February; 2009, March). The 2009 CHIP reauthorization also included financing for new programs to conduct quality assessment and assurance in CHIP. The legislation discusses potential goals for quality efforts. None address transition for adolescents with ongoing health conditions, although the quality activities could address this topic.

At age 18, SSI eligibility (and thus access to Medicaid) changes in two main ways: 1) parental income is no longer considered for the child; and 2) disability is determined by adult rules rather than child/adolescent rules. The first of these provisions may increase the number of young people eligible for SSI, although many may not be aware of their eligibility; the second change typically excludes a number of young people who previously had SSI coverage. The Social Security Administration has recently initiated a number of pilot programs to help adolescent SSI recipients make the transition to adulthood. These include maintaining eligibility of any adolescent with an individualized education program (IEP) and providing services and systems to assist youth with chronic health conditions and disabilities to make a successful transition from school to work (Social Security Administration, 2007). To some degree, these pilot projects also aim to help youth with chronic health conditions and disabilities maintain their SSI (and thus Medicaid) eligibility through the transition period.

In contrast to Medicare, which offers fairly limited coverage of long-term institutional care and assistive technology and no coverage of personal assistance services, Medicaid's benefit package covers more of these items and services for its impoverished elderly recipients as well as younger enrollees. This benefit package is especially helpful to children, youth, and young adults with disabilities who have Medicaid insurance (Rosenbaum, 2002). Furthermore, under the 1915(c) Home and Community-Based Services waivers, states can provide extensive long-term benefits, such as case management, home health aides, personal assistive services, respite care, and home modifications—in most cases with the intent of preventing costly hospitalization and institutionalization. States have substantial flexibility in the numbers of waiver recipients (and their ages and conditions), as well as the scope of services provided. As of 2009, 48 states and the District of

Columbia offered such waivers (Centers for Medicare and Medicaid Services, n.d.). CHIP benefits packages more closely resemble private insurance, with limited long-term care and assistive technology coverage. A persisting issue is that states set rules for Medicaid and CHIP and thus adolescents and young adults cannot assume similar benefits across state borders.

Parental Health Insurance Through the Transition

Some young adults with chronic health conditions and disabilities can continue private coverage through their parents' employer-based health insurance for a few years while in postsecondary education. This coverage, though, typically ends with graduation or completing specified years of schooling. This approach seems paradoxical, however, because most colleges have insurance options for attendees, while youth not enrolled in school do not have such group insurance options. Several policy proposals have been advanced to expand these parental insurance coverage options, and some states have begun to extend the ages to which they apply. Few figures are available about use of parental employer-based health coverage as children make the transition from adolescence to young adulthood.

In the absence of extensive data quantifying this problem, an anecdote involving Marianne, a 21-year-old woman with cystic fibrosis, highlights the critical insurance issues for young adults with complex health needs. Marianne must take prescription medications to maintain her breathing and nutritional supplements and enzymes to replace some functions of her pancreas (cystic fibrosis affects both pulmonary and pancreatic functioning). She attends a local community college, works part-time as a salesperson in a dress store, and shares an apartment with a high school friend attending the same college. Marianne is quite independent and knowledgeable about her medications and treatments. Her lung care involves daily respiratory therapy to clear the mucus. Her roommate learned how to perform these treatments, although a professional respiratory therapist makes home visits weekly to ensure Marianne's treatments are working well. During the infectious disease season in winter months, Marianne needs more respiratory therapy and sometimes emergency care and hospitalization.

Because she is still in junior college, Marianne retains health insurance through her parents' policy, which considers her a dependent. The private insurance covers her medications, respiratory therapist home visits, and periodic acute care services and hospitalizations. When she graduates, she is unclear about what coverage she will have. Marianne worries that the types of jobs she might get will not offer health insurance or might exclude coverage of her cystic fibrosis as a preexisting condition. Marianne plans to explore SSI in case she cannot get her own insurance after her parents' health insurance can no longer cover her.

Costs of Care

In general, people with chronic health conditions and disabilities and substantial impairments generate higher health care costs than do other people (DeJong et al., 2002; Kuhlthau, Perrin, Ettner, McLaughlin, & Gortmaker, 1998). They typically generate much higher median total health care expenditures than do other people and also pay more out of pocket for their care. For instance, working-age people with major lower extremity mobility difficulties generated $7,389 in median total health expenditures in 2000, compared with $408 for people with no impairment (Iezzoni & O'Day, 2006, p. 58). People reporting any major impairment paid a median $510 out of pocket for health care in 2000, compared with $92 for people without any impairments (Iezzoni & O'Day). Medicaid costs average three to nine times higher for children with SSI coverage than for those without (Kuhlthau et al., 1998). Children with chronic health conditions have three times greater health care expenditures than children without such health care needs (Newacheck & Kim, 2005).

People with disabilities generally visit health care providers more often than do others. More people with major disabilities are hospitalized at least once in the previous year (25.6% compared with 6.9% for people not reporting disabilities; data from 2000), although the vast majority had only one stay (Iezzoni & O'Day, 2006, p. 59). They were also much more likely to have at least one physician office, clinic, or physical or occupational therapist visit, and if they have at least one, their mean number of total visits is higher than for people without disabilities. Among children, those with chronic health conditions have four times the rate of hospital use, three times the rate of physician visits, and seven times the rate of other health care visits compared to those without (Newacheck & Kim, 2005).

Insurance does not necessarily cover all costs, leaving people to pay out of pocket for uncovered expenses. In addition, striving to control health care costs and maintain quality, certain new insurance products (e.g., health savings accounts) aim at structuring incentives to motivate consumers to appreciate the costs of care. These plans typically have low premiums and cover limited services, but provide a specified pool of dollars from which consumers can draw to cover other health care expenses. At the end of the year, consumers can retain unexpended dollars. The expectation is that consumers—by putting their own dollars at risk—will shop around for the best health care value (a meld between cost and quality). Obviously, such plans will hold few attractions for people with significant health care needs. Because of their low premiums and potential for saving money, these plans are most popular among young healthy adults who do not anticipate requiring health care services beyond minimal episodic care. Such plans offer inadequate benefits and possibly pose considerable hazards for adolescents with chronic health conditions and disabilities making the transition into adulthood.

FINDING SOURCES OF CARE

As they make the transition into adulthood, youth with chronic health conditions and disabilities will confront the challenges older people with such conditions often face daily: trying to make a coherent health care network out of disconnected, scattershot parts. People with disabilities and significant health care needs must weigh many factors in choosing their care providers, ranging from costs and health insurance stipulations to physical location and accessibility of facilities to clinicians' technical knowledge, attitudes, and communication approaches. The experiences of Davey, now in his 30s, highlight the complexities of trying to find care. Davey started looking while in his 20s, with many health care needs and few resources: in Davey's own words, he has a hearing disability, glaucoma, major depression, and severe knee problems (Iezzoni, Killeen, & O'Day, 2006). When he first moved to the rural community where he currently lives, it took him 5 years to find a primary care physician. He was poor, unemployed, and only had Medicaid insurance. The first challenge was finding a physician who would accept Medicaid, which typically pays lower fees than other insurers. Many physicians told Davey up front that they refused Medicaid recipients. Davey also had trouble finding a physician who would make appropriate specialist referrals and then manage his care, while treating him like a whole person.

According to the 2001 Medical Expenditure Panel Survey, relatively large numbers of people with disabilities, especially young adults, reported not having a usual source of health care: a particular doctor's office, clinic, health center, or other care setting where they seek care and medical advice. Among people age 18 through 44 reporting major disabilities, 20.5% did not have a usual source of care; neither did 10.6% of their counterparts 45 to 64 years of age (Iezzoni & O'Day, 2006, p. 54). Roughly 36% of working-age people without a usual source of care attributed this absence to high costs, while nearly 10% said they did not know where to go to get care. Uninsured people reported not having a usual source of care much more often than those with insurance. Among working-age people reporting any major sensory or physical impairment, 52.6% of uninsured individuals said they had no usual source of care, compared with 14.2% of those with any private insurance.

Little information is available about the experiences of people with chronic health conditions and disabilities trying to find health care services, but a national telephone survey (Hanson, Neuman, Dutwin, & Kasper, 2003) conducted in late 2002 and early 2003 of working-age people with disabilities produced troubling findings: Although the majority of survey respondents said that they have a regular doctor, one in four reported having had trouble finding a doctor who understands their disability. The uninsured were also more likely than those with health insurance to say they have no regular doctor and to report trouble finding a doctor who understands their disability. When it comes to finding a doctor who accepts their insurance, 17% of the sample reported this problem, with higher rates (22%) among those covered by Medicaid.

Difficulties finding physicians certainly relate directly to current payment policies, which generally do not reimburse providers adequately for the full costs of caring for people with chronic health conditions and disabilities (Eichner & Blumenthal, 2003; Institute of Medicine Committee on a National Agenda for the Prevention of Disabilities, 1991; Institute of Medicine Committee on Disability in America, 2007). Nationwide, a handful of programs specialize in caring for adults with disabilities (Blanchard & Hosek, 2003; Reis, Breslin, Iezzoni, & Kirschner, 2004). These programs typically share the following traits: dedicated clinicians committed to caring for people with disabilities; effective advocacy by local disability rights organizations; and special funding arrangements, primarily philanthropy (e.g., from foundations, disease-specific advocacy groups, or large health care institutions), in addition to partnerships with payers (e.g., customized contracts with Medicaid). These programs also often rely heavily on nonphysicians, such as nurse practitioners, and providing care in homes, especially to people with significant physical impairments.

These kinds of specialized programs unfortunately are limited in scope and size and thus do not offer a widespread solution. Without continuing special financial arrangements, such programs would lose money and not be sustainable over time. Starting new programs specializing in care for individuals with chronic health conditions and disabilities also can require capital expenditures to build accessible environments and acquire appropriate equipment. In addition, "Many of these programs provide care to an underserved population with needs that have been largely overlooked in the past. Expanding access to such a population will result in initially high costs" (Blanchard & Hosek, 2003, pp. 23–24). Savings may ultimately occur as patients receive more preventive services and wellness care that mitigate or postpone costly secondary conditions. Nonetheless, "Unless risk-adjusted payments that reflect the higher treatment costs…are widely adopted, these programs are likely to remain small" (Blanchard & Hosek, p. xiv).

One small study in western Pennsylvania found that women with disabilities had trouble finding physicians who understood their needs or even agreed to provide care: some physicians deny them service if they cannot, for example, mount an examination table without assistance, or even refuse to see them solely because of their disability, both of which cases are in violation of the Americans with Disabilities Act (Blanchard & Hosek, 2003, p. 9). Assuming that the physician has adequate technical knowledge and skills to care for such patients, refusing to accept or treat people solely because of disability is clearly illegal. When physicians have insufficient knowledge, making referrals to other clinicians is appropriate and legal. Among more than 100 adults with disabilities interviewed by Iezzoni and O'Day (2006), no interviewees reported that physicians outright refused to care for them because of their disability, with one exception: obstetrical care for pregnant women with major mobility difficulties. Their stories suggested that these refusals fit into a broader societal discomfort with women wheelchair users becoming mothers, as well as concerns about their skills for medically managing the pregnancy and delivery.

The 2007 Institute of Medicine report *The Future of Disability in America* highlights concerns about the minimal training primary care physicians generally receive for caring for people with chronic health conditions and disabilities (Institute of Medicine Committee on Disability in America, 2007), despite learning voluminous information about many disabling diseases (e.g., cardiac diseases, asthma, diabetes, arthritis) (Hoenig, 1993; Iezzoni, 2003; Institute of Medicine Committee on Disability in America, 2007). Not surprisingly, primary care physicians can feel inadequately knowledgeable to treat adults with congenital conditions (e.g., cerebral palsy, spina bifida) and may refuse to accept them as patients. These reservations reflect the dawning scientific understanding about the complexities of aging from childhood into later adulthood with these conditions:

> There is a growing body of literature about aging issues and secondary conditions among people with congenital and childhood-onset mobility impairments. Systematic studies of secondary conditions have only recently been initiated. . . . Much of the conventional wisdom in this area has been communicated through the network of people with disabilities. . . . Health-care providers and consumers have limited knowledge from which to base decisions regarding adult health issues and anticipated changes in function in these individuals with disabilities (Turk & Weber, 2005, p. 1519).

Pediatric facilities where people with childhood disabilities have had long-term relationships can and at times do refuse to continue providing care after a certain age. This can make adults with childhood disabilities unsure where to turn for health care services. Another anecdote from Iezzoni and O'Day (2006) exemplifies the human cost and emotional consequences of these difficulties. Janice, in her late 30s, is a health law attorney in a large city. Born with spina bifida, she ambulates using two forearm crutches and has dealt with disability issues since her earliest memories. When her parents tried to enroll young Janice in public elementary school, she was turned away: "They said I was a fire hazard because I couldn't climb stairs" (p. 69). Janice had to attend a special school for 3 years before the public schools allowed her to register. Janice had numerous surgeries during her childhood, such as a shunt to avoid further hydrocephalus; a urostomy; and many hip, ankle, and foot operations. Her parents took her to a clinic for children with disabilities. "Through college and even law school, I stuck with the pediatricians back home, Janice admitted" (p. 70). She went on to say,

> In real life, I became a grownup and got a job, then I started looking around for an adult doctor. I don't think I did a very good job despite all my expertise and understanding. To be perfectly honest, just like everyone else in their twenties, even if you have a disability, you think you're going to live forever! Plus, I had trouble finding anyone who had a clue about what to do about my disability. (p. 70)

Since she turned 30 years old, Janice noted that she has had aches and pains that you don't usually get until your forties or fifties (p. 70). Needing to address these issues, she began a serious search for doctors who understood her needs. "It takes an enormous investment of time and energy to make sure I get what I need and that it's not fragmented, said Janice. This takes time away from my career and my personal life" (pp. 70–71). She now sees an urologist who has carved out a niche caring for people with disabilities within her broader urological practice. However, although Janice is well educated and connected within the local health care community, she has not yet found a primary care physician to coordinate her complex care, and she still sees a pediatric orthopedist. This makes her concerned she is not getting the best health care.

QUALITY OF CARE

People with chronic health conditions and disabilities are particularly susceptible to substandard health care in the United States and often slip through the gaps crisscrossing health care delivery systems. People with common chronic conditions frequently do not receive routine, recommended health care services. One study found that adult Americans receive, on average, roughly half of recommended health care services (McGlynn et al., 2003). Healthy People 2010, which outlines national public health priorities, explicitly reported that people with chronic health conditions and disabilities often get inadequate health care (U.S. Department of Health and Human Services, 2000). Studies repeatedly show lower rates of screening services, such as Pap tests, mammography, and colonoscopy, among people with disabilities, although rates do vary by disability type. Misconceptions about their lives and preferences contribute to troubling disparities in the services they receive, especially an underemphasis on health promotion and disease prevention activities; thus, as a potentially underserved group, people with disabilities would be expected to experience disadvantages in health and well-being compared with the general population (U.S. Department of Health and Human Services, pp. 6-3, 6-5). On July 26, 2005, the 15th anniversary of the signing of the ADA, the U.S. Surgeon General issued a Call to Action, warning that people with disabilities can lack equal access to health care. Observing that every life has value and every person has promise (Carmona & Cabe, 2005), the Call to Action aimed to ensure, among other things, that

- People nationwide recognize that individuals with disabilities can lead long, healthy, and productive lives;
- Health care providers attain the knowledge and tools to screen, diagnose, and treat people with disabilities with dignity as whole persons; and
- Health care and related services are fully accessible to maximize the independence of people with disabilities. (Carmona & Cabe, 2005; U.S. Department of Health and Human Services, 2005)

The Institute of Medicine Committee on Quality of Health Care in America (2001) warns that fundamental restructuring is required to rectify the many shortfalls of the health care delivery system. Major changes should ensure that health care is

- Safe—avoids injuring patients
- Effective—based on scientific evidence of benefit
- Patient-centered—respectful of patients' preferences, needs, and values
- Timely—reduces waits and harmful delays
- Efficient—avoids waste of equipment, supplies, ideas, and energy

- Equitable—equal quality regardless of patients' personal characteristics (Institute of Medicine Committee on Quality of Health Care in America, pp. 41–42)

Each of these goals holds special relevance for people with chronic health conditions and disabilities (Iezzoni, 2002). Patient centeredness—the primacy of the experience of patients, their loved ones, and the communities in which they live, seeing the experience of patients as the fundamental source of the definition of quality—should come first (Berwick, 2002). Many people with disabilities have experienced others defining and circumscribing their options, in many aspects of daily life. Concerns that health care providers may consciously or subconsciously denigrate and devalue their quality of life raises fears about being deprived therapeutic options.

The Institute of Medicine's other five health care reform goals also carry particular resonance for people with chronic health conditions and disabilities. People with complex diagnoses or multiple coexisting conditions are more susceptible to safety risks (e.g., they often consume more medications, have more invasive procedures, spend more time within the health care system). They also can suffer dangerous consequences from neglect in care settings (e.g., developing pressure ulcers). People with disabilities, as well as children, are typically excluded from the randomized clinical trials that assess the efficacy and effectiveness of therapeutic interventions, such as new medications or surgical procedures. Therefore, minimal evidence exists about people with their clinical conditions that direct evidence-based care. The lack of scientific evidence is likely especially marked for children with chronic health conditions. In addition, scientific evidence about assistive technologies and rehabilitation services to prevent or delay functional declines is fairly sparse.

Delays and waits affect all patients, but, at the most basic level, people who depend, for example, on overbooked and financially strapped paratransit systems often find themselves arriving late for office visits or missing appointments altogether. This situation frustrates both patients and clinicians. While parents provide transportation to health care encounters for their children, as adolescents make the transition to adulthood, getting to and from health care visits may pose significant problems, especially for people who cannot drive. Studies suggest that people with certain chronic health conditions and disabilities are significantly less likely than others to receive selected screening and preventive services. Without appropriate screening tests, serious diseases such as breast, cervical, and colon cancer may be diagnosed at later, less treatable stages of disease. Avoiding waste of time and energy is critically important for people with physical impairments. With short appointment times, however, young people with chronic health conditions and disabilities may need to make multiple trips to the doctor to address fully their health care concerns. Traveling to multiple settings to see multiple providers can be exhausting. Finally, achieving equity for people with ongoing health conditions and disabilities is very pertinent, as suggested by the commentary of Healthy People 2010.

RECOMMENDATIONS

By necessity, this chapter has been brief, providing only an overview of problems that vex the U.S. health care delivery system and may be especially problematic for young adults with chronic health conditions making the transition into the adult service sector. As have others, we have concentrated here primarily on the problems—the barriers that young people with chronic health conditions and disabilities face in transition—rather than on successful models or programs. We are tempted to start our recommendations with pleas for widespread reforms of the U.S. health care system, as eloquently articulated in the Institute of Medicine Committee on Quality Health Care in America's *Crossing the Quality Chasm* (2001) and with concerns reprised in *The Future of Disability in America* (Institute of Medicine Committee on Disability in America, 2007). Although youth with chronic health conditions do face specific problems with health care services as they make the transition to adulthood, seemingly intractable problems are rife across U.S. health care, and many subpopulations of people fail to get the high quality services Americans might expect. Indeed, as these young adults move into middle and older ages and themselves begin developing common conditions of aging, they will likely face continuing challenges with obtaining the coordinated, comprehensive, patient-centered care they need.

As in the adult world, examples of care models designed to provide comprehensive, patient-centered care to people with chronic health conditions and disabilities tend to be found in small practices. Relatively few initiatives have yet brought the most successful models to scale, expanding beyond panels of several hundred patients or enrollees. Thus, we base our recommendations primarily on promising models with only limited evaluation, insufficient experimentation in multiple settings, and relatively small caseloads.

Our first recommendation is that adolescents and young adults with ongoing conditions and disabilities should have a designated medical home. The responsibility of the medical home is to provide coordinated, continuous, patient-centered care. The overarching principle of the medical home (American Academy of Pediatrics Medical Home Initiatives for Children With Special Needs Project Advisory Committee, 2002) carries intuitive appeal and, rhetorically at least, has formed the foundation upon which pediatric settings have built effective care environments for children with chronic health conditions. Basic components of the medical home include

- Central focus on primary care

- Emphasis on coordinated, holistic care, which focuses on the whole patient and involves referrals to specialists and community services whenever necessary

- Including patients as coequal collaborators in care decisions and providing patients information sufficient to support their fully informed decision making

- Creation of comprehensive patient registries to track patient outcomes, monitoring the results of interventions and treatment side effects

- Application of science-based evidence, whenever available, to guide therapeutic decisions

Medical home principles could frame efforts to support successful transitions for older adolescents into adult care settings and, in the cases in which that home requires a transfer of provider, it should share some responsibility for the transition process occurring. Recently, medical home concepts have gained traction among adult clinical leaders. For example, the American Academy of Pediatrics, the American Board of Internal Medicine, the American Osteopathic Association, and the American Association of Family Medicine (2007) endorsed the medical home concept in a joint statement. Despite these endorsements of guiding principles, actual implementation of the medical home is challenging, both for adults and for children. Various aspects of this approach may generate additional uncompensated expenses beyond those incurred in routine practice, and considerable organizational sophistication is needed for full implementation.

For children, the relative rarity of individual disabling conditions has led to the model being implemented around ongoing or chronic conditions in general, rather than for specific conditions, with the exception of a few common conditions such as asthma and attention-deficit hyperactivity disorder (National Initiative for Children's Healthcare Quality, 2005). For adults, nascent medical home initiatives have focused primarily on improving care for common adult chronic conditions (e.g., diabetes). The adult medical home practice may broaden, however, with the recognition that many adults with such common conditions as diabetes often have multiple coexisting diagnoses: a more comprehensive patient-centric, rather than diagnosis-centric, model is both more clinically relevant and consistent with basic medical home tenets.

Having medical home programs in place will not ensure adequate transition of youth with chronic health conditions and disabilities to adult health care. Nonetheless, such programs can provide a home base for effective transition, with clear lines of responsibility for various aspects of care. Other essential components include mechanisms to improve communication between care settings and among providers, patients, and families. Some improvements in coordinated and comprehensive communication can come from better use of secure electronic health information. The role of the longitudinal, electronic medical record—and giving patients and, as appropriate, families access to these health records—is an important area that merits further exploration.

One key component is not always explicit in the medical home but is fundamental to the management of many with ongoing health needs and disabilities: the designation of a contact person within the medical home who is available and to whom the young adult can turn for assistance. That person should be responsible for helping with obtaining necessary services and problem solving. One approach for accomplishing this is the navigator concept, which operationally designates a single person (not necessarily the physician) who is responsible for helping the consumer identify necessary services and coordinate the care that is needed. Conceived initially to assist adults from socioeconomically disadvantaged backgrounds to find their way through the complex health care system after receiving a serious diagnosis, such as of breast or colon cancer, navigators are becoming increasingly popular.

Patient navigators need not be health care professionals and could even be community peers. Key to their success, however, is their detailed knowledge of local health care resources and an understanding of the types of services people need in different clinical circumstances. Navigators serve as the patient's advocate and reinforce the need for patients to follow-up and adhere to care recommendations. Similar models exist in child and adolescent health using a range of professionals and nonprofessionals, although few have had substantial uptake and spread in large parts of the health care system (c.f. Chernoff, Ireys, DeVet, & Kim, 2002; Stein & Jessop, 1984). Several state maternal and child health programs have established care coordination programs built on this model. Establishing navigators for youth with disabilities who are making the transition into the adult care system and involving peers who themselves have had successful transition experiences could improve transition. This approach clearly requires evaluation prior to widespread adoption, as well as some means of ongoing payment for these services. Health insurers do not generally pay for the services of a navigator or peer counselor.

A third component of an improved transition system involves enhanced training of both professionals and consumers. One important challenge to improving transitions for adolescents into their new role as adult consumers of health care involves training consumers in responsible decision making and enhancing health literacy. Pediatricians might start preparing younger adolescents for increasing self-responsibility, so that changes in these decision-making roles occur in a planned way over time rather than suddenly at age 18. This will be challenging, especially in busy practices and recognizing that payors do not currently compensate health care professionals for these types of services (i.e., enhancing health literacy among their patients). Nonetheless, increasing evidence indicates that early planning for transition—beginning before adolescence—can enhance the specification of health decision-making tasks, the distribution of responsibilities, and increasing self-responsibility and self-confidence of young people with chronic health conditions and disabilities (McDonagh, 2006). Clinicians could work with patients and families to specify service plans and individualized goals, with plans for periodic monitoring and updating. These plans should include attention to transition planning for several years prior to age 18.

Beyond endeavoring to improve the responsiveness of individual practice settings and the capabilities of individual patients, broad systemic improvements require attention, including work force preparation. Current adult care providers receive little training about ongoing conditions of childhood and their long term sequelae. This lack of training may present a major obstacle to clinicians' assumption of responsibility for young adults with ongoing conditions (Peter et al., 2009). To feel comfortable caring for these patients, adult clinicians need enhanced training in both specific health conditions that previously were not seen by internists and chronic care management. Other clinicians, such as nurse practitioners working alongside physicians in adult settings, also need this enhanced training.

We anticipate that state-of-the-art care for many conditions will continue to require highly specialized knowledge and familiarity with highly specific issues. In is not realistic or feasible to expect that the typical primary care clinician could develop adequate expertise in every unusual issue confronted by his or her patients with ongoing health conditions and disabilities. Clinicians who see a single patient with a rare condition will never have the same level of expertise as one who sees many with that condition. Mechanisms such as telemedicine, web-based consultations, or other ways to enhance systematic sharing of information through health information technologies could facilitate sharing of expertise with specialists. These technologies might allow the primary care provider in a medical home that may be quite distant from a specialized center to care effectively for a patient with conditions outside their immediate expertise. The exponential growth of adolescents making the transition to adult care providers heightens the priority of smoothing the logistics for primary care providers to determine where to turn for help and how to get it. Legal (e.g., malpractice) and financial (e.g., health insurance coverage) implications must also be addressed.

Finally, it is critical to enhance or supplement health insurance especially during the period of late adolescence and young adulthood. A promising option would be to extend Medicaid and CHIP to age 25 for people with chronic health conditions and disabilities who do not qualify for SSI. Applying additional resources to improve the quality of health care transitions for youth with ongoing conditions is a related high priority.

REFERENCES

Adams, S.H., Newacheck, P.W., Park, M.J., Brindis, C.D., & Irwin, C.E. (2007). Health insurance across vulnerable ages: Patterns and disparities from adolescence to the early 30s. *Pediatrics, 119,* e1033–e1039.

American Academy of Family Physicians, American Academy of Pediatrics, American College of Physicians, & American Osteopathic Association. (2007). *Joint Principles of the Patient-Centered Medical Home.* Retrieved December 12, 2007, from http://www.medicalhomeinfo.org/Joint%20Statement.pdf

American Academy of Pediatrics Medical Home Initiatives for Children With Special Needs Project Advisory Committee. (2002). The medical home. *Pediatrics 110,* 184–186.

Americans with Disabilities Act (ADA) of 1990, PL 101-336, 42 U.S.C. §§ 12101 *et seq.*

Baker, J.L., Olsen, L., & Sorensen, T.I. (2007). Childhood body-mass index and the risk of coronary heart disease in adulthood. *The New England Journal of Medicine, 357,* 2329–2337.

Berwick, D.M. (2002). A user's manual for the IOM's Quality Chasm report. *Health Affairs (Project Hope), 21,* 80–90.

Blanchard, J., & Hosek, S. (2003). *Financing health care for women with disabilities.* RAND Health White Paper WP-139. Santa Monica, CA: RAND.

Carmona, R.H., & Cabe, J. (2005). Improving the health and wellness of persons with disabilities: A call to action. *American Journal of Public Health, 95,* 1883.

Centers for Medicare and Medicaid Services. (n.d.). HCBS waivers—Section 1915 (c). Retrieved February 1, 2009, from http://www.cms.hhs.gov/MedicaidStWaivProg DemoPGI/05_HCBSWaivers-Section1915(c).asp

Chernoff, R.G., Ireys, H.T., DeVet, K.A., & Kim, Y.J. (2002). A randomized, controlled trial of a community-based intervention for families of children with chronic illness: Pediatric outcomes. *Archives of Pediatrics & Adolescent Medicine, 156,* 533–539.

Coupey, S.M., & Wager, M. (1987). Issues of sexuality in chronically ill adolescents. In M. Wolraich, & D.K. Routh (Eds.), *Advances in developmental and behavioral pediatrics* (Vol. 9). Greenwich, CT: JAI Press.

DeJong, G., Palsbo, S.E., Beatty, P.W., Jones, G.C., Knoll, T., & Neri, M.T. (2002). The organization and financing of health services for persons with disabilities. *The Milbank Quarterly, 80,* 261–301.

DeNavas-Walt, C., Proctor, B.D., & Smith, J.C. (2008). *Income, poverty, and health insurance coverage in the United States: 2007.* U.S. Census Bureau, Current Population Reports, P60–235. Washington, DC: U.S. Government Printing Office.

Eichner, J., & Blumenthal, D. (2003). *Medicare in the 21st century: Building a better chronic care system.* Final report of the Study Panel on Medicare and Chronic Care in the 21st Century. Washington, DC: National Academy of Social Insurance.

Hanson, K.W., Neuman, P., Dutwin, D., & Kasper, J.D. (2003). Uncovering the health challenges facing people with disabilities: The role of health insurance. *Health Affairs.* Retrieved December 8, 2009, from http://content.healthaffairs.org/cgi/content/full/ hlthaff.w3.552v1/DC1

Health Insurance Portability and Accountability Act (HIPAA) of 1996, PL 104-191, 42 U.S.C. §§ 201 *et seq.*

Hoenig, H. (1993). Educating primary care physicians in geriatric rehabilitation. *Clinics in Geriatric Medicine, 9,* 883–893.

Iezzoni, L.I. (2002). The canary in the mine. *Archives of Physical Medicine and Rehabilitation, 83,* 1476–1478.

Iezzoni, L.I. (2003). *When walking fails. Mobility problems of adults with chronic conditions.* Berkeley, CA: University of California Press.

Iezzoni, L.I., Killeen, M.B., & O'Day, B.L. (2006). Rural residents with disabilities confront substantial barriers to obtaining primary care. *Health Services Research, 41*(4, Pt. 1), 1258–1275.

Iezzoni, L.I., & O'Day, B.L. (2006). *More than ramps: A guide to improving health care quality and access for people with disabilities.* New York: Oxford University Press.

Institute of Medicine Committee on a National Agenda for the Prevention of Disabilities. (1991). *Disability in America: Toward a national agenda for prevention.* Washington, DC: National Academies Press.

Institute of Medicine Committee on Disability in America. (2007). *The future of disability in America.* Washington, DC: National Academies Press.

Institute of Medicine Committee on Quality of Health Care in America. (2001). *Crossing the quality chasm: A new health system for the 21st century.* Washington, DC: National Academy Press.

Institute of Medicine Committee on the Consequences of Uninsurance. (2001). *Coverage Matters. Insurance and health care.* Washington, DC: National Academies Press.

Institute of Medicine Committee on the Consequences of Uninsurance. (2002a). *Care without coverage. Too little, too late.* Washington, DC: National Academies Press.

Institute of Medicine Committee on the Consequences of Uninsurance. (2002b). *Health insurance is a family matter*. Washington, DC: National Academies Press.

Kaiser Family Foundation. (2009, February). *Children's Health Insurance Program Reauthorization Act of 2009 (CHIPRA)* (Publication No. 7863). Menlo Park, CA: Author.

Kaiser Family Foundation. (2009, March). *The role of section 1115 waivers in Medicaid and SCHIP: Looking back and looking forward* (Publication No. 7874). Menlo Park, CA: Author.

Kuhlthau, K., Perrin, J.M., Ettner, S.L., McLaughlin, T.J., & Gortmaker, S.L. (1998). High-expenditure children with Supplemental Security Income. *Pediatrics, 102,* 610–615.

Macon, T., Miller, J.E., Gaboda, D., Simpson, T., & Cantor, J.C. (2007). Is there differential retention of children with special health care needs in the State Children's Health Insurance Program? *Pediatrics 120,* e1217–e1224.

McDonagh, J.E. (2006). *Growing up ready for emerging adulthood*. Birmingham, UK: Birmingham Children's Hospital, University of Birmingham.

McGlynn, E.A., Asch, S.M., Adams, J., Keesey, J., Hicks, J., DeCristofaro, A., & Kerr, E.A. (2003). The quality of health care delivered to adults in the United States. *The New England Journal of Medicine, 348,* 2635–2645.

Moss, K., & Burris, S. (2007). *The employment discrimination provisions of the Americans with Disabilities Act: Implementation and impact*. Washington, DC: National Academies Press.

National Initiative for Children's Healthcare Quality. (2005). *Spread of the medical home concept. Comprehensive final report to the Maternal and Child Health Bureau*. Retrieved December 12, 2007, from http://www.nichq.org/NR/rdonlyres/83AFF39E-BF99-40B3-8803-442623776043/0/MHLC_2_Final_Report_Final.pdf

Newacheck, P.W., & Halfon, N. (2000). Prevalence, impact, and trends in childhood disability due to asthma. *Archives of Pediatrics and Adolescent Medicine, 154,* 287–293.

Newacheck, P.W., & Kim, S.E. (2005). A national profile of health care utilization and expenditures for children with special health care needs. *Archives of Pediatrics and Adolescent Medicine, 159,* 10–17.

Olson, L.M., Tang, S.F., & Newacheck, P.W. (2005). Children in the United States with discontinuous health insurance coverage. *The New England Journal of Medicine, 353,* 382–391.

Perrin, J.M., & Stein, R.E. (1991). Reinterpreting disability: Changes in supplemental security income for children. *Pediatrics, 88,* 1047–1051.

Peter, N.G., Forke, C.M., Ginsburg, K.R., & Schwarz, D.F. (2009). Transition from pediatric to adult care: Internists' perspectives. *Pediatrics, 123,* 417–423.

Reis, J.P., Breslin, M.L., Iezzoni, L.I., & Kirschner, K.L. (2004). *It takes more than ramps to solve the crisis in healthcare for people with disabilities*. Chicago: Rehabilitation Institute of Chicago.

Rosenbaum, S. (2002). Medicaid. *The New England Journal of Medicine, 346,* 635–640.

Silver, E.J., Westbrook, L.E., & Stein, R.E. (1998). Relationship of parental psychological distress to consequences of chronic health conditions in children. *Journal of Pediatric Psychology, 23,* 5–15.

Sipski, M.L., Alexander, C., & Sherman, A. (2005). *Sexuality and disability*. Philadelphia: Lippincott-Raven Publishers.

Social Security Administration. (2007). *Annual report of the Supplemental Security Income program*. Washington, DC: Author.

Stein, R.E., & Jessop, D.J. (1984). Does pediatric home care make a difference for children with chronic illness? *Pediatrics, 73,* 845–853.

Stein, R.E., Shenkman, E., Wegener, D.H., & Silver, E.J. (2003). Health of children in Title XXI: Should we worry? *Pediatrics, 112,* e112–e118.

Thyen, U., Kuhlthau, K., & Perrin, J.M. (1999). Employment, child care, and mental health of mothers caring for children assisted by technology. *Pediatrics, 103,* 1235–1242.

Turk, M.A., & Weber, R.J. (2005). *Congenital and child-onset disabilities: Age-related changes and secondary conditions in mobility impairment.* Philadelphia: Lippincott-Raven Publishers.

U.S. Census Bureau. (2006). *Current population survey: Annual social and economic supplement, 2006.* Retrieved July 31, 2007, from http://www.census.gov/hhes/www/cpstc/cps_table_creator.html

U.S. Department of Health and Human Services. (2000). *Healthy people 2010: Understanding and improving health and objectives for improving health* (2nd ed., Vols. 1–2). Washington, DC: U.S. Government Printing Office.

U.S. Department of Health and Human Services. (2005). *The Surgeon General's call to action to improve the health and wellness of persons with disabilities.* Washington, DC: Author.

Yu, H., Dick, A.W., & Szilagyi, P.G. (2006). Role of SCHIP in serving children with special health care needs. *Health Care Financing Review, 28,* 53–64.

5

Transportation

Vehicles for Participation by Youth with Disabilities and Chronic Health Conditions

Bryna Helfer

Transportation is a critical consideration for all youth when thinking about living independently in the community. Having a way to "get around" is often the deciding factor for where you live, where you work, and where you play. One of the first things adolescents want to do is to go out without their parents—visit friends, shop, make independent decisions, and accept personal responsibility. Obtaining a driver's license is a rite of passage for many of America's youth. However, there are many individuals with disabilities that do not have access to automobiles and will rely on public transportation for that same sense of freedom and independence (Project ACTION, 2005).

The U.S. Bureau of Transportation Statistics (2002) found that six million people with disabilities have difficulties obtaining the transportation they need, and research conducted by the National Organization on Disability (2000) established that nearly one third of people with disabilities report having inadequate access to transportation. However, research has also shown that having accessible modes and learning independent means of mobility increased self-determination for people with disabilities (Moon & Hernandez, n.d.; West, Barcus, Brook, & Rayfield, 1995). Independent use of transportation is "one of the survival skills that people with disabilities must learn in order to become truly autonomous in their communities" (Samberg, 1996, p. 543). Independent travel "requires a coordination of planning and action that many individuals perform every day and take for granted, but which people with disabilities must consider with care" (Denver, 1989, p. 13).

> Tony is a 19 year old who uses a power wheelchair for his mobility and who recently graduated from high school. He is living at home with his parents, and they drive him to community college classes and other destinations whenever he needs to go anywhere. During high school, he received door to door transportation on a daily basis. He was not introduced to public transportation services or to complementary paratransit services available under the Americans with Disabilities Act (ADA) of 1990 (PL 101-336). With the right training, he could easily increase his transportation options and his independence.

Without the opportunity to learn the necessary skills, behaviors, and strategies, many students with disabilities will have fewer postschool options. The inability to travel, or lack of knowledge about how to access the range of transportation options in the community, frequently translates into difficulties finding employment and participating in postsecondary educational/vocational training, recreation, leisure, and other community activities (Project ACTION, 2005). As youth make the transition to adulthood, it is important that they identify their transportation options as they consider college, volunteer experiences, work opportunities, and going out with friends. Youth should be encouraged to consider the "family of transportation" options for "getting around."

The family of transportation options includes walking, biking, driving, riding with friends and family, using the bus or subway, getting a paratransit ride (if eligible), using taxi services, and using volunteer driver programs that might be available in the community. Regardless of how someone "gets around," it is important for youth to explore their transportation options as they explore where they will live, work, learn, and play.

THE MYRIAD OF TRANSPORTATION OPTIONS AND CHALLENGES

The challenge with having access to transportation is that there might be a significant number of options or no options at all, depending on whether someone lives in a large city, a suburban area, a small town, or a rural community. Some youth with disabilities or special health care needs may be able to drive themselves if they have access to a car. Thinking about a pedestrian/bike friendly community may be another option for some youth. However, for many youth with disabilities and/or special health care needs, alternative transportation options will be important. Understanding those options can often be daunting, as there are often many complex and difficult rules to navigating the varying types of transportation options that could potentially be available.

There are approximately 64 federal programs that support transportation services for people with disabilities and others who do not drive because of limitations. Unfortunately, the transportation services provided in a community are often determined based on an individual's disability, age, destination, or funding agency (Government Accountability Office, 2003). Because of the "maze" and the challenges of finding the "right" transportation services, the Federal Interagency Coordinating Council on Access and Mobility (CCAM) is working on policies and programs that can enhance the possibilities of having a simplified point of access for individuals who need a ride. The CCAM was created as a result of a President's Executive Order on Human Service Transportation in 2004 (Exec. Order No. 13330, 1994). In its early stages, the CCAM launched United We Ride, a federal interagency initiative to promote coordinated transportation systems across the country (Federal Interagency Coordinating Council on Access and Mobility, 2005). In 2009, United We Ride is working to improve access to a coordinated system of transportation services in states and communities across the country.

A FAMILY OF TRANSPORTATION OPTIONS

On any given day, Americans use a broad range of transportation options to get around. For example, those people living in a large city may choose to drive their car, take a taxi, or use public transportation. Transportation options will vary from community to community; and from individual to individual. Larger communities might have a robust public transportation system that includes a subway, an extensive fixed route bus system, regular taxi service, and other options outlined in this chapter. However, suburban and/or rural communities might have limited or no access to transportation services. Individuals might own a car or be able to afford a taxi ride or alternatively need to use the lower priced public transportation option. For these reasons, it is important for young adults to learn about the available transportation services options and build the necessary skills to use them.

It is critical that youth also develop the necessary skills in areas related to planning, directions, time management, decision making, and problem solving in order to enhance independence and safety. Community mobility involves learning certain social and communication skills such as recognizing and responding to emergency situations, knowing how to ask for help, and independently knowing when not to interact with other people (Moon & Hernandez, n.d.; National Information Center for Children with Disabilities, 1996).

The following sections outline the various transportation options available in communities around the country and considerations for utilizing these.

School Transportation

Although transportation is an integrated aspect of school for all youth with disabilities, too often youth with disabilities and/or special health care needs do not develop the skills necessary to utilize the transportation options available (e.g., driving, pedestrian access, public transportation). Part 300 (16) of the Individuals with Disabilities Education Act (IDEA) of 1990 (PL 101-476) includes transportation as a related service: 1) travel to and from school and between schools; 2) travel in and around school buildings; and 3) specialized equipment (e.g., special or adapted buses, lifts, and ramps), if required to provide special transportation for a child with a disability. Unfortunately, this provision is often implemented by offering a "door to door" or "special bus" for students. This type of transportation segregates students with disabilities from others, typically does not provide access to activities that occur after school (e.g., choir, band, student clubs, sports), and limits a student's exposure to the necessary skills for safe community mobility that are learned and developed over time. As a result, as youth graduate from the school system, they are often unprepared for utilizing the available transportation options in their communities.

Recognizing Options for Driving

Most teenagers look forward to their sixteenth birthday and driving. For youth with disabilities, driving may not be an option. It is important for youth to have the chance to consider the option of driving. Driver education classes are often available through local high schools. However, McGill and Vogtle (2001) identified that youth with disabilities are often not given the chance to participate in drivers' education with their peers at school. They recommend that parents and school systems need to be proactive regarding the driving needs of students with disabilities by establishing policies and programs for this population's special needs.

> Julia just turned 16 years old with spina bifida and uses a manual wheelchair for her mobility. She is taking the classroom component of driver education at school with her peers. The school has helped her access driver rehabilitation services for training on the use of hand controls. The school has also been working with vocational rehabilitation to help her explore potential funding support for modifications on the family's vehicle.

Licensing Depending on age, a graduated or restricted license may be required before a student can apply for a full-privilege driver's license. Although the questions on the exam may vary, all states require that new drivers study the rules of the road in order to pass the state's required written test. Individuals must pass written tests before they are issued an instruction permit or a driver's license. Youth and parents can find practice tests for the state where they live at http://www.dmv.org. If needed, individuals with disabilities should request reasonable accommodations necessary for taking the exams.

Driver Education and Driver Rehabilitation Services For youth with learning disabilities, considerations should be made for assisting the student with getting reasonable accommodations and accessing alternative assessments during the testing process. For youth with physical disabilities, it will be important for them to have a chance to receive an assessment to evaluate their potential for driving. Driver rehabilitation specialists perform comprehensive evaluations to identify the adaptive equipment most suited to an individual's needs (National Highway Traffic Safety Administration, 1999).

Vehicle Modifications Some individuals with disabilities need specific types of modifications made to and/or adaptive equipment added to their motor vehicles to meet their transportation needs (National Highway Traffic Safety Administration, 2007). This may include lifts, wheelchair securements, hand controls, brake extenders, special mirrors, and other equipment that is available. It is recommended that individuals explore the background of dealers regarding experience with adapting vehicles and checking references (National Highway Traffic Safety Administration, 1999).

Riding with Family and Friends

Some teens and young adults may be without either a license or a car. In these cases, it is not unusual for individuals to get rides from friends, parents, or family members. There are some considerations when exploring options for arranging rides: 1) If a teen or young adult needs unique assistance (e.g., sitting in the front seat to avoid dizziness; needing someone to walk the individual directly to the destination, as opposed to dropping a teen or youth off at the curb), it will be important to identify these needs and discuss them with the individuals providing a ride; 2) individuals who use a wheelchair, walker, or cane will want to check with the individual providing a ride regarding space and discuss the level of assistance he or she may need to transfer in and out of the car; and 3) for individuals who use wheelchairs who cannot transfer out of the chair, it will be important to have access to a vehicle with a lift. In some cases, the family may own such a vehicle and may be willing to have other people drive. Families should ensure that the individual driver has a current license and that he or she will be covered on the insurance policy.

It is also very important that teens or young adults fully recognize that they should never be expected to get into a vehicle with someone who has been drinking. In this case, the teen or youth should discuss a backup plan prior to going out and be prepared to implement the plan if necessary.

Public Transportation Options

Public transportation can be a viable option for individuals who do not have access to a private vehicle; however, it can vary by community. Communities often have "fixed route" service available, where vehicles run on regular, predetermined, prescheduled routes, with no variation. Fixed-route services typically use large vehicles like buses, printed schedules or timetables, and designated bus stops where passengers board and get off the vehicle (Federal Transit Administration, 2007).

More than a decade after the advent of the ADA, accessible public transportation continues to offer many advantages to people with disabilities. Since the passage of the ADA in 1990, transit systems' buses and trains have become increasingly accessible. Accessibility means the extent to which places and equipment, including transit vehicles, are barrier-free and can be used by people who have disabilities, including those who use wheelchairs (Project ACTION, 2000). The American Public Transportation Association (2007) reports that 96% of all public fixed route buses have low floor or lift access. The more young adults know about using buses and trains, the more they can control their schedule and move freely about their community (Project ACTION, 2000).

ADA Complementary Paratransit Services

Under the ADA, transit agencies must provide ADA complementary paratransit services for individuals who have functional limitations that prevent them from using the fixed route system. Transit systems must provide ADA complementary paratransit services within three fourths mile of the fixed route services for individuals who cannot independently get to the bus, get on the bus, or independently and safely navigate the route of the bus (PL 101-336). Transit agencies are only required to offer ADA complementary paratransit services during regular fixed route service hours. Therefore, if the community only has fixed route bus service available from 9 a.m. to 5 p.m. for the general public, those are the same hours of operation for ADA complementary paratransit services. However, the U.S. Federal Transit Administration (2007) released guidance for the New Freedom Program, which provides funding for transit agencies to provide services beyond those required in the ADA, like the three-fourths-mile radius and hours of operation.

> Dan is 22 years old and has a job at a local recreation center, is active in Special Olympics, and also sings in a local church choir. He lives just one half mile from the bus stop. However, because of the challenges and distance required for crossing several complex streets to get to the bus stop, he is eligible for paratransit services in his local community. Dan makes his own reservations and gets picked up at the curb outside of his apartment. This option has significantly increased Dan's independence and mobility within the community.

If a student was receiving "door to door" service or getting a ride on a "special bus" during his or her school years, that does not automatically translate to eligibility for ADA complementary paratransit services. Eligibility for ADA complementary paratransit service is based on an individual's functional ability to use the fixed route service. Transit agencies often conduct an in-person assessment to determine an individual's eligibility. This assessment often includes evaluating an individuals' ability to get to the bus and get on the bus. The assessment will also include an evaluation of his or her ability to independently and safely navigate the fixed route system.

Complementary paratransit services under the ADA are not *complimentary*—in other words, these services are not free. In fact, the ADA allows transit authorities to charge up to two times the fare of a regular fixed route fare for the general public. Therefore, if the fare for a bus token to ride from the grocery store to the downtown business district is $1, then the transit authority can charge up to $2 for the same ride on paratransit.

Individuals using ADA complementary paratransit services often have to make advance reservations, be open to a negotiated pick up time, and adhere to cancellation policies. While ADA complementary paratransit services provide access regardless of destination for those individuals who are eligible, it does not offer as much flexibility as taking the fixed route bus for riders. Therefore, for individuals who can learn to use the fixed route system safely, even if only for a few familiar routes, more opportunities for community participation open.

Other Transportation Options

Public transportation services (e.g., subway, fixed route bus, ADA complementary paratransit) may only be available on specific days or at specific hours. Therefore, it is important for youth to explore all of the options for "getting around."

University Transportation Many universities provide campus transportation. When exploring college and university options, it will be important for college-bound youth to ask about available transportation options, including the accessibility of transportation services, the hours of operations, the routes that the service covers, and the location of bus stops. This is especially noteworthy for youth who will depend on university transportation for getting around campus.

Specialized Van Services Many social service and disability-specific programs provide special transportation services for individuals involved in targeted programs. For example, a community-based rehabilitation program or vocational training program may provide specialized transportation to and from the program each day for the period of enrollment. However, this is typically limited service for only program-specific activities.

Medicaid Transportation Individuals who receive health insurance through Medicaid may be eligible for nonemergency medical transportation to travel to medical and other related health appointments. It will be important for youth to explore the eligibility and availability of service in the state where they are living and receiving health services.

Taxi Service Although more common in urban settings, many communities have taxicabs available for transportation in the community. Accessible taxicabs are becoming more available, though they are still not as popular as regular cars. Therefore, it is especially important to research taxi options—especially when traveling to unfamiliar cities or towns. In most cases, reservations for accessible taxicabs should be made in advance to ensure availability.

Volunteer Services Many communities, especially those in rural areas, are launching volunteer driving programs. These programs are often coordinated through nonprofit organizations, including Centers for Independent Living.

PAYING FOR TRANSPORTATION SERVICES

The CCAM has identified several dozen programs that provide some financial support for a bus pass, a taxi voucher, or for gas mileage to get to and from specific types of programs and services. It is important that each individual explores these options for each program from which he or she receives services. For example, if an individual is a consumer of vocational rehabilitation services, he or she should ask his or her rehabilitation counselor if reimbursement for transportation is an eligible expense to get to and from job-related training and services (United We Ride, n.d.). In addition, there are other reduced fare programs for individuals with disabilities that are required by law.

Half-Price Fare Options for People with Disabilities Public transit systems that receive federal grant funding for public transportation in urban communities must certify that the rates charged to older adults and individuals with disabilities during nonpeak hours for fixed-route transportation will not exceed one half of the rates generally applicable to other people at peak hours. These same grant recipients also must provide half-fare rates to any person presenting a Medicare card issued to that person (Safe, Affordable, Flexible, Efficient Transportation Equity Act: A Legacy for Users [PL 109-59], Section 5307). Local transit authorities have information regarding application and dissemination processes.

Costs for ADA Complementary Paratransit Services As stated previously, "complementary" paratransit services under the ADA does not mean "free." In fact, the ADA allows transit authorities to charge up to two times the fare of a regular fixed route fare for the general public. Therefore, if the fare for a bus token to ride from the grocery store to the downtown business district is $1; then the transit authority can charge up to $2 for the same ride on paratransit.

Bus Tokens or Transit Pass Support As indicated earlier, many social service and/or disability-related programs will support the costs of a bus token or transit pass to support individuals who need transportation to get to and from the service or supports provided by the specific program. For example, some individuals may be eligible for a transit pass to get to or from job training if they are a consumer of employment services.

Gas Mileage Reimbursements Similar to bus tokens or transit pass support, a few programs will support reimbursement for mileage. The reimbursement rates may vary from agency to agency and between geographic regions. In addition, some programs may require specific documentation. It will be important to explore this with the agencies where an individual receives support.

Support for Vehicle Modification Very few public programs support the costs of a private vehicle and/or modification for a private vehicle. However, in some cases, individuals receiving services from either the U.S. Department of Veterans Affairs and/or Rehabilitative Services may be eligible for gaining support in this area. Typically, the support is based on the connection to the goals and objectives for returning to work and community activities.

THE IMPORTANCE OF NAVIGATION

Luis is 15 years old and enrolled in special education in the New York City school system. He is enrolled in the travel training program where he is learning the necessary skills so that he can safely walk to the bus stop, get on the bus, pay his fare, identify his stop, exit the bus, and successfully get to his final destination.

Regardless of how an individual travels in the community (e.g., drive, walk, bike, bus, train), it will be important for youth to learn the necessary skills to safely navigate to and from destinations. Students without disabilities learn navigational skills at an early age as they learn to cross the street, ride their bike, and use the general education school bus; however, it is unclear when students with disabilities are introduced to these skills.

Sohlberg, Fickas, Lemoncello, and Hung (2009) validated a model of community transportation knowledge and skills to ground future work and provide a framework for assessment and treatment of necessary travel skills. The resulting model, the Activities of Community Transportation (ACTs), is the first such model to be introduced. Three "ACTs Wheels" present a general, theoretical framework to address community navigation steps, requisite supports, and person-centered skills required for successful community transportation using fixed route or paratransit public transportation systems.

IDEA 1990 (§ 300.39) defines travel training as the following:

> Providing instruction, as appropriate, to children with significant cognitive disabilities, and any other children with disabilities who require this instruction, to enable them to (1) Develop an awareness of the environment in which they live; and (2) Learn the skills necessary to move effectively and safely from place to place within that environment (e.g., in school, in the home, at work, and in the community).

The field of travel instruction and training emerged in the 1990s and focuses on comprehensive, intensive instruction to teach individuals with impairments other than visual challenges to safely and independently travel on public transportation (Groce, 1996). The explicit goal of travel training is to help people "develop autonomy and practice their right to move freely through a community" (Newbigging & Laskey, 1995, p. 75). Many transportation agencies and/or local disability organizations (e.g., Independent Living Centers) also make "travel training" available to help individuals with disabilities build the necessary skills to utilize public transportation in their community. Instructional elements often include 1) orientation to the student's immediate environment and landmarks, 2) learning routes of travel and street crossing skills, 3) understanding fixed route schedules, 4) identification of transportation vehicles and transit stops, 5) skills required for paying fares, 6) interacting with transit operators and other passengers, and 7) emergency procedures (Project ACTION, 2004).

RECOMMENDATIONS

As discussed throughout this chapter, there are a variety of strategies and approaches for getting around the community. However, the key challenge is helping youth build the necessary skills so that they can utilize the options available. To do this, introduction to community mobility skills must start at a younger age and continue throughout the transition years. Therefore, school systems must rethink the opportunities for integrating community skills for all students, especially for youth with disabilities and/or special health care needs. In this regard, the following recommendations are put forward:

1. Ensure that travel training is included as part of a student's individualized transition plan. As discussed in this chapter, it is critical that students develop the necessary skills to safely navigate the community. While these skills should be developed throughout a child's development, travel training will facilitate the development of specific skills related to navigating the community and public transportation systems. School districts can conduct travel training directly or alternatively partner with local transportation agencies.

2. Include eligible students with disabilities in driver education programs. For students with disabilities who have driving as an option, students should be included in driver education classroom sessions and, to the extent possible, in the driving component as well. Schools should work closely with driver

rehabilitation specialists to ensure successful outcomes for students with disabilities.

3. Include students with and without disabilities onto the same school buses and routes. School districts often provide door-to-door service in a vehicle that is separate from school transportation provided for other students. Although this may be an appropriate strategy for supporting some students with disabilities, it significantly limits students' ability to build the necessary skills that are obtained throughout a child's developmental sequence. There are several strategies for schools to consider as they integrate general education and special education transportation:

   a. Extending Use of Small Buses: School districts can explore options for integrating general education students onto the special education buses by creating a pick up point near the special education student's home and having students with and without disabilities ride the small bus.

   b. Expanding Access to General Education Transportation: Include students with disabilities in general education bus routes provided for all students. This may require the utilization of a lift-equipped vehicle for general education routes or the addition of a monitor. Including students with disabilities on general education school buses will help to facilitate community mobility and navigation skills throughout their school experiences.

   c. Bus Attendants: Many students with disabilities are able to ride the regular school bus with support provided by an aide, who can be an instructional assistant or a volunteer. Some local education agencies also use older students to provide this service.

   d. Bus Stop Monitors: For students who may need assistance with going to the bus stop or waiting at the bus stop independently, there may be consideration for adding a bus stop monitor. Bus stop monitor positions may be filled by parents or community volunteers. Bus stop monitors will facilitate safe travel for all students.

   e. Buddy System: Sometimes students with disabilities just need a "buddy" to walk with them to and from the bus stop. Schools might consider building a buddy system for facilitating safe travel for school transportation.

   f. Positive Behavior Supports: Recognizing that the school day begins at the bus stop is a first important step to ensuring that all students have a safe and positive experience. Many schools are implementing positive behavior support programs that include the integration of strategies on the bus.

REFERENCES

Americans with Disabilities Act (ADA) of 1990, PL 101-336, 42 U.S.C. §§ 12101 *et seq.*

American Public Transportation Association. (2007). *Public transportation fact book.* Washington, DC: Author.

Bureau of Transportation Statistics. (2002). *Freedom to travel.* Washington, DC: U.S. Department of Transportation.

Denver, R.B. (1989). A taxonomy of community living skills. *Exceptional Child, 55,* 395–404.

Exec. Order No. 13330, 69 Fed. Reg. 9185 (February 26, 2004).

Federal Interagency Coordinating Council on Access and Mobility. (2005). *Report to the President.* Washington, DC: Author.

Federal Transit Administration. (2007). *New Freedom program guidance circular C 9045.1.* Washington, DC: U.S. Department of Transportation.

Government Accountability Office. (2003). *Transportation-disadvantaged populations.* Washington, DC: Author.

Groce, M.M. (1996, June 9). A model of a travel training program—the New York City Board of Education Travel Training Program. *NICHCY transition summary,* 10–13.

Individuals with Disabilities Education Act (IDEA) of 1990, PL 101-476, 20 U.S.C. §§ 1400 *et seq.*

McGill, T., & Vogtle, L. (2001). Driver's education for students with physical disabilities. *Exceptional Children, 67*(4), 455–466.

Moon, M.S., & Hernandez, G. (n.d.). *Teaching community mobility skills to adolescents and young adults with disabilities.* College Park, MD: University of Maryland.

National Highway Traffic Safety Administration. (1999). *Adapting motor vehicles for people with disabilities.* Washington, DC: U.S. Department of Transportation.

National Highway Traffic Safety Administration. (2007). *Research notes: Estimating the number of vehicles adapted for use by persons with disabilities.* Washington, DC: U.S. Department of Transportation.

National Information Center for Children and Youth with Disabilities. (1996, June 9). *NICHCY transition summary.* Washington, DC: Author.

National Organization on Disability. (2000). *N.O.D./Harris survey of Americans with disabilities.* Washington, D.C: Author.

National Resource Center on Human Service Transportation. (2007). *Transit pass toolkit.* Washington, DC: Community Transit Association of America.

Newbigging, E.D., & Laskey, J.W. (1995). Riding the bus: Teaching an adult with a brain injury to use a transit system to travel independently to and from work. *Brain Injury, 10,* 543–550.

Project ACTION. (2000). *Rights and responsibilities of transit customers with disabilities.* Washington, DC: Easter Seals.

Project ACTION. (2004). *Competencies for the practice of travel training and travel instruction.* Washington, DC: Easter Seals.

Project ACTION. (2005). *Public transportation, a route to freedom.* Washington, DC: Easter Seals.

Safe, Affordable, Flexible, Efficient Transportation Equity Act: A Legacy for Users, PL 109-59, 49 U.S.C.

Samberg, S.K. (1996). Travel training for people with physical disabilities. *National Information Center for Children and Youth with Disabilities Transition Summary.* Volume 9(June), 13–15.

Social Security Act of 1935, PL 74-271, 42 U.S.C. §§ 301 *et seq.*

Sohlberg, M.M., Fickas, S., Lemoncello, R., & Hung, P.F. (2009). Validation of the Activities of Community Transportation (ACTs) model of community navigation for individuals with cognitive impairments. *Disability and Rehabilitation, 31*(11), 887–897.

United We Ride. (n.d.). *Community transportation options directory.* Washington, DC: Federal Interagency Coordinating Council on Access and Mobility.

United We Ride. (2007). *Family of services fact sheet.* Washington, DC: Federal Interagency Coordinating Council on Access and Mobility.

West, M., Barcus, J.M., Brook, V., & Rayfield, R.G. (1995). An exploratory analysis of self determination of persons with disabilities. *Journal of Vocational Rehabilitation, 5,* 357–364.

6

Housing

Choosing, Getting, and
Keeping Homes as Young Adults with
Disabilities and Chronic Health Conditions

Valerie Fletcher

In most societies, adulthood is measured by increasing degrees of independence and responsibility. For a good portion of the 20th century, common rites of passage in American society included acquiring a car and eventually moving into a place of one's own alone or with a partner, likely a spouse. Images of those simpler times are fodder for nostalgia movies but not particularly relevant or resonant for most Americans today. The changing social context has upended familiar expectations. No one is immune from today's more ambiguous and complex reality, but the path can be especially difficult for young people with disabilities and chronic health conditions.

The 21st century transition stage includes the need to remain in school years longer to earn even a modest living wage, a major shift in cultural demographics, a more eclectic mix of mores and values, and even a burgeoning sense of responsibility that personal life choices affect the planet and its sustainability. The nation is more culturally and linguistically diverse than ever before, though tougher immigration laws and a faltering economy have slowed rates of immigration.

In 2008, the U.S. Census Bureau reported that the overall minority population was 34% of the total population and predicted that white children would be a minority in 2023, with the full population following in 2042. In May of 2009, the Census Bureau announced a correction. The nation's minority population continues to expand, but it has slowed down. New projections, expected for release in 2009, may result in shifting the calendar forward 10 years for the minority tipping point (Yen, 2009).

It is important to recognize that young people from multicultural communities are represented among young people with disabilities and chronic health conditions in larger proportions than even their growing numbers would predict. For example, in most states, African American children are identified at 150% to 400% the rate of white children in the disability categories of mental retardation and emotional disturbance (Civil Rights Project, 2002). In a chronic health condition area like HIV infection, African American youth between 13 and 24 years of age account for 55% of all HIV infections in the age group (Centers for Disease Control and Prevention, 2008).The pattern of over-representation of African American and Latino students in special education over white or Asian students has come to be known as "disproportionality" (Deninger, 2008). The Individuals with Disabilities Education Improvement Act (IDEA) of 2004 (PL 108-446) responded with a set of new requirements for documentation in an attempt to generate better data and help to correct at least some of the subjective decisions about diagnoses that contribute to the problem (U.S. Department of Education, 2005).

Additional changing patterns in American society include sharp changes in household composition. Reports based on the 2000 census tell parts of the story of shifting patterns of how we live. Young people with disabilities and serious health conditions, like their age peers, are less likely today to have a married parent nuclear family household and yet more likely to remain longer in the parental home.

- Families represented 81% of households in 1970 but only 69% in 2000 (U.S. Census Bureau, 2000).

- In 2000, 56% of men and 43% of women ages 18–24 lived at home with one or more parents (U.S. Census Bureau, 2000).

- Married-couple households declined dramatically from 40% of households in 1970 to only 24% in 2000 (Fields & Casper, 2001). The majority (55%) of married couple households lived in suburban areas (Fields & Casper, 2001).

The great majority of young people, including people with disabilities or chronic health conditions, will make it into work and a home and a social support system by the time they are 25. Young people with disabilities and chronic health conditions have also become more diverse in the type and complexity of functional issues that they experience and in the complexity of challenges they must overcome when making the transition to adulthood. In *On Your Own Without a Net: The Transition to Adulthood for Vulnerable Populations,* the authors report a projection based on existing patterns that at least a million and a half—5–7% of the total—will not (Osgood, Foster, Flanagan, & Ruth, 2006, pp. v–viii). The book classifies seven vulnerable populations: youth involved in the criminal justice system, youth formerly in the criminal justice system, runaway and homeless youth, special education students, young people in the mental health system, and youth with physical disabilities. Given the populations, people with disabilities or chronic health conditions comprise a high proportion of the total. These young people are not so much making a transition as reeling from being severed from what slim supports they have had when they reach the legal age of adulthood. These youth are not embedded in social networks that can support their evolving identities so much as in health and human service systems with arbitrary dates of cut-off (Osgood et al., 2006, pp. v–viii). For this portion of the transition population, a stable home may always have been elusive and more critical than ever if they are to survive and have the opportunity to thrive as adults.

STATEMENT OF GOALS AND EXPECTATIONS

The World Health Organization's *International Classification of Functioning, Disability and Health (ICF)* with its contextual or "biopsychosocial model" definition of disability and health frames the issues. In the model, health conditions (diseases, disorders, and injuries) must be understood first in the context of internal personal factors such as gender, age, social background, education, behavioral pattern, and character (World Health Organization, 2002). The other context is external and includes the physical, information, and communication environments as well as social and policy environments. Disability occurs at the intersection of the individual and each of these environments. The ICF contextual definition invites attention to the powerful opportunity to shape environments to minimize disability and enhance strengths. It focuses the worthy challenge of figuring out housing. There is a clear outcome to pursue regardless of obstacles and confusion along the way: the right home diminishes the negative aspects of functional limitation and supports you in your particular pursuit of happiness. Three overarching principles, responsive to the contextual definition of disability, characterize the best models currently in place and should guide planning for innovation and expansion:

1. Person-centered decision making: Person-centered choice isn't guaranteed to be successful, but it has proven the most resilient process for finding success eventually. For some young people, it may work best and perhaps only work at all if they and those that care about them invest in learning to recognize and express what they need and want.
2. Flexibility in choice: Flexibility accommodates differences in types of dwelling and in social circumstance (e.g., living alone, with a partner or roommates, with extended family). It includes an assumption of flexible supports that are more or less intensive in relation to need. Flexibility is also a principle that can frame policy and practice to respect the disparate values, priorities, and cultures of youth and their families.
3. Interdependence between housing and transportation: For want of addressing the issues in tandem, many other choices will be blocked or compromised. Americans have a long habit of not wanting to consider the inevitable tie between transportation and housing. In the United States, our large landmass and historically inexpensive fuel has allowed us to avoid making sustainable choices about

where we live. It can be too costly a habit for young people with disabilities or chronic health conditions. Failure to pay serious and simultaneous attention to transportation in relation to housing can condemn a young person to a long roster of disabling contexts: dependence upon family, friends, or caregivers for transportation anywhere and everywhere; isolation; constrained choices of work and leisure; excessive drain by transportation costs on personal budget. No housing choice is a solution without a reliable, cost-effective transportation plan.

In order to keep clear the distinctive issues of young people with disabilities or chronic health conditions, it is important to keep in mind the broader patterns of young adults in the United States now. Today's twenty-somethings are taking longer to settle down and figure out their lives. University of Maryland developmental psychologist Jeffrey Arnett calls it "emerging adulthood…a time of instability, self-focus, exploration and perceived possibility" (Arnett, 2004). Transition is becoming longer and more complex for most everyone, and we should recognize the impact of these shifts on those young people with disabilities and chronic health conditions.

HOUSING OPTIONS AND WHAT WE KNOW NOW

This section looks at current trends in housing and transportation, housing models with access to services, and additional models for youth with disabilities and chronic health conditions.

Housing and Transportation

The nation's economic crisis that began in 2008 and the central factor of the untenable behavior of the housing sector is an opportunity to identify policy opportunities for young people with disabilities. We can no longer pretend that housing and transportation are separate choices. There are critical lessons to learn from a study by the Center for Housing Policy of the National Housing Conference with funding provided by the John D. and Catherine T. MacArthur Foundation. *A Heavy Load: The Combined Housing and Transportation Burdens of Working Families,* by Barbara J. Lipman (2006), sounds an alarm important to heed in evolving best-practice transition models. The focus of the report is on the impact for working families of the dual costs of housing and transportation and the folly of failing to analyze them together. The research pays particular attention to the burden on households with incomes of $20,000 to $35,000—an income bracket common to a majority of young people with and without disabilities. Ignoring these facts puts at risk the hope of both financial stability and quality of life. Among the shocking and relevant findings are as follows:

• For every dollar saved on housing by locating further from work or other necessary destinations, a household spends 77¢ more on transportation.

- On average, the study found that families in the 28 metropolitan areas analyzed for the report spend 57% of their incomes on the combined costs of housing and transportation with roughly 28% going for housing and 29% going for transportation.

- For the lowest income group—households with $20,000 to $35,000—the proportions vary from 54% to 70% of income in combined costs of housing and transportation for people that live in exurban locations distant from employment centers.

From the perspective of the housing crisis that began in the fall of 2008, the alarming news of 2006 looks like an early warning that still did not predict how bad things could get. Given the present crisis in housing and the calls for more sustainable solutions, it is an ideal moment to model innovation that pairs housing and transportation (e.g., transit-oriented development) for this group of young people by providing incentives to developers or preference to transitional youth for units in transition-oriented developments.

Housing Models with Access to Service

Packaging housing and services together was once the norm for community living and the desirable alternative to institutional care. Prior to the mid to late 1980s, public policy advocacy for people with disabilities promoted a "continuum of care," a model in which people moved to different settings as their needs changed. Services were attached to the residence (United Cerebral Palsy, 2009). It is now widely considered a regressive model, unnecessarily burdensome to people with disabilities and perceived as perpetuating segregation. It has been supplanted with a supported housing approach in which the person has stable conventional housing with rights of tenancy. Flexible services increase or decrease in response to personal need. The vision of supported housing spans disability groups including those that focus on developmental disabilities, mental health, and HIV/AIDS.

There is substantial national consensus that the housing solution that people with disabilities and their families and advocates want is a home of one's own, ranging from a rental apartment secured independently or through a non-profit provider to an owned single family home, with supports and services provided through person-based flexible models. In a public policy fact sheet, the organization for people with intellectual and developmental disabilities known as The Arc (2006) calls a home of one's own "the cornerstone of independence" and advocates an end to the crisis of too little decent, safe, affordable, and accessible housing.

The Substance Abuse and Mental Health Services Administration of the U.S. Department of Health and Human Services frames its mission today in terms of a "recovery oriented system" that promotes consumer-driven and consumer-operated approaches. It stipulates that its ambitious and progressive goal rests upon stable housing. Without it, no amount of community service can support recovery: "Housing is perhaps the first line of treatment for people with psychiatric disabilities" (Denton & Bianco, 2001).

Supportive housing may be a clear advocacy preference today, but there remain many variations on housing with less flexible support services. Waves of deinstitutionalization in the 1970s gave birth to the community system of human service providers. They were surrogates for government services funded almost exclusively by state agencies, and the services were sometimes supplemented by Social Security and/or Medicaid. These providers created and managed the system. State health and human service agencies licensed the programs, controlled access to these expensive supports exclusively for people who met their eligibility requirements, and paid or contributed to the cost of services. Community providers have, in most states, evolved services that are a mix of the old continuum of care model with more flexible supportive housing programs.

Providers most often have had to become sophisticated housing developers in order to package an ever-expanding number of resources necessary to make the housing affordable. The prime national resource is the U.S. Department of Housing and Urban Development (HUD)'s Section 811 Supportive Housing for Persons with Disabilities program. Section 811 funds are always for people with very low incomes (at or below 50% of the area median income) and can be used in two ways. Providers can develop and own the housing, or 811 funds can be used to create tenant-based rental assistance to give eligible people with disabilities over the age of 18 the opportunity to rent housing in the private rental market (The Arc, 2006).

Additional Models

Other housing models include intermediate care facilities for people with mental retardation (ICFs/MR), private-pay shared homes, and state-licensed private homes. These are discussed next.

Intermediate Care Facilities for People with Mental Retardation
Given the continuing crisis of too few desirable options, the nation still uses the most restrictive of the housing and support models, ICFs/MR, an optional Medicaid benefit. As of 2009, all 50 states have at least one ICF/MR and approximately 129,000 people with intellectual limitations and other related conditions live in an ICF/MR. Many residents also are not ambulatory, have seizure disorders, have psychiatric conditions, or have sensory impairments. Residents must qualify for Medicaid. Although the number of residents remains high, these facilities have greatly decreased in size since the 1970s. By 1997, 70% of them had 4–8 residents versus a pre-1977 average of 185 residents per facility (Centers for Medicare and Medicaid Services, 2006).

Private-Pay Shared Homes
A range of private firms, some local and some national, have provided housing with supports to families with adult children with disabilities that can afford to pay out of pocket. The model has met the needs

of a small portion of families, mostly with young adult children with intellectual limitations and some with other conditions. Supports are often a mix of paid staff, natural community supports, and coordination with publicly funded services.

State-Licensed Private Homes Given the chronic gap in affordable community housing options, every state has a range of housing models that stretch the inadequate inventory of housing options for people with disabilities eligible for some level of state services. Though known by slightly different names in each state (e.g., board and care homes, adult foster care), they are characterized by a couple of elements: private homeowners provide housing and basic supports like meals and laundry for one to a few individuals with disabilities in exchange for payment, most commonly from Supplemental Security Income (SSI) and/or Social Security Disability Insurance (SSDI) income. The state licenses the homes and may have an additional service relationship with the resident. This model is most common among older adults, many of whom have no families but like a family environment. The location of care is most often in urban or town centers, an asset for ready access to transportation. There may be potential for shared living arrangements with some of the same characteristics for a portion of young people interested in this kind of shared home. It would require reframing the program model but, in light of the projected pattern of baby boomers across the cultural spectrum with large homes and too little retirement income, there may be potential for this low-cost use of existing resources.

IMPEDIMENTS

Barriers to finding appropriate housing solutions for youth with disabilities and chronic health conditions are discussed in this section.

Affordability

Beginning in 1998, the Technical Assistance Collaborative, Inc., and the Consortium for Citizens with Disabilities have produced a series of reports entitled *Priced Out: The Housing Crisis for People with Disabilities*. The housing crisis that began in 2008 may have shocked the nation, but people with disabilities have had a perennial crisis in affordable housing. The 10th edition offers the following conclusions:

- Escalating rents are unaffordable in all places—on average across the nation, people with disabilities pay 112.1% of SSI payments for a modest one-bedroom unit. That's an increase from 69% in 1998.

- The geography of the crisis is large and expanding—219 housing markets across 41 states had modest one-bedroom rents exceeding 100% of monthly SSI.

- Discretionary state SSI supplements are not the answer. Even in Alaska, with the highest rate of supplements to SSI, people with disabilities receiving SSI still paid 80.6% of their monthly income for a modest one-bedroom unit (Cooper, Korman, O'Hara, & Zovistoski, 2009).

Since the passage of the Community Development Act in 1992, owners were allowed to restrict "elderly and disabled housing" to allowing "elder-only housing" in the most affordable HUD-assisted public housing developments and in privately owned, federally assisted units. Together, units already unavailable and those projected to be lost amount to as many as 300,000 units of affordable housing (National Alliance on Mental Illness, 2001).

There are two current primary tools for making ordinary housing affordable. The most significant and flexible tool is HUD's Housing Choice Vouchers (formerly Section 8), which can be used to bridge the gap between market rate and affordable. Competition with other Americans struggling with poverty guarantees that long waiting lists—sometimes stretching for many years—are the norm for these vouchers. HUD policy changed in 2005 to create an option to link Project-Based Vouchers with permanent supportive housing for people with significant disabilities (Cooper et al., 2009). In addition, fiscal year 2008 and 2009 appropriations bills included funds for an estimated 7,500 new Housing Choice Vouchers for nonelderly people with disabilities. For anyone trying to live on Social Security disability funds, these vouchers are the most efficient housing solution (Cooper et al., 2009).

Because a significant proportion of Housing Choice Vouchers are administered at the local public housing authority (PHA) level, waiting lists are town-specific. The more desirable the place, often inclusive of the availability of good transportation options, the longer the waiting list.

The other funding tool is HUD's Section 811 Supportive Housing for Persons with Disabilities program, a model more restrictive than Housing Choice Vouchers but especially valuable in that it is a financial tool for developing or purchasing affordable and accessible community housing that remains available long-term only to people with disabilities. An effort to reinvigorate and modernize the 811 program, called the Frank Melville Supportive Housing Investment Act, was reintroduced in Congress in March of 2009 and passed in the U.S. House of Representatives in July 2009. Its passage would substantially boost the community integration vision for people with disabilities (Cooper et al., 2009).

Accessibility

Accessibility in housing comprises two distinct issues. The first is a civil right to freedom from discrimination for people with disabilities and equal access to the housing of their choice as long as they meet the same economic guidelines as anyone else. People with disabilities are considered a "protected class" because of historical patterns of being denied full access to resources such as housing. The Fair Housing Act, originally passed in 1968, was comprehensively amended in 1988 (Fair Housing Amendments Act [FHAA] of 1988, PL 100-403) to include discrimination against people with disabilities or because of familial status, specifically the presence of a child under 18 (Fair Housing Accessibility FIRST, n.d.).

The second issue of housing accessibility equates to physically accessible design that accommodates primarily people who use wheelchairs. It is common for accessible units, especially if they were built for unknown residents, to align with standards but not often to exceed them. Laws and codes at the federal, state, and sometimes at the municipal level govern the requirements for architectural accessibility in housing. The most expansive requirement for accessible housing as a civil right derives from the FHAA that applies to all rented or owned properties of four units or more and designed and constructed for first occupancy after March 13, 1991. The FHAA covers multifamily homes containing four or more units in buildings that have one or more elevators, and all ground floor units in buildings containing four or more units, without an elevator. It also covers rooms in places in which people share kitchens and baths including dormitories, transitional shelters, time shares, and student housing. Rental and privately owned housing such as condominiums are covered. The FHAA can be confusing. The design standards are only one aspect for the FHAA protections for people with disabilities. Among the most important provisions in FHAA that can benefit any resident or prospective resident with a disability are "reasonable accommodation" and "reasonable modification."

A *reasonable accommodation* is a request to waive or change policies, practices, procedures, or services to allow greater accessibility and use of the premises by a person with a disability. Reasonable accommodations could mean allowing an assistive animal in a no-pets building, constructing additional handicap parking spaces, or relocating a tenant to a more accessible unit. A reasonable accommodation can only be denied if it causes an undue administrative or financial burden or changes the basic nature of the program.

A *reasonable modification* is a physical alteration to the unit or residential common use area to allow greater accessibility and use of the building by a person with a disability. Responsibility for payment for the reasonable modification will depend on which fair housing law or ordinance offers the higher standard of accessibility. Some states mandate that property owners assume all costs for the reasonable modification depending on the number of units in the building or development. FHAA mandates that the costs for a reasonable modification lie with the resident making the request.

Free information and technical assistance for all U.S. states and possessions is available during business hours at the Fair Housing Accessibility FIRST Design and Construction Resource Center: 888-341-7781 (voice/teletypewriter).

Finding Existing Accessible Units   HUD requires that PHAs that administer Housing Choice rental vouchers provide assistance to people with disabilities to find accessible housing. But HUD does not define or dictate what it considers appropriate assistance. The assistance could be newspaper listings, a list of property owners that the PHA often uses, a detailed database, or coordination with knowledgeable nonprofit agencies to assist people with disabilities looking for accessible units.

There is a National Accessible Apartment Clearinghouse serving the 50 states that can be accessed on the Internet at http://www.accessibleapartments.org/website/article.asp?id+4. An increasing number of states have created web-based accessible housing search registries as a free program that serves both people looking for accessible units and apartment owners and managers with apartments to rent. Examples include Massachusetts' Accessible Housing Registry (http://www.massaccesshousingregistry.org), Maryland's Affordable and Accessible Housing Registry (http://www.dhcd.state.md.us/Website/programs/aahr/aahr.aspx), and New York's Housing Search service (http://nyhousingsearch.gov).

It is the potential tenant's responsibility to assess the accessibility features to make sure that they meets his or her needs. There are many variations of accessible features, with many designed for a particular individual and not aligned with standardized guidelines. Visiting each unit is the only way to ensure that the accessibility features work.

Renovation for Accessibility   Renovating a home for accessibility is a challenge in two categories: paying for the work and finding the information to do it right. A person with a disability may have state or local fair housing rights that will require that a property owner or manager pay for modifications under certain circumstances. Although the Fair Housing Amendments Act of 1988 requires that owners of rental properties and condo or homeowner associations must allow a resident with a disability to modify his or her home to meet his or her accessibility needs, if the building is a "covered multi-family dwelling," the resident is expected to pay for the renovations.

There are many sources for reliable information on modifications that will deliver the best results for particular types of limitations and, for a growing portion of the country, there are reliable referrals for competent contractors. The National Resource Center on Supportive Housing and Home Modification at the University of Southern California Ethel Percy Andrus Gerontology Center is the most efficient link to reliable resources; it can be accessed on the Internet at http://www.usc.edu/dept/gero/nrcshhm/directory. It is important to track information to align with individual needs. It is becoming easier to find home modification information that addresses sensory impairments and cognitive limitations as well as motor impairments.

Paying for home modification is increasingly feasible with a variety of states offering very low interest loans. There are some scholarships as well as volunteer programs such as a national program for architecture students through the American Institute of Architecture Students, called Freedom by Design, or some local Rotary Clubs or fire departments that will do some work at no cost, especially if the modifications are to an existing single family home. Finding information requires digging at the state level. State vocational rehabilitation agencies are still more likely to know of available options than state or local housing agencies.

"Visitability," a Policy Tool for Accessibility Visitability is a narrower variation of universal design intended only for homes and has been adopted by a variety of municipalities. Coined by a wheelchair-using advocate from Atlanta named Elinor Smith, visitability stipulates a few essential features that make it possible for people with mobility limitations to visit their family, friends, and neighbors:

- One zero-step entrance, at the front, back, or side of the house

- All main floor doors, including bathrooms, with at least 32 inches of clear passage space

- At least a half bath, preferably a full bath, on the main floor.

The term *visitability* derives from the frustration of people living in accessible apartments or homes but unable to visit neighbors, friends, and family because those homes are not accessible. A bill known as the Inclusive Home Design Act has been sponsored annually in the U.S. House of Representatives for some years, seeking to make visitability a requirement of single family homes built with some level of federal support. More information about visitability can be accessed at http://www.concretechange.org.

Assistive Technology Options at Home Assistive technology (AT) proliferates annually in both the number and sophistication of available products. Many young people with disabilities or chronic health conditions have their AT needs provided via school systems until they turn 22. At age 22, locating sources and paying for their AT needs is key to their transition to independence. The Assistive Technology Act Amendments of 2004 (PL 108-364) required states to improve access to and acquisition of AT in four areas: education, employment, community living, and telecommunications and information technology. States must submit 3-year plans that describe their plan to spend 60% of the AT Act funds for state-level activities and 40% on state leadership activities. Though federal AT Act funds cannot be used directly to pay for assistive technology for individuals, all of the states have developed programs focused on state systems able to purchase, lease, or otherwise acquire and pay for assistive technology. Most states have chosen to create alternative financing programs, but there are many other additional models intended to make it easier to locate and afford AT products all at the state level. States generally provide device loan programs, device reutilization programs, device demonstration programs, and state financing activities. Contact information for any state AT program can be accessed at http://www.resna.org/taproject/at/stateprograms.html. Although every state has a program, the quality of marketing and public awareness varies considerably.

An alternative to the state programs is the Digital Federal Credit Union (DCU) that affords people with disabilities the opportunity to access the services of a financial institution that are sometimes difficult to access. One option is the Access Loan for any product, device, or building modification designed to assist someone with a disability for amounts ranging from \$1,500 to \$25,000, with pay-back terms up to 72 months (Digital Federal Credit Union, 2009).

PRECEDENTS AND OPPORTUNITIES FOR A NEW HOUSING STRATEGY

Young people with disabilities and chronic health conditions had their own housing crisis before the nation's housing situation lurched from an impossible bubble to national calamity. No one would choose the situation in which we found ourselves in 2009, but desperate times are catalysts and opportunities to change how we think and act. There has never been enough funding to meet the need, and the needs of these young people will be in competition with a growing chorus of competitors for attention. We need clarity about needs and advocacy for models that include elements that not only make sense for young people with disabilities and chronic health conditions but that also can shape the entire national housing agenda. Inevitably, there will be a need to test ideas and model innovation. The transition population could be positioned as a manageable subset with which to test new models.

Data Mining Opportunity

In one way, these young people are unique: children with disabilities and chronic health conditions in the United States are a subset of the population that is most likely to be known, about whom information has been gathered by the educational system and, for many, by the health care, human service, or custody systems. It is possible, at least at the point at which one is arbitrarily deemed to be an adult and cut off from the supports for children, for policy analysts to witness the daunting impediments and yawning gaps in support that they face. These young people are at the far edges of the spectrum of growing up in America. If we can find ways to facilitate their successful transition, we are likely to identify supports that work for everyone.

Integrate Universal Design into the Sustainability Agenda

Universal design is a framework for both policy and personal choice. The quest for places to live that are designed to accommodate functional limitations of any kind is daunting. An assumption persists that there is housing and there is special housing. For young people with disabilities and chronic health conditions who are making the transition to independence, "special" is an identity most want to leave behind. Universal design is a way of thinking that gets beyond assumptions that differences in functional ability are rare or fixed or that differing functional ability occurs in a couple of narrow categories such as wheelchair users and people who are blind. Universal design offers a framework for the design of places, things, information, communication, and policy that focuses on the user, on the widest range of people operating in the widest range of situations without special or separate design. Universal design, also called inclusive design, design for all, and human-centered design, aligns with the contextual definition of disability in recognizing the power of the choices we make about the design of environments to minimize limitations and enhance everyone's experience (Institute for Human Centered Design, 2009).

There are an increasing number of universally designed model projects. The original pattern of market-rate single family homes is giving way to more innovation in multi-family projects and in some that are environmentally sustainable and universally designed. There is progress in many states and cities in mounting policy initiatives to expand universal design to new construction in multifamily developments as well as single-family homes. There are models ripe for replication, although many of the best examples are located outside the United States. One example in the United States is University Neighborhood in Berkeley, California, which offers a new downtown complex of 29 attractive, light-filled, affordable units, all with enhanced usability features and 14 of which are fully accessible for residents using wheeled mobility. Also, Erick Mikiten, AIA, an architect with a disability, designed Lincoln Street Apartments in Fremont, California, which has 11 units of affordable housing in walking distance to the town center for young adults with intellectual limitations.

Universal design expands the potential value of ordinary housing stock for people across the spectrum of age. Most of the work in universal design in housing remains focused on features that respond to mobility and dexterity limitations. In pushing for more attention to universal design, we need to promote research and replication of design features that are also responsive to people with sensory and/or cognitive issues. It is important to make the link for developers and policy makers between environmentally sustainable design and universal design. "Green" features include good lighting, acoustics, indoor air quality, and customizable controls. Those are overlapping features with inclusive or universal design. We have witnessed a stunning growth of environmentally sustainable values in all kinds of housing since 2004 and can expect to see that evolve more seriously as a national priority. The 2009 federal stimulus funds set a high priority on environmental sustainability for both new and renovation projects. Policy-makers and the public must be reminded that sustainability is a three-legged stool: environmental, social, and economic. Universal design provides a robust core of practical design features that can define a revitalized understanding of socially sustainable design and development.

In framing a vision of truly sustainable housing in these times, it is important to consider renovation as well as new construction. A great deal of our existing housing stock, especially subsidized housing, is in poor repair. Taking what we already have and making it better is a hallmark of green design and has been an early priority of the Obama administration and the stimulus funds. The American Recovery and Reinvestment Act (ARRA) of 2009 (PL 111-5) allocates federal funds for a wide range of housing initiatives, including innovative partnerships between HUD and the U.S. Department of Energy (DOE). The new partnership will allocate

$16 billion in economic recovery funds to retrofit existing homes and provide guidance to public and assisted housing on weatherization and energy efficiency renovations (DOE, 2009), creating models of renovation that start from a commitment to make projects that are environmentally, socially, and economically sustainable.

Link Transportation and Housing

More transit-oriented development (TOD) should be promoted, and young people with disabilities and chronic health conditions should be prioritized to get to the top of the waiting list. Although focused most around urban corridors, TOD is a core concept of a national movement to move beyond the choking state of our car-centric nation, sometimes called livable communities. The website for an organization called Transit Oriented Development lists common components of TOD (Transit Oriented Development, n.d.):

- Walkable design with pedestrian as the highest priority
- Train station as prominent feature of town center
- A regional node containing a mixture of uses in close proximity including office, residential, retail, and civic uses
- High density, high-quality development within 10-minute walk circle surrounding train station
- Collector support transit systems including trolleys, streetcars, light rail, and buses, etc.
- Designed to include the easy use of bicycles, scooters, and rollerblades as daily support transportation systems
- Reduced and managed parking inside 10-minute walk circle around town center/train station

There is a lot to admire in the vision of TOD and livable communities, but few in the movement have endorsed universal design or the infusion of inclusive design into an understanding of socially sustainable development. The opportunity is ripe. Youth with disabilities and chronic health conditions are a reasonable advocacy priority.

Borrow and Reinvent Some Promising Practices from the Adult Side

Medicaid's Program of All-Inclusive Care for the Elderly (PACE) model is centered around the belief that it is better for the well-being of seniors with chronic care needs and their families to be served in the community whenever possible. It is a popular and successful program begun in the Chinese community in San Francisco in the 1970s and now a common Medicaid waiver program across the country. It would seem to have particular appeal for replication and tailoring to youth with chronic health conditions. PACE packages medical care, social services including nutrition and exercise, housing, and transportation into a single person-centered approach. It would be easy to see the potential of "medical home" programs being the hub of a PACE-style model for young people with the most complex needs.

Adult foster care is among the few elastic elements of a too-small collection of housing options for adults with disabilities. Facilities vary greatly in quality, but the model could be reinvented for a new time with program changes appropriate to serving young people. A large, new crop of empty-nester baby boomers across the nation overwhelmingly want to age in place but are suddenly finding that they don't have the retirement accounts or part-time work opportunities they'd assumed. Matched with home modification loan funds where needed, it is likely that there would be enough interest in this 77-million-strong population to generate an attractive collection of options to help grow an additional housing resource for young people with disabilities.

The Fair Share Strategy

At any point in life, the housing challenge for people with disabilities or chronic health conditions can be predicted to be daunting at best. The time is ripe for a strategy that thinks and advocates differently. Times of crisis and inevitable change offer opportunities to reframe the agenda. It may be an opportunity to pursue a *fair share strategy.* The strategy is rooted in providing information to people with disabilities, families, other advocates, local decision-makers, and other community residents about the spectrum of housing needs in communities, especially for those with very low incomes (Denton & Bianco, 2001). Real numbers of young people with disabilities and chronic health conditions needing housing could be generated town by town and could be used to educate the local community about the critical importance of linking housing and transportation. The information, organized to be easy to understand and widely disseminated, would be much more likely to shape local policy and priorities for opportunities like Community Development Block Grants or priorities for set-asides in local projects. It might also wake up communities to the benefits of visitability and universal design and the value of integrating inclusive or socially sustainable design into "green" projects. Maybe the nation is ready for a housing agenda that is driven by a vision of social equity in which young people with disabilities can give voice to their dreams.

REFERENCES

American Recovery and Reinvestment Act (ARRA) of 2009, PL 111-5.

The Arc. (2006). *Public policy fact sheet: Housing for people with disabilities, the crisis escalates.* Retrieved June 1, 2009, from http://www.nacdd.org/pages/2009%20Fact% 20Sheets/Housing_-_Fact_Sheet_2009_Seminar.doc

Arnett, J. (2004). *Emerging adulthood: The winding road from the late teens through the twenties.* New York: Oxford University Press.

Assistive Technology Act Amendments of 2004, PL 108-364, 29 U.S.C. §§ 3001 *et seq.*

Centers for Disease Control and Prevention. (2008). *HIV/AIDS among youth: CDC HIV/ AIDS fact sheet.* Washington, DC: U.S. Government Printing Office.

Centers for Medicare and Medicaid Services. (2006). *Intermediate care facilities for the mentally retarded (ICF/MR).* Retrieved January 11, 2008, from http://www.cms.hhs.gov/CertificationandComplianc/Downloads/ICFMR_Background.pdf

The Civil Rights Project, University of California Los Angeles. (2002). *Racial inequity in special education: Executive summary for policy makers.* Retrieved May 15, 2009, from http://www.civilrightsproject.ucla.edu/research/specialed/IDEA_paper02.php

Cooper, E., Korman, H., O'Hara, A., & Zovistoski, A. (2009). *Priced out in 2008: The housing crisis for people with disabilities.* Boston: Technical Assistance Collaborative.

Deninger, M. (2008). *Disproportionality: A look at special education and race in the Commonwealth.* Malden, MA: Massachusetts Department of Education.

Denton, A., & Bianco, C. (2001). Housing. In C. Bianco & S. Wells (Eds.), *Overcoming barriers to community integration for people with mental illness* (Sec. 3, pp. 27–31). Washington, DC: U.S. Department of Health and Human Services.

Digital Federal Credit Union. (2009). *DCU access loans.* Retrieved May 15, 2009, from http://www.dcu.org/prodserv/loans/access.html#about

Fair Housing Accessibility FIRST. (n.d.). *History.* Retrieved May 15, 2009, from http://www.FairHousingFirst.org/fairhousing/history.html

Fair Housing Amendments Act of 1988, PL 100-403, 42 U.S.C. §§ 3601 *et seq.*

Fields, J., & Casper, L.M. (2001). *America's families and living arrangements.* Washington, DC: U.S. Census Bureau.

Individuals with Disabilities Education Improvement Act (IDEA) of 2004, PL 108-446, 20 U.S.C. §§ 1400 *et seq.*

Institute for Human Centered Design. (2009). *Universal design in housing.* Retrieved June 8, 2009, from http://www.humancentereddesign.org/index.php?option=Home

Lipman, B.J. (2006, October). *A heavy load: The combined housing and transportation burdens of working families.* Retrieved from http://www.nhc.org/pdf/pub_heavy_load_10_06.pdf

National Alliance on Mental Illness. (2001). *A housing toolkit.* Arlington, VA: Author.

Osgood, D.W., Foster, E.M., Flanagan, C., & Ruth, G.R. (2006). *On your own without a net: The transition to adulthood for vulnerable populations.* Chicago: University of Chicago Press.

Transit Oriented Development. (n.d.). *Components of Transit Oriented Design.* Retrieved November 30, 2009, from http://www.transitorienteddevelopment.org/tod.html

United Cerebral Palsy. (2009). *Housing options, supported living.* Retrieved June 1, 2009, from http://www.ucp.org/ucp_channeldoc.cfm/1/13/79/79-79/6180

U.S. Census Bureau. (2000). Living together, living alone: Families and living arrangements. In *Population profile of the United States* (pp. 5-1–5-3). Washington DC: U.S. Government Printing Office.

U.S. Department of Education. (2005). *IDEA–Reauthorized statute, disproportionality, and overidentification.* Retrieved May 15, 2009, from http://www.ed.gov/policy/speced/guid/idea/tb-overident.pdf

U.S. Department of Energy. (2009). *Press release: Secretaries Donovan and Chu announce partnership to help working families weatherize their homes.* Retrieved June 7, 2009, from http://www.energy/gov/news2009/6956.htm

World Health Organization. (2002). *Toward a common language for functioning, disability and health.* Geneva: WHO.

Yen, H. (2009, May 14). Growth of Hispanic, Asian population slows unexpectedly, census reports [Electronic version]. *The Washington Post.* Retrieved May 14, 2009, from http://www.washingtonpost.com/wp-dyn/content/article/2009/05/13/AR2009051303821_pf.html

III

Goals for
Seamless Transitions

7

Communities for All

Community Participation by Adolescents and Young Adults with Disabilities

Laurie E. Powers, David R. Johnson, and Josie Badger

Sally Matthews, who has Down syndrome, is the 25-year-old daughter of Susan and George Matthews. At birth, there were several concerns regarding her physical health, related to a congenital heart condition and diagnosed seizure disorder. Both conditions required regular medical attention during Sally's preschool years but stabilized, which permitted her to explore preschool opportunities in her community. The preschool they selected included students with and without disabilities, and Sally developed lasting friendships with several of the children in this program. Even during these very early years, Susan and George Matthews had a vision for Sally, a vision that virtually every family holds for its children. They wanted Sally to experience a rich life, surrounded by a loving, extended family, meaningful friendships with individuals with and without disabilities, positive inclusive school experiences with teachers who would recognize her unique capabilities, and opportunities for Sally to make important choices about her future and where she would live, work, and participate in her community.

This chapter was prepared for the National Center for Birth Defects and Developmental Disabilities, Centers for Disease Control and Prevention. The opinions expressed herein do not necessarily reflect those of the funder.

Sally completed her entire education in the same community and school district. She attended general education classes throughout her school career and was involved in many extra-curricular activities, such as soccer, student council, and choir. She was also an active member of her church and participated in several youth groups. While in high school, she participated in several career development experiences, which included a service learning experience at a local nursing home and a part-time job stocking shelves at a local retail store. Through these experiences, she learned to navigate her community and use public transportation, developed important job skills, and learned how to work effectively with her coworkers as part of a team. She also developed an understanding of what kind of job she might pursue following graduation. Her medical condition remained relatively stable throughout her adolescence; however, she was required to take a regimen of medications to control seizures related to her epilepsy. Sally's parents and her pediatrician at the local health clinic worked closely with her to address her ongoing health care needs. Her pediatrician also worked with the Matthews family to help Sally make a smooth transition from pediatric to adult family practice health services.

Following completion of high school, Sally continued her retail-store job and increased her work hours to full-time, enough to begin receiving health care, dental, and other employee benefits. She has several goals that she wants to accomplish over the next few years: She wants to attend a local community college to pursue training as a dietary technician and obtain employment working with nursing home residents. She is also looking at someday living independently and is currently on a waiting list for a supported living apartment near her family home. In the meantime, she continues to be an active member of her community. She is a member of her church choir and social groups, shops independently, meets with friends and e-mails them regularly, holds a membership in a local fitness club, and is currently exploring becoming a member of a local community theater group. For Sally, the community is a place where she shares her interests, develops interpersonal relationships, and plays out her role as an active and productive community member with others. To achieve this level of community participation has, however, required considerable effort by Sally, along with support from schools and adult community service organizations, her family, as well as friends and neighbors.

HISTORICAL PERSPECTIVES ON PEOPLE WITH DISABILITIES LIVING IN THE COMMUNITY

National expectations and commitments regarding access and support for community participation have mainly been associated with moving people out of institutions and into community housing (Lakin, Gardner, Larson, & Wheeler, 2005). These commitments are, however, much broader today and expressed in such concepts as self-determination and self-advocacy (Powers, Dinerstein, & Holmes, 2005; Shoultz & Ward, 1996; Wehmeyer, Gragoudas, & Shogren, 2006); the rights and responsibilities of individuals with disabilities to make their own choices and decisions about their lives (Abery & Stancliffe, 1996; Sands, Bassett, Lehmann, & Spencer, 1998); participating in inclusive educational and transition services (Benz, Lindstrom, & Yovanoff, 2000; Hasazi, Furney, & DeStefano, 1999; Johnson, Stodden, Emanuel, Luecking, & Mack, 2002); gaining access to meaningful employment (Mank, 2007; Wehman & Revell, 1996); and access to essential transportation services (National Council on Disability, 2004). Access to and support for community participation, however, has been a relatively recent development in the evolution of services for individuals with disabilities and their families.

Historically, dramatic shifts have occurred in how this nation has provided individuals with disabilities access to integrated, satisfying community lives. The movement toward community is best described as a shift from isolation to segregation to integration and inclusion and most recently to a focus on community participation as an interdependent exchange among community members. Each of these periods in our history takes on significance in understanding the movement toward increased community participation opportunities.

The Era of Isolation

In 18th-century America, individuals with significant disabilities and chronic conditions were cared for at home by family and, in some cases—particularly for people with severe cognitive, physical, sensory, and medically fragile conditions— by entire communities. Individuals with disabilities were afforded care and treatment, based on a sense of moral obligation, religious beliefs, and other factors. This perspective treats people with disabilities as helpless victims needing care and protections and relied heavily on charity and benevolence, rather than justice and equality. This period of isolation justified the exclusion of individuals with disabilities from all facets of community participation, including education, employment, and citizenship.

The Period of Segregation and Exclusion

By the mid-19th century, shifting public attitudes and the complexity of an increasingly urbanized society fostered the development of institutions for individuals with severe physical, sensory, intellectual, and mental health disabilities. The concept of the "medical model" emerged during this period as the dominant approach in the development and delivery of services. The medical model is based on the premise that the problems and difficulties experienced by individuals with disabilities are largely related to their physical, sensory, or intellectual impairments. Disability is viewed as intrinsic to the individual. That is, it is a part of the individual's own physical make-up that results in reducing the individual's quality of life, capacity to care for oneself, and other disadvantages. The medical model defined disability in the clinical framework of diseases, thus providing major roles for the medical and health professions to cure such problems and establish ways to make the individual as "normal" as possible.

Institutions for individuals with disabilities were established to be parallel to the hospital systems for people with acute illness. This separation of illness and family and community became a paradigm for care for individuals with intellectual disabilities, severe physical and sensory disabilities, and degenerative diseases and for elderly people with declining ability to care for themselves (Allen & Mor, 1998).

Movement Toward Integration and Inclusion

By the mid-1960s, the movement toward community-based services began, based on the recognition that societal barriers and prejudice needed to be overcome to support the community participation of individuals with disabilities. *Integration* and *inclusion* are terms used by individuals with disabilities and other disability-rights advocates to advance the idea that all people should freely have access to educational opportunities, living arrangements, employment, and other responsibilities of citizenship, the same as any community member without disabilities.

One of the major hallmarks of this shift toward community-based services was deinstitutionalization. The movement from institution to community, however, was neither well planned nor successful for many individuals with disabilities during the early years of deinstitutionalization. In June 1977, for example, an estimated 207,356 people with intellectual and other developmental disabilities receiving residential services lived in public and private institutional settings. By 2003, just 72,474 remained in these institutional settings (Prouty et al., 2004). During this same period, the number of residents in "community" settings with 15 or fewer residents has increased from 40,424 people to an estimated 329,804 people, with about 90% of the increase occurring in settings with 6 or fewer residents (Prouty et al., 2004).

The shift from institutional to community living among people with disabilities has been facilitated by the design and third-party payment for medical devices that can be maintained at home and transported about the community. Previously, many life-sustaining medical devices were too large, heavy, and complicated to be taken from medical facilities, often causing individuals to be confined to a facility or even one room. Over the past decades, many devices such as ventilators have become portable, allowing individuals who are reliant on them to be able to leave medical institutions and join community life. Third-party coverage for tilt-and-lift power wheelchairs has expanded individuals' capacities for self-care. These devices have increased users' life expectancies and promoted their quality of life (Tecklin, 2007). In turn, individuals' desires for community living and support have increased.

The inclusion of individuals with disabilities in communities has also been stimulated by the disability rights movement, which seeks access to public education, employment, housing, transportation, and the economic independence of individuals with disabilities through new peer-based support models, federal legislation, court actions, presidential executive orders, and other developments. For example, the independent living movement, catalyzing the establishment of Centers for Independent Living across the United States, has promoted the delivery of peer-based support for community living as well as the provision of consumer-directed personal assistance services (DeJong, Batavia, & McKnew, 1992). Hundreds of national, local, and state advocacy organizations are active in monitoring and shaping the direction of long-term services for people with disabilities (Dybwad & Bersani, 1996; Shapiro, 1993). Growing advocacy in the psychiatric disability community is focused on initiatives such as ending forced treatment and adapting personal assistance services for individuals with psychiatric disabilities (Lefley, 1996; Pita, Ellison, & Kantor, 1999).

Visions of Interdependent Community Living

Various definitions of *interdependence* emphasize mutual dependence as well as sharing a common set of principles, values, and goals with others (e.g., Merriam-Webster, 2008). The concept differs distinctly from *dependence,* in that an interdependent relationship implies that all participants are reliant on one another. While American society has been historically rooted in "radical individualism" heralded by such values as self-sufficiency, increasing recognition is being given to our interdependence and the value of social capital that each person brings to society (Partington, 2005). That is, we are involved in daily reciprocal exchanges between friends, neighbors, families, coworkers, and the like. We share a common connectedness and have shared responsibilities toward a common good in our communities.

While early perspectives on inclusion and integration in disability reflected the concept of interdependent community living, these efforts often reflected an underlying assumption that individuals with disabilities would be the primary beneficiaries of their participation in typical community contexts. Early approaches also communicated an assumption of inherent benefit to individuals with disabilities in being with individuals without disabilities.

In contrast, disability policy and practice during the last 2 decades has increasingly recognized benefits of inclusion that come to all parties through acknowledging and supporting their interdependent relationships. Emerging perspectives on inclusion also acknowledge the mutual benefit realized through interaction with all others, with and without disabilities. Initiatives reflective of these shifts include universal access in computing, engineering, and architecture where accessibility is designed to benefit all citizens (Akoumianakis & Stephanidis, 2003); programs to engage volunteers with disabilities in national and community service (National and Community Service Act of 1990); recognition of the complementary benefits of peer-based support and community participation (e.g., President's New Freedom Commission on Mental Health, 2003); and a new definition of disability put forth through the *International Classification of Functioning, Disability and Health* (*ICF*; World Health Organization, 2001). According to the ICF, health change and disability are universal human experiences affected by personal and environmental facilitators and barriers as well as by health condition factors. From this perspective, disability status itself is determined by examining functional relationships among health condition factors and contextual factors, including the physical, social, and attitudinal environment, personal and social background, coping approaches, and others. Increasing adoption of interdependence principles and models has potential to fundamentally change the way truly inclusive communities are defined and accessed by the next generation of young people.

CHANGING DEFINITIONS OF COMMUNITY

As reflected in the preceding discussion, the concept of "community" and what it means for individuals to fully participate have been highly debated and the focus of considerable study. Traditionally, community has been regarded as a geographical place within which citizens engage in many varied activities. A common understanding of community for individuals with disabilities has been to view it as the opposite of segregation or isolation in specialized programs or facilities that provide services only to children, youth, and adults with disabilities. Today, however, definitions of community have evolved to become much broader. Community can no longer be defined merely in terms of a geographic location. There are many subcommunities of people with shared experience (e.g., gender, age, disability, interests) and even technology-supported virtual communities that are all part of the broader understanding of community.

COMMUNITY LIVING BY ADOLESCENTS AND YOUNG ADULTS

In comparison to extensive research conducted on employment and postsecondary education for young people with disabilities, limited study has focused on community living. Even less research has been conducted to directly ask young people with disabilities about their expectations or experiences. One such study (Powers, Hogansen, Geenen, Powers, & Gil-Kashiwabara, 2008) surveyed 242 youth in special education; broad agreement was expressed for the importance of completing high school, having a good doctor and health insurance, receiving support from family and teachers, and attending individualized education program (IEP) meetings. The youth agreed that worries about safety make their families reluctant to permit them to do activities, particularly for young women. The youth consistently rated the importance of transition activities higher than their opportunity to engage in each activity. Likewise, findings from the first youth-directed, participatory action survey confirmed youths' desires for inclusion and confirmed that, while youth with disabilities generally value transition experiences identified as important by professionals, they have limited opportunity to participate in them (Powers et al., 2007).

Transition Planning for Community Living

The Individuals with Disabilities Education Improvement Act (IDEA) of 2004 (PL 108-446) requires that transition planning be undertaken for all youth with disabilities. Specifically, IDEA regulations mandate that transition planning be conducted for students ages 16 and older, that students be invited to their transition-planning meetings, that decisions be based on students' interests and preferences, and that transition planning include adult services and independent living or community participation.

Unfortunately, findings suggest IDEA transition planning mandates related to preparation for community living may not be realized in practice. For example, Everson, Zhang, and Guillory (2001) examined 329 transition plans, finding they generally followed IDEA's mandates for addressing postschool activities such as postsecondary education, vocational training, integrated employment, and continuing or adult education. However, the plans were less likely to address other community transition issues, such as postschool living arrangements, financial or income needs, homemaking needs, transportation, community resources, recreation and leisure, health or medical services, relationships, advocacy, and legal needs. Likewise, Powers, Gil-Kashiwabara, Powers, Geenen, Balandran, and Palmer's (2005) analysis of 399 IEP transition plans revealed student exposure to practices associated with successful community living was disappointing, ranging from a low of 1% for mentoring, to 4% for learning how to request services, to 7% for self-determination education, despite the findings that mentoring, self-advocacy, and self-determination skill development appear to support postschool community living outcomes (McLearn, Colasanto, Schoen, & Shapiro, 1999; Powers, Sowers, & Stevens, 1995; Wehmeyer & Schwartz, 1997). Of the transition plans analyzed, 36% included medical services goals, 40% included housing goals, 33% had independent living goals, and 32% had adult services goals; 19% of all goals had evidence of student desires or interests. Only 6.4% of goals listed made reference to accommodations or supports needed by students to achieve the goal.

Community Living Transition Outcomes

For more than 2 decades, families, professionals, and self-advocates have led efforts to improve transition outcomes of youth with disabilities, and data collected in 2003 for the National Longitudinal Transition Study-2 (NLTS2) suggests that some important progress is being made while areas of need remain (Wagner, Newman, Cameto, & Levine, 2005). With regard to community living outcomes, post-high-school findings from youth at wave 2 of the study (2003) indicated that 1) about three quarters of youth were living with their parents, a similar rate to that of the general population of youth, 2) two thirds of the youth could drive, 3) about 12% of out-of-school youth were living with a spouse or roommate outside of their parents' home, 4) two thirds of youth were reported to have annual incomes of $5,000 or less, 5) about 10% of youth were receiving government benefits, 6) about one third of youth had personal checking accounts and almost one in five had a credit card in his or her own name, and 7) 8% of out-of-school youth with disabilities were parents, a rate of parenting similar to that for the general population. Participation in passive leisure activities, such as watching TV or listening to music, and participation in community groups or volunteer activities declined for youth after leaving high school. In contrast, out-of-school youth with disabilities were seeing friends more often than they were 2 years earlier. Almost two thirds of youth with disabilities who were 18 or older were registered to vote, a rate similar to that for the general population of youth. As a whole, the arrest rates of young adults with disabilities were not significantly different from their peers in the general population.

Demographic Disproportionality   Gender, disability, and ethnic and racial diversity are factors associated with disproportionality in community living outcomes. For example, it is clear that students with particular disabilities, such as emotional or behavioral disturbance, as well as ethnically and racially diverse youth, do not fare as well as others in making the transition to adulthood (U.S. Department of Education, 2002; Wagner, Newman, Cameto, Garza, & Levine, 2005). For example, NLTS2 findings indicate youth with emotional disturbance experienced the largest increase in their rate of parenting since leaving high school. They are likely to see friends often, yet they are unlikely to take part in organized community groups or volunteer activities, or to be registered to vote. More than three fourths of youth with emotional disturbance had been stopped by police, 58% have been arrested at least once, and 43% had been on probation or parole. Youth with intellectual disabilities were as likely as any other category of youth to be living on their own and to be parenting. Relatively few had driving privileges or checking accounts. Youth with intellectual disabilities and those with multiple disabilities were among the least likely to take part in organized community groups or volunteer activities. Youth with hearing impairments were significantly less likely than youth with disabilities as a whole to frequently get together with friends. Caucasian youth with disabilities were more likely than African American youth to have driving privileges and a personal checking account, as were youth from households with incomes of more than $50,000 per year. Other research has documented the high value placed on transition success by ethnically and racially diverse youth and their families, exceeding the expectations of professionals (Geenen, Powers, Lopez-Vasquez, & Bordani, 2003; Gil-Kashiwabara, Hogansen, Geenen, Powers, & Powers, 2007). For example, Geenen et al. reported that parents of African American, Latino/a, and Native American youth reported higher levels of involvement in their children's transition preparation than did parents of Caucasian youth. Gil-Kashiwabara et al. found that Latina youth and parents expressed higher educational aspirations than Caucasian youth and their parents.

Evidence also documents poorer community living transition outcomes for young women in comparison to young men (Educational Equity Concepts, 1993; Froschl, Rubin, & Sprung, 1999; Stoddard, Jans, Ripple, & Kraus, 1998). NLTS2 findings indicate girls with disabilities were significantly more likely than boys to be supporting themselves on less than $5,000 per year. Boys accounted for almost all of the difference in rates of involvement in the criminal justice system, compared to youth with disabilities overall.

Life Circumstances Certain life experiences are associated with poorer community living transition outcomes. Foremost is poverty, which intersects with disability and various other sociodemographic characteristics to impede transition success (Lustig & Strauser, 2007). Having dropped out of high school is a second factor associated with poor outcomes. For example, NLTS2 findings indicate that, in comparison to youth who completed high school, youth who dropped out were more likely to support independent households and children, and they were less likely to have a driver's license or a checking account and to be registered to vote (Wagner, Newman, Cameto, & Levine, 2005). Dropouts with disabilities were significantly more likely to be involved in the criminal justice system than youth with disabilities who finished high school.

Another life circumstance that seriously affects youth's adult outcomes is being in foster care. Of approximately 550,000 children in foster care, 30%–45% experience a disability (Advocates for Children of New York, 2000; Courtney, Piliavin, & Grogan-Kaylor, 1995; Geenen & Powers, 2007). Most such children live in poverty before entering state custody (Harden, 2004). They are disproportionately children of color (e.g., 38% are African American; Chipungu & Bent-Goodley, 2004) and children with mental health issues (American Academy of Pediatrics, 1994). The National Evaluation of Title IV-E Independent Living Programs for Youth in Foster Care, the only study that specifically examined outcomes of foster youth with disabilities, found these youth were significantly less likely to 1) be employed, 2) graduate from high school, 3) have social support, and 4) be self-sufficient, when compared to their foster peers without disabilities (Westat, 1991).

Having a history of incarceration also seriously impedes community living for young adults. Following release, approximately 50% of incarcerated youth with disabilities return to the correctional system, and very few obtain education or employment (Bullis & Cheney, 1999; Ensminger & Juon, 1998; Myner, Santman, Cappelletty, & Perlmutter, 1998). However, compared to their peers without disabilities, youth with disabilities have been shown to be less likely to return to the correctional system if they become engaged in community activities and supports (Bullis, Yovanoff, Mueller, & Havel, 2002).

SHIFTING POLICIES AND FEDERAL ROLES

Community participation has been a highly valued goal for individuals with disabilities over the past several decades. Since the 1970s, the United States has demonstrated its commitment to this goal through federal legislation, including the Americans with Disabilities Act (ADA) of 1990 (PL 101-336), the Developmental Disabilities Assistance and Bill of Rights Act of 1987 (PL 100-146), the Developmental Disabilities Assistance and Bill of Rights Act Amendments of 2000 (DD Act; PL 106-402), and the Rehabilitation Act of 1973 (PL 93-112); court decisions (e.g., *Olmstead v. L.C.*, 1999); national policy initiatives (e.g., President's New Freedom Initiative); reports of national panels such as the Healthy People 2010 Objectives; and other developments.

The ADA of 1990 recognized the interests of people with disabilities in avoiding segregation and underscored their rights to accommodations for community inclusion. ADA's Title II and Title III forbid discrimination in government-operated programs and in public accommodations, prohibit denial of services or benefits on the basis of disability, and require equal opportunity for people with disabilities to participate in, or benefit from, a service or activity that is offered to the general public. Based upon ADA Title II regulations that require services in the most integrated setting (28 C.F.R. Sec. 130 [d], integration regulation; Sec. 450, preamble), a milestone event in the evolution of community-based services for people with disabilities was the Supreme Court ruling on *Olmstead v. L.C.* (1999). Through *Olmstead v. L.C.*, the right of individuals with disabilities to live and receive supports where they desire was affirmed. Since the *Olmstead* decision, numerous systems change initiatives have been launched to support states in expanding home and community-based long-term services for people with diverse disabilities (Tritz, 2005).

The DD Act acknowledges that disability "does not diminish the right of individuals with developmental disabilities to live independently, to exert control and choice over their own lives" (101[a][1]), and that the goals of the nation properly include the goal of providing individuals with developmental disabilities with the information, skills, opportunities, and support to live in homes and communities in which individuals can exercise their full rights and responsibilities as citizens (101[a][16][B]). The DD Act also emphasizes that services, supports, and other assistance should be provided in a manner that demonstrates respect for individual dignity, personal preferences, and cultural differences.

The Individuals with Disabilities Education Improvement Act (IDEA) of 2004 (PL 108-446) specifically stresses the critical importance of engaging families, community service agencies, and other public and private entities in decisions concerning the school and postschool needs of students with disabilities. IDEA defines transition services as a coordinated set of activities for a child with a disability that includes instruction, related services, community experiences, the development of employment and other postschool adult living objectives, and, if appropriate, acquisition of adult living skills and functional vocational evaluation. Engaging students and families in active discussions concerning their individual community participation goals while still in school and following graduation is an important requirement of the transition services provisions of IDEA.

The New Freedom Commission on Mental Health report, issued during the George W. Bush administration, featured "Goal 2: Mental Health Care Is Consumer and Family Driven," which emphasized the development of personalized, highly individualized health management programs that will help lead the way to appropriate treatment and supports that are oriented toward recovery and resilience: "Consumers, along with service providers, will actively participate in designing and developing the systems of care in which they are involved" (President's New Freedom Commission on Mental Health, 2003).

Finally, the Healthy People 2010 report of the Centers for Disease Control and Prevention expressed the importance of community-based living in the following statement:

> Institutionalization and other forms of congregate care are inconsistent with positive public health policy and practice. They diminish people's opportunities to realize essential features of human well-being: choice, control, ability to establish and pursue personal goals, family and community interaction, privacy, freedom of association, and the respect of others. (National Center on Birth Defects and Developmental Disabilities, 2003, p. 181)

National Commitments

Growing emphasis on expanding access to community options and providing community-based, long-term services to people with diverse disabilities signals an important paradigm shift from diagnostically defined medical care approaches to individualized services that maximize self-determination, quality of life, equity, and opportunity for full community participation. These national public policies and initiatives outline a clear, although yet to be fully realized, national commitment to

- Increasing self-determination and personal control in decisions affecting individuals with disabilities and their families;
- Providing opportunities to live, participate, and receive needed services in one's own community;
- Promoting structural, attitudinal, and social access to create communities that welcome full participation by individuals with disabilities;
- Improving the quality of life for individuals and families as they define it for themselves;
- Investing in each individual's potential and capacity to contribute in age-related roles as productive, respected community members;

- Assuring access to sufficient, high-quality health and social supports to ensure each person's health, safety, rights, and well-being; and
- Supporting families as the most permanent unit of development, protection, and assistance in promoting the community participation of their child with a disability. (Lakin & Turnbull, 2005, p. 3)

National commitment to ensuring physical access to and participation in community life is now well established within our attitudes, public policies, and responsibilities as professionals. Fully achieving these objectives and goals is the next frontier.

SERVICE AND SUPPORTS: DELIVERY PERSPECTIVES

In line with evolution at the policy level, advancements have been made in formal and informal support and services to support youths' transition to community living.

Formal Services and Supports

Community response to disabilities has often centered on providing an array of formal or specialized educational and community services that prepare individuals to live as independently as possible, support their participation in community living and employment, and provide financial supports needed for medical, health, and mental health services. Over the years, different conceptualizations and disability classification systems have been established as the dominant criteria for determining eligibility for children, youth, and adults with disabilities for community services. Early methods relied on diagnostic approaches through behavioral or medical criteria and evaluations. During the late 1990s and into the 2000s, a greater emphasis has been placed on matching an individual's functional needs and abilities with the requirements of community environments such as schools, workplaces, recreational programs, and residential settings. Rather than applying a deficits approach and documenting the things an individual cannot do, functional abilities and life support perspectives focus on skills and abilities that an individual possesses and the types of supports needed for successful participation in an individual's specific environmental context (Odom, Horner, Snell, & Blacher, 2007).

Informal Supports

The term *natural supports* was first introduced in the literature by Nisbet and Hagner in 1988 and has since been discussed and applied with varying meanings in relation to supporting the community participation of individuals with disabilities. In addition to employment, natural support approaches and strategies have been used successfully in environments such as public schools, recreational programs, and residential settings (Nisbet, 1992; Pearpoint, 1990; Perske, 1988). The idea of natural supports is certainly not new. Each of us relies to some extent on others to support aspects of our daily life. What is important is that the informal role of family, friends, neighbors, and other community members be acknowledged as a valued source of support in promoting the community participation of individuals with disabilities. Most people, with or without disabilities, rely extensively on a wide range of natural supports that exist in virtually every community, large or small.

Estimates of the proportion of long-term support for individuals with disabilities provided by family members ranges from 79% to 90% (Kennedy, LaPlante, & Kaye, 1997; Rutgers University and World Institute on Disability, 1992). A growing body of evidence suggests that families make a significant difference in the health status, mental health, and quality of life of people with long-term support needs. Concern has been expressed that support from family members may inhibit individual decision making and control. However, Benjamin, Matthias, and Franke (1998) found that individuals who received their support from family members reported feeling safer, having greater choice about when and how services were provided, and having a stronger desire to direct their providers' work than did individuals who received services from nonfamily members.

While informal supports are central to many youths' success in community living, as mentioned earlier in our discussion of youth in foster care, some youth do not have these supports in their lives. Furthermore, many informal supporters require assistance to carry out their functions. What happens when a family member becomes ill, needs to go to work, or is otherwise unable to fulfill the responsibility? Service provider agencies also often require a youth and his or her family member to contact the provider, fill out paperwork, attend follow up appointments, and more. What happens when family members or other informal supporters are not able to assist youth with these tasks? There are few accommodations available for natural support providers, and it is unfortunately the youth and caring family members who suffer in these situations.

Much attention is focused on youth within their families of origin; however, little research has focused on practices that promote youths' formation of intimate relationships, marriage/partnerships, and relationships with neighbors and other community members developed through religious activities, social clubs, and other avenues. Interestingly, while the importance of personal relationships for well-being is universally acknowledged for people as a whole, concerns about vulnerability and safety, along with minimization of the importance of such relationships, are dominant in the disability literature (Powers et al., 2005).

Effective Support Practices

Syntheses of findings suggest effective practices for promoting youth's transition to community living include 1) transition preparation and planning, 2) experiences in community environments, and 3) supports to ensure success in community settings (Kohler, 1998; Kohler & Chapman, 1999; Kohler & Troesken, 1999). Specific effective practices that have been identified include 1) student involvement in transition planning (Halpern, Yovanoff, Doren, & Benz, 1995; Powers et al.,

2001); 2) student-centered life planning coupled with community career and service experiences in youth-chosen areas (Hagner & Dileo, 1993; Mank, 1994; Sowers, McAllister, & Cotton, 1996); 3) culturally responsive transition supports (Chesapeake Institute, 1994; Geenen et al., 2003; Harry, 1992); 4) instruction in skills such as self-advocacy, independent living, and self-determination (Benz, Yovanoff, & Doran, 1997; National Center for Disability Services, 1991; Powers et al., 2001; Wehmeyer & Schwartz, 1997); 5) relationships with supportive adults or mentors (Campbell-Whatley, 2001; McLearn et al., 1999; Powers et al., 1995); 6) support for family involvement in transition planning and preparation (Halpern et al., 1995; Morningstar, Turnbull, & Turnbull, 1995; Powers, Turner, Matuszewski, Wilson, & Loesch, 1999); and 7) interagency collaboration (Hasazi et al., 1999). Research findings also suggest that person-directed service and support models, such as consumer-directed personal assistance, cash and counseling, and brokered support, are associated with enhanced quality of life, personal control, satisfaction with services, and reduced unmet need (see review by Powers, Sowers, & Singer, 2006).

CHALLENGES AND OPPORTUNITIES FOR COMMUNITY LIVING

While significant progress has been achieved in community living by people with disabilities, key challenges and opportunities remain for full participation to become a reality for many young people.

Fostering Welcoming Communities

In laying the framework for fostering accessible communities, the Americans with Disabilities Act of 1990, Titles II and III, forbids discrimination in government-operated programs and in "public accommodations," prohibits denial of services or benefits on the basis of disability, and requires equal opportunity for people with disabilities to participate in or benefit from a service that is offered to the general public. Title II prohibits state and local governments from discriminating against individuals with disabilities and sets forth structural access requirements for public entities. Unlike Section 504 of the Rehabilitation Act of 1973, which only covers programs receiving federal financial assistance, Title II extends to all activities of state and local governments, whether or not they receive federal funds. Title II ensures that individuals with disabilities are not excluded from services, programs, and activities because buildings are inaccessible. Title III was included in the ADA following testimony before Congress that many individuals with disabilities led isolated lives and did not frequent places of public accommodation, because the individual's physical limitations were not accommodated. Physical barriers come in many different forms, including architectural, transportation, and communications. The "public accommodations" at issue under Title III cover virtually every category of businesses, including retail establishments, schools, hotels, medical and recreational facilities, museums, and other places of public gathering. Major challenges remain, however, in realizing the spirit and intent of Titles II and III of the ADA.

A particular obstacle confronting youth with disabilities is getting around the community. According to the 2003 National Transportation Availability and Use Survey, about one in four individuals with disabilities needs help from another person and/or some sort of assistive equipment, such as a cane, walker, or wheelchair to travel outside the home (U.S. Department of Transportation, Bureau of Transportation Statistics, 2003). The same study also revealed that nearly one in eight people with disabilities, or about six million, has difficulty getting needed transportation help because public transportation in the area is limited or nonexistent, or because the individual does not have a car or has a disability that makes transportation difficult to use or has no one available to give assistance, among other reasons. More than half of the homebound—1.9 million— are people with disabilities. Of these nearly two million people, 560,000 indicated that they never leave home because of transportation difficulties. Nationally, compliance with ADA's transportation provisions is still under considerable scrutiny, with efforts by state and local governments progressing, in some locales, slowly. Providing accessible, affordable, reliable, and safe transportation is, however, an absolute requirement for creating opportunities for individuals with disabilities to fully participate in their communities in schools, workplaces, recreational programs, and shopping for their personal needs. Lack of funding, lack of coordination among primary transportation providers, disparate levels of authority, and other factors have all contributed to inefficiencies in making universally accessible transportation systems available.

Beyond structural access, fostering of welcoming communities requires continuing attitudinal shift toward increasing value for diversity, universal access, and contributions of all community members to quality of life for everyone. Historic labeling of people with disabilities based on medical diagnosis or "special needs" has been counterproductive to promoting inclusion of people with disabilities from a social justice perspective, the dominant model embraced by other marginalized groups. Opportunities exist for people in general and disability communities to further encourage the reframing of disability as diversity, and to link disability inclusion with other social justice movements seeking to expand opportunity for full participation by all people.

Promoting attitude change regarding the capacities of youth with disabilities is essential for shifting paradigms of disability. Most fundamental is encouraging expectations that youth with disabilities will be successful community members. Encouraging findings from the NLTS2 indicate that 41% of youth reported they were hopeful about the future "most or all of the time" and an additional 23% reported being hopeful "a lot of the time" (Wagner, Newman, Cameto, Levine, & Marder, 2007). In contrast, 12% reported "rarely or never" feeling hopeful about the future. These levels suggest many youth with disabilities expect to live productive and fulfilling lives. In contrast, research on teachers and transition professionals' expectations for youth with disabilities suggests they question youth's capacities for success, particularly youth who experience significant disabilities and/or who are racially or culturally diverse (Geenen et al., 2003; Wehmeyer, 2005). Thus, a challenge exists in fostering hope and increasing expectations in the hearts and minds of professionals who work with youth.

Youth Capacity-Building and Family Support

The effectiveness of the ADA, IDEA, and other policy initiatives is not only linked to the appropriate provisions made by school districts, state and local government entities, and businesses and employers, but also to individuals with disabilities who learn about their rights, advocate for themselves and apply their community living knowledge and skills. Yet, as already highlighted, many youth have little access to experiences and resources validated as important for transition success (Everson et al., 2001: Powers et al., 2008; Powers et al., 2007). Challenges that impede youth access to such opportunities include instructional requirements that limit individualized, flexible learning by all youth, including those with disabilities; inadequate teacher and professional preparation to implement effective transition practices; difficulty in implementing model practices on a large scale; and lack of coordination between educational and adult service agencies. We also have a long way to go in embracing beliefs and practices that prepare youth to be active change agents in their lives (Squire, in press).

Families traditionally have been the core unit and foundation of American society, and youth with disabilities identify support from their families as most critical for their transition success (Powers et al., 2007). It is estimated that in the year 2000 the total spending for family support services from state developmental disabilities agencies in the United States exceeded $1 billion (Blacher & Hatton, 2007; Parish, Pomeranz-Essley, & Braddock, 2003). There is a growing empirical basis documenting the benefits of policies and programs that support families in helping their child with a disability to achieve positive life outcomes (Armstrong, Biernie-Lefcovitch, & Ungar, 2005; Bromley, Hare, Davison, & Emerson, 2006; Pruchno & McMullen, 2004). Further attention is needed to identify specific factors that influence the well-being and achievement of positive outcomes of youth with disabilities receiving transition assistance from their families, including approaches to provide culturally responsive support to families and to build partnerships with family members in supporting youth. Additionally, new support models are needed for youth who do not have support from their families to ensure they have ongoing relationships and guidance from supportive adults who are in the youths' lives because they care for them.

Adoption of Individualized, Person-Directed Support Approaches

Innovative approaches for understanding disability from a functional perspective and for identifying, mobilizing, and creating opportunities and supports for youth, both formal and informal, have been developed and validated in the last decade (e.g., person-centered or directed planning, mentorship and other natural supports, personal assistance services, cash and counseling, peer-delivered services). Yet, most of these resources have yet to be made available to the majority of young adults with disabilities.

We have many new capacity-building and support tools to facilitate full community participation that warrant deployment. In many respects, the greatest challenge is redirecting the momentum of highly established, large service systems, founded and funded on professional rehabilitation principles that focus on "fixing" the person. In order to effectively support youth with disabilities to create opportunities for full community participation, existing funding structures and professional roles must be realigned to make a place for these new approaches. For example, as pervasive as natural supports are, and as commonly used by most people, we often think of extraordinary measures to incorporate natural supports into the lives of individuals with disabilities, usually after first considering formal, specialized services provided by professional, paid supports (Allen, 1999).

Fostering Interagency Collaboration

The importance of interagency collaboration to support young people in the achievement of postschool outcomes was recognized in early analyses of transition concepts and challenges (e.g., Halpern, 1985; Will, 1984) and remains as a critical practice among professionals at the community level (e.g., Hasazi et al., 1999; Johnson et al., 2002). Continuing national attention to interagency collaboration is due, in part, to research that has documented that students with disabilities and families were not receiving the information and assistance necessary to support a successful transition to work, postsecondary education, and community life (Johnson, McGrew, Bloomberg, Bruininks, & Lin, 1997).

Difficulties in interagency collaboration are not insurmountable and can be overcome. A wide range of community participation goals can be achieved for students who are still attending school, as well as upon graduation, through strengthened interagency efforts. Several research-based strategies include 1) using written interagency agreements between education and adult community service providers that structure collaborative transition services focused on students' participation in community-based service learning, work experiences, and recreational programs; 2) establishing key positions (e.g., job coaches, direct support professionals) jointly funded by schools and adult agencies to support the community participation of students; 3) developing and delivering interagency- and cross-training in special education, rehabilitation, and other adult agency professionals that addresses key community participation and inclusion strategies; and 4) providing a secondary curriculum that helps students to identify and reach transition goals related to their community participation in work, postsecondary education, and community living environments (e.g., Benz, Lindstrom, & Latta, 1999; Benz et al., 2000; Hasazi et al., 1999; Johnson et al., 2002). The challenge is to use what research reveals about effective collaboration strategies that lead to improved transition planning practices in schools and communities. To make this happen, educators and human service professionals will need to continue examining the use of legislation and policy as instruments of change and improvement and to replicate existing evidence-based collaboration models (Hasazi et al., 2005).

Participating in Virtual Communities

The promise of emerging electronic and information communications technologies has never held greater potential for enhancing the integration and independence of youth with disabilities in communities. Americans now have at their disposal a plethora of versatile Internet-based and digital communication technologies that offer innovative and creative ways to communicate and receive information in virtually every walk of life (National Council on Disability, 2006). Improvements to our nation's communication technologies can have a liberating effect on the lives of people with disabilities by offering new opportunities for enhanced independence, increased mobility, and greater choices in products and services (National Research Council, 2001). Virtual communities available on the Internet offer many new opportunities for individuals with disabilities to expand social networks, engage in self-advocacy efforts, access natural supports independent of others, purchase goods and services, and accomplish many other personal needs. Online discussion and support groups are currently available that cover every imaginable subject area. Google, Yahoo, and MSN, for example, offer online discussion groups and forums that include opportunities for regular e-mail exchanges as well as real-time exchanges between parties. Electronic mailing lists, e-mentoring, news groups, blogs, wikis, and other venues also extend opportunities for individuals with disabilities to engage with other community members in new forms of communication and information exchange. Participation in virtual community is particularly important for more than two thirds of adolescents who use the Internet for private communication, finding information and downloading music, and participating in public discussions (Gross, 2004). Internet use has been less among children and youth with disabilities compared with their peers without disabilities. However, the digital divide is narrowing. The National Center for Educational Statistics (2004) reported that approximately half of children and youth with disabilities were using the Internet in 2001; most likely, the proportion of users has increased since then. Challenges for youth with disabilities and chronic health conditions in accessing computers, paying for Internet access, navigating the Internet, and using online resources require ongoing attention.

RECOMMENDATIONS FOR ACHIEVING MEANINGFUL COMMUNITY PARTICIPATION

We envision a future when young people with disabilities make the transition from school into typical community lives where, as they choose, they spend time with family, friends, and other supportive adults; develop intimate relationships; get around the community; run errands; participate in recreational activities; attend religious and social groups; volunteer; become parents; cast their ballots and run for political office; and IM with friends from another town on the Internet. Individualized supports are available, based on each young person's goals and needs, although supports sometimes are not needed because most of the community is designed to be universally accessible. Fostering this reality will require many policy and practice improvements incorporating the following key recommendations.

Increase Universal Access to the Community

Continuing efforts, enforcement activities, and incentives are needed to expand community access by youth with disabilities and ongoing health conditions. For example, in the area of transportation, a promising development has been a collaborative effort between the Federal Transit Authority and the U.S. departments of Health and Human Services, Labor, and Education, which recently launched "United We Ride," a national 5-year initiative to reduce barriers and improve the coordination of transportation services within communities (Easter Seals, 2004). Other universal access initiatives in computing, engineering, and architecture are underway to benefit all citizens (Akoumianakis & Stephanidis, 2003), including accessible housing construction being promoted by the National Association of Home Builders in response to increasing demands for housing that supports aging in place. Potential exists for the disability and aging communities to join forces in advancing community access.

Clearly, technology has the potential to accelerate the community participation of youth with disabilities in many new ways. Public laws and regulations requiring the incorporation of accessible design and safeguards for individuals with disabilities in all new technology are critical, and must be enforced now rather than later. As novel ways to exchange communication and information continue to radically change the way that everyone works, learns, shops, and participates in civic affairs, additional legislation is critical to ensure that Americans with disabilities have equal access to these technologies (National Council on Disability, 2006). Working now to ensure that new Internet-based, digital, and video technologies are being developed for the broadest possible audience of end-users will minimize costly future needs for retrofitting the technology for individuals with disabilities.

Finally, in the area of attitudinal access, antistigma campaigns are underway by mental health, self-advocacy organizations, centers for independent living, ADAPT, and mental health consumer/survivor organizations. These groups are working to increase public awareness of the capacities and rights of individuals with disabilities to participate in accessible communities. Encouraging professionals to challenge their assumptions and adopt functional assessment and support approaches in their work with people with disabilities will also increase their understanding and responsiveness.

Promote Youth Self-Determination

A variety of strategies have been shown to promote self-determination among youth (Powers, Deshler, Jones, & Simon, 2006; Ward & Kohler, 1996). At an individual level, youth self-determination is fostered when young people can make key decisions—such as choosing their courses, extracurricular activities, and career goals—and can actively participate in their transition planning. At a collective level, self-determination is promoted by supporting youth to participate in leadership activities (e.g. peer mediation, youth leadership, community service programs), as well as making decisions related to curriculum content, scheduling, governance, and community engagement activities. To make informed decisions, youth must be able to access information about available options as well as their strengths and accommodation needs. Experiential learning is a cornerstone of promoting self-determination, and therefore a key part of virtually every model. Because self-determination skills are generic and intended to be learned and applied across settings, it is important to provide multiple opportunities for students to practice their newly learned skills in different environments. Mentoring and peer support can also promote youth's self-determination, as do encouragement and support from family members and other supportive adults (Powers et al., 1999; Sands et al., 1998).

Self-determination efforts in education have taught us several important lessons, the first being that self-determination should be addressed systematically through formal infusion into the curriculum, as well as through the identification and expansion of opportunities and support for its expression, such as from mentors and experienced peers (Powers et al., 1995; Ward, 1996). A second lesson is that self-determination can be expressed by students with diverse disabilities, including those with significant cognitive disabilities. Third, self-determination instruction and opportunities must begin when children are very young to reverse the cycle of dependency, control by others, and feelings of inability that too often characterize individuals with disabilities. Finally, expression of self-determination is fostered by having real opportunities to make decisions and direct one's life, not by a "readiness" approach that requires youth to demonstrate specified levels of competence before they can participate in self-direction activities. Foremost, promoting self-determination requires that we believe in the capacities of youth to be change agents in their lives as well as in our own capacities to support them.

Implement New Perspectives and Approaches for Supporting Families

A first step toward better supporting families is to adopt a definition that encompasses the true depth and diversity of what families are today in our communities. Over the years, we have relied on the legal definition of families as those who are related by blood or marriage or by legal adoption or foster parent relationship (Turnbull et al., 2005). A second definition—one that more richly encompasses the multiple, interdependent dimensions and diverse characteristics of today's families—identifies the family unit in terms of individuals providing support for one other on a regular basis (Poston et al., 2003). This definition recognizes the family as highly idiosyncratic, with unique ways of characterizing itself, determining membership, carrying out member functions, and evolving over the lifespan (Turnbull, Turnbull, Erwin, & Soodak, 2006). In examining family services and support needs, Turnbull et al. (2005) identified four trends. First, most families favor inclusive community opportunities for their children. Second, families often lack inclusive options for their youth and adult members with disabilities to participate in the community. A third trend is the desire of ethnically and racially diverse families for increased participation in policy development and service delivery. A fourth trend is a lack of qualified personnel to provide quality, inclusive, and culturally responsive services and supports for individuals with disabilities and their families (Turnbull et al., 2005). Particularly lacking are what might be termed "personalized supports" or those services that support the psychological, social, and economic needs of families (respite care, financial subsidies, in-home supports, transportation, others). Additional concerns have been raised by families regarding the lack of service coordination that occurs to help them plan for and arrange needed transition and adult services (Johnson et al., 2002). Despite some progress, services and supports for families remain uneven and inconsistent in their availability and quality within and across states. Renewed commitment is needed to make these opportunities and supports available to families.

Accelerate *Olmstead* Implementation

In *Olmstead v. L.C.,* 527 U.S. 581, 119 S. Ct. 2176 (1999) the Supreme Court interpreted Title II of the ADA to require states to place qualified individuals with disabilities in community settings, rather than in institutions, whenever treatment professionals determine that such placement is appropriate, the affected people do not oppose such placement, and the state can reasonably accommodate the placement, taking into account the resources available to the state and the needs of others with disabilities. The full intent and goals have not, however, been fully realized for many individuals with disabilities. Under Title II of ADA and the *Olmstead* decision, states should move forward in the development of comprehensive plans for placing qualified people with disabilities in less restrictive community settings. Congress in Title II of ADA should also clarify and define the roles that other federal agencies (e.g., the U.S. Departments of Labor, Transportation, Health and Human Services, and others) should play in supporting governors and their states in carrying out these plans. Historically, public policy has funded institutional living as the norm, requiring states to request waivers to use Medicaid funds for community-based services. It is time to formally reverse this policy by funding community-based services in all states and requiring states to obtain waivers for institutional care.

Expand Person-Directed Services and Supports

Person-directed service models are at the forefront of efforts to enhance the quality of long-term services and supports for people with disabilities. Person-directed services can be designed to provide for varying levels of control, including 1) direct cash payments and counseling for individuals who are responsible for all facets of funding and service management, 2) fiscal intermediary programs that assume responsibility for administrative employment functions (i.e., payroll, taxes, paperwork) while customers manage their services, 3) supportive intermediary programs that assist customers with activities such as service coordination, brokering supports, or screening and training care providers, 4) self-directed case management programs that actively involve customers in decisions regarding their services but retain control over the management of funds and services, and 5) spectrum service programs in which customers can choose among a range of the above support options (Flanagan, Green, & Eustis, 1996). Most person-directed programs offer customers only one of these options rather than a range of supports (Scala & Mayberry, 1997). Three of the most dominant types of person-directed services in the United States are personal assistance services, brokered support, and the Cash and Counseling program for users of Medicaid with disabilities (Powers et al., 2006). These service models typically provide customers with individualized budgets they can use to purchase needed accommodations and supports, including personal assistant services, in conjunction with some form of service coordination or technical assistance.

Use of person-directed services and supports are associated with enhanced quality of life, personal control, satisfaction with services, and reduced unmet need (see review by Powers et al., 2006). Individuals who have a choice of support provider often choose family members and report higher levels of safety (Benjamin et al., 1998; Foster, Brown, Phillips, Schore, & Carlson, 2003). While person-directed service models have been demonstrated and validated for adults and families of children with mobility, developmental, or sensory disabilities and for elders, very little attention has been given to evaluating the benefits of these approaches for individuals with mental health disabilities, and few demonstrations have been targeted specifically to facilitate the transition of young adults with disabilities to community living.

To truly facilitate community living, services and supports definitions must be expanded beyond providing activities of daily living and instrumental activities of daily living care at home to include support for community-based social, leisure, and civic involvement. Individuals' support funds must be available to make structures accessible; purchase adaptive equipment; hire family, neighbors, and coworkers to provide personal assistance that includes physical, emotional, and social support; obtain education about community living options and accommodations; and other key assistance. Professionals must learn to redirect their helping efforts toward providing information and facilitation for youth, families, and community members. Essential to youths' success, receipt of disability and health benefits must no longer be tied to personal limitation so that youth are afraid they will lose essential supports if they are successful in assuming valued roles in their communities. If young people with disabilities are to have the chance to rise out of poverty, benefit restrictions that limit personal savings also must be replaced by "buy-in models" in which young people are encouraged to work and acquire wealth, while paying taxes and contributing toward their benefit costs.

Increase Funding for a Skilled Direct Support Work Force

Even when young people have the opportunity to live in the community and to determine and direct their supports, one of the biggest obstacles they face is the lack of skilled, stable direct support workers. We must provide young people with disabilities and ongoing health conditions and their families with access to stable, skilled support providers who can work in partnership with them to optimize their community participation. Unfortunately, many direct support workers do not receive living wages, benefits, training, and respectful working conditions that are essential to keeping them in the work force and providing stable, quality services and supports that meet youths' needs. Access to high quality, accessible, and affordable training for direct support workers is immediately needed. Furthermore, funding and policies that advance new infrastructure development (e.g., public entities that provide benefits to workers who are employed by individuals) are needed that enable states to provide competitive pay and benefits for workers. Congress should increase funding available to states for direct support worker training, wages, and benefits by enacting legislation such as the Direct Support Professionals Fairness and Security Act reintroduced as H.R. 868 in Congress in 2009.

COMMUNITIES FOR ALL

Ultimately, full participation by young people with disabilities will be achieved through structuring and supporting communities that recognize and address the diverse needs of the children, youth, adults and elders that live in them. Community development efforts most likely will be catalyzed by the efforts of youth themselves and their families, advocates, and supporters who become informed and educate themselves and others about youth contributions and needs. Creation of welcoming communities will be realized through high expectations, knowledge and ingenuity of community members, and creative and efficient use of resources that promote social sustainability for all.

REFERENCES

Abery, B., & Stancliffe, R. (1996). The ecology of self-determination. In D.J. Sands & M.L. Wehmeyer (Eds.), *Self-determination across the life span: Independence and choice for people with disabilities* (pp. 111–146). Baltimore: Paul H. Brookes Publishing Co.

Advocates for Children of New York. (2000). *Educational neglect: The delivery of educational services to children in New York City's foster care system.* Retrieved June 15, 2004, from http://www.advocatesforchildren.org/ppubs/2005/fostercare.pdf

Akoumianakis, D., & Stephanidis, C. (2003). Universal access. Theoretical perspectives, practice, and experience: 7th ERCIM International Workshop on User Interfaces for All, Paris, France. In *Lecture Notes in Computer Science* (Vol. 2615), Berlin: Springer.

Allen, J.B. (1999). Enhancing recovery through linkage with indigenous natural supports. Retrieved December 12, 2007, from http://www.power2u.org/downloads/Local Communities and Natural Support Systems 2a-Mental Health.doc

Allen, S., & Mor, V. (1998). *Living in the community with disability: Service needs, use, and systems.* New York: Springer.

American Academy of Pediatrics. (1994). Health care of children in foster care: Policy statement. *Pediatrics, 93,* 335–338.

Americans with Disabilities Act (ADA) of 1990, PL 101-336, 42 U.S.C. §§ 12101 *et seq.*

Armstrong, M.I., Biernie-Lefcovitch, S., & Ungar, M.T. (2005). Pathways between social support, family well-being, quality of parenting, and child resilience: What we know. *Journal of Child and Family Studies, 14,* 269–281.

Benjamin, A.E., Matthias, R.E., & Franke, T. (1998, September). *Comparing client-directed and agency models for providing disability-related supportive services at home* (Report prepared for the Assistant Secretary for Planning and Evaluation, U.S. Department of Health and Human Services). Los Angeles: University of California School of Public Policy and Social Research.

Benz, M.R., Lindstrom, L., & Latta, T. (1999). Improving collaboration between schools and vocational rehabilitation: The youth transition program model. *Journal of Vocational Rehabilitation, 13,* 55–63.

Benz, M.R., Lindstrom, L., & Yovanoff, P. (2000). Improving graduation and employment outcomes of students with disabilities: Predictive factors and student factors. *Exceptional Children, 66,* 509–529.

Benz, M.R., Yovanoff, P., & Doren, B. (1997). School-to-work components that predict postschool success for students with and without disabilities. *Exceptional Children, 63,* 151–165.

Blacher, J., & Hatton, C. (2007). Families in context: Influences on coping and adaptation. In S.L. Odom, R.H. Horner, M.E. Snell, & J. Blacher (Eds.), *Handbook of developmental disabilities* (pp. 531–551). New York: Guilford Press.

Bromley, J., Hare, D.J., Davison, K., & Emerson, E. (2006). Mothers supporting children with autistic spectrum disorders: Social support, mental health status and satisfaction with services. *Autism, 8,* 409–423.

Bullis, M., & Cheney, D. (1999). Vocational and transition interventions for adolescents and young adults with emotional or behavior disorders. *Focus on Exceptional Children, 31(7),* 1–24.

Bullis, M., Yovanoff, P., Mueller, G., & Havel, E. (2002). Life on the outs: Examination of the facility-to-community transition of incarcerated youth. *Exceptional Children, 69,* 7–22.

Campbell-Whatley, G. (2001). Mentoring student with mild disabilities: The "nuts and bolts" of program development. *Intervention in School and Clinic, 36,* 211–216.

Chesapeake Institute. (1994). *National agenda for achieving better results for children and youth with serious emotional disturbance* (Report for the U.S. Department of Education, Office of Special Education and Rehabilitative Services). Washington, DC: Author.

Chipungu, S.S., & Bent-Goodley, T.B. (2004, Winter). Meeting the challenges of contemporary foster care. *The Future of Children, 14(1),* 74–93.

Courtney, M., Piliavin, I., & Grogan-Kaylor, A. (1995). *The Wisconsin study of youth aging out of out-of-home care: A portrait of children about to leave care.* Madison, WI: University of Wisconsin-Madison, School of Social Work.

Courtney, M.E., Dworsky, A., Ruth, G., Keller, T., Havlicek, J., & Bost, N. (2005). *Midwest evaluation of the adult functioning of former foster youth: Outcomes at age 19.* Chicago: Chapin Hall Center for Children at the University of Chicago.

DeJong, G., Batavia, A.I., & McKnew, L.B. (1992, Winter). The independent living model of personal assistance in national long-term-care policy. *Aging and Disability,* 89–95.

Developmental Disabilities Assistance and Bill of Rights Act Amendments of 1987, PL 100-146, 42 U.S.C. §§ 6000 *et seq.*

Developmental Disabilities Assistance and Bill of Rights Act Amendments of 2000, PL 106-402, 42 U.S.C. §§ 6000 *et seq.*

Direct Support Professionals Fairness and Security Act of 2009, H.R. 868, 110th Cong. (2007).

Dybwad, G., & Bersani, H.A. (1996). *New voices: Self-advocacy by people with disabilities.* Cambridge, MA: Brookline Books.

Easter Seals, Project Action. (2004, Spring). *Leaders at forum gather to proclaim: "United We Ride:" Project ACTION Update (Accessible Transportation in our Nation).* Retrieved June 12, 2004, from http://projectaction.easterseals.com/site/DocServer/spring 2004pdf.pdf?docID=5264

Educational Equity Concepts. (1993). *A report on women with disabilities in postsecondary education* (Issue Paper No. 1). New York: Author.

Ensminger, M.E., & Juon, H.S. (1998). Transition to adulthood among high-risk youth. In R. Jessor, *New perspectives on adolescent risk behavior* (pp. 365–391). New York: Cambridge University Press.

Everson, J.M., Zhang, D., & Guillory, J.D. (2001). A statewide investigation of individualized transition plans in Louisiana. *Career Development for Exceptional Children, 24(1),* 37–49.

Flanagan, S.A., Green, P.S., & Eustis, N. (1996, November). *Facilitating consumer-directed personal assistance services (CD-PAS) through the use of intermediary service models: Eleven states' experiences.* Paper presented at the annual meeting of the Gerontological Society of America, Washington, DC.

Foster, L., Brown, R., Phillips, B., Schore, J., & Carlson, B.L. (2003, March 26). Improving the quality of Medicaid personal assistance through consumer direction. *Health Affairs,* Web exclusive. Retrieved October 29, 2009, from http://content .healthaffairs.org/cgi/reprint/hlthaff.w3.162v1

Froschl, M., Rubin, E., & Sprung, B. (1999). *Connecting gender and disability.* Newton, MA: Women's Educational Equity Act (WEEA) Equity Resource Center, Education Development Center.

Geenen, S.J., & Powers, L.E. (2007). Tomorrow is another problem: The experiences of youth in foster care during their transition to adulthood. *Children and Youth Services Review, 29,* 1085–1101.

Geenen, S., Powers, L.E., Lopez-Vasquez, A., & Bersani, H. (2003). Understanding and promoting the transition of minority youth. *Career Development for Exceptional Individuals, 26(1)*, 27–46.

Gil-Kashiwabara, E., Hogansen, J., Geenen, S., Powers, K., & Powers, L.E. (2007). Improving transition outcomes for marginalized youth. *Career Development for Exceptional Individuals, 30(2)*, 80–91.

Gross, E.F. (2004). Adolescent Internet use: What we expect, what teens report. *Applied Developmental Psychology, 25*, 633–649.

Hagner, D., & Dileo, D. (1993). *Workplace culture, supported employment and people with disabilities.* Cambridge, MA: Brookline Books.

Halpern, A.S. (1985). Transition: A look at the foundations. *Exceptional Children, 51(6)*, 479–486.

Halpern, A.S., Yovanoff, P., Doren, B., & Benz, M.R. (1995). Predicting participation in postsecondary education for school leavers with disabilities. *Exceptional Children, 62(2)*, 151–164.

Harden, B.J. (2004). Safety and stability for foster children: A developmental perspective. *The Future of Children: Children, Families and Foster Care, 14(1)*, 31–47.

Harry, B. (1992). *Cultural diversity, families, and the special education system: Communication and empowerment.* New York: Teachers College Press.

Hasazi, S.B., Furney, K.S., & DeStefano, L. (1999). Implementing the IDEA transition mandates. *Exceptional Children, 65(4)*, 555–566.

Hasazi, S., Johnson, D.R., Thurlow, M., Cobb, B., Trach, J., Stodden, R., Leuchovius, D., Hart, D., Benz, M., DeStefano, L., & Grossi, T. (2005). Transitions from home and school to the roles and supports of adulthood. In K.C. Lakin & A. Turnbull (Eds.), *National goals and research for persons with intellectual and developmental disabilities* (pp. 65–92). Washington, DC: American Association on Mental Retardation and The Arc of the United States.

Individuals with Disabilities Education Improvement Act (IDEA) of 2004, PL 108-446, 20 U.S.C. §§ 1400 *et seq.*

Johnson, D.R., McGrew, K., Bloomberg, L., Bruininks, R.H., & Lin, H.C. (1997). *Policy research brief: A national perspective on the postschool outcomes and community adjustment of individuals with severe disabilities.* Minneapolis, MN: University of Minnesota, Institute on Community Integration.

Johnson, D.R., Stodden, R.A., Emanuel, E.J., Luecking, R., & Mack, M. (2002). Current challenges facing secondary education and transition services for youth with disabilities: What research tells us. *Exceptional Children, 68(4)*, 519–531.

Kennedy, J., LaPlante, M.P., & Kaye, H.S. (1997). *Need for assistance in the activities of daily living.* Disability Statistics Abstract (18). Washington, DC: U.S. Department of Education, National Institute on Disability and Rehabilitation Research.

Kohler, P.D. (1998). Implementing a transition perspective of education: A comprehensive approach to planning and delivering secondary education and transition services. In F.R. Rusch & J. Chadsey (Eds.), *High school and beyond: Transition from school to work* (pp. 179-205). Belmont, CA: Wadsworth.

Kohler, P.D., & Chapman, S. (1999, March). *Literature review on school-to-work transition.* Retrieved November 7, 2009, from http://homepages.wmich.edu/~kohlerp/pdf/ Lit%20Review%20on%20STW%20Transition.pdf

Kohler, P.D., & Troesken, B.J. (1999). *Improving student outcomes: Promising practices and programs.* Chicago: National Transition Alliance for Youth with Disabilities.

Kraemer, B.R., & Blacher, J. (2001). Transition for young adults with severe mental retardation: School preparation, parent expectations, and family involvement. *Mental Retardation, 39,* 423–435.

Lakin, K.C., Gardner, J., Larson, S., & Wheeler, B. (2005). Access and support for community lives, homes, and social roles. In K.C. Lakin & A. Turnbull (Eds.), *National goals and research for persons with intellectual and developmental disabilities* (pp. 179–215). Washington, DC: American Association on Mental Retardation and The Arc of the United States.

Lakin, K.C., & Turnbull, A. (Eds.). (2005). *National goals and research for people with intellectual and developmental disabilities.* Washington, DC: American Association on Mental Retardation and The Arc of the United States.

Lefley, H. (1996). *Family caregiving in mental illness.* Thousand Oaks, CA: Sage.

Lustig, D.C., & Strauser, D.R. (2007). Causal relationships between poverty and disability. *Rehabilitation Counseling Bulletin, 50(4),* 194–202.

Mank, D. (1994). The underachievement of supported employment: A call for reinvestment. *Journal of Disability Policy Studies, 5(2),* 1–24.

Mank, D. (2007). Employment. In S.L. Odom, R.H. Horner, M.E. Snell, & J. Blacher (Eds.), *Handbook of developmental disabilities* (pp. 390–409). New York: Guilford Press.

McLearn, K.T., Colasanto, D., Schoen, C., & Shapiro, M.Y. (1999). Mentoring matters: A national survey of adults mentoring young people. In J.B. Grossman (Ed.), *Contemporary issues in mentoring.* Retrieved April 8, 2002, from http://www.ppv.org/content/reports/issuesinmentoring_pdf.htm

Merriam-Webster. (2008). *Merriam-Webster's collegiate dictionary* (11th ed.). Springfield, MA: Author.

Morningstar, M.E., Turnbull, A.P., & Turnbull, H.R. (1995). What do students with disabilities tell us about the importance of family involvement in the transition from school to adult life? *Exceptional Children, 62(3),* 249–260.

Myner, J., Santman, J., Cappelletty, G.G., & Perlmutter, B.F. (1998). Variables related to recidivism among juvenile offenders. *International Journal of Offender Therapy and Comparative Criminology, 42(1),* 65–80.

National and Community Service Act of 1990 (as amended through PL 106-170, approved December 17, 1999).

National Center for Disability Services. (1991). *A demonstration project to identify and teach skills necessary for self-determination.* Albertson, NY: Author.

National Center for Educational Statistics. (2004). *Computer and Internet use by children and adolescents in 2001.* Washington, DC: U.S. Department of Education Institute of Education Sciences.

National Center on Birth Defects and Developmental Disabilities. (2003). *Healthy People 2010: Disability and secondary conditions.* Atlanta, GA: Centers for Disease Control and Prevention.

National Council on Disability. (2004, December 2). *Newsroom: Livable communities for adults with disabilities.* Retrieved October 14, 2007, from http://www.ncd.gov/newsroom/publications/2004/LivableCommunities.htm

National Council on Disability. (2006, December 19). *Newsroom: The need for federal legislation and regulation prohibiting telecommunications and information services discrimination.* Retrieved December 10, 2007, from http://www.ncd.gov/newsroom/publications/2006/discrimination.htm

National Research Council. (2000, February). *Broadband: Bringing home the bits.* Washington, DC: National Academy Press. Retrieved from http://books.nap.edu/html/broadband/ch3.htlm

National Research Council. (2001). *Educating children with autism.* Committee on Educational Interventions for Children with Autism, Division of Behavioral and Social Sciences and Education. Washington, DC: National Academy Press.

Nisbet, J. (Ed.). (1992). *Natural supports in school, at work, and in the community for people with severe disabilities.* Baltimore: Paul H. Brookes Publishing Co.

Nisbet, J., & Hagner, D. (1988). Natural supports in the workplace: A reexamination of supported employment. *Journal of the Association for Persons with Severe Handicaps, 13,* 260–267.

Odom, S.L., Horner, R.H., Snell, M.E., & Blacher, J. (2007). The construct of developmental disabilities. In S.L. Odom, R.H. Horner, M.E. Snell, & J. Blacher (Eds.), *Handbook of developmental disabilities* (pp. 3–14). New York: Guilford Press.

Olmstead v. L.C., 527 U.S. 581 (1999).

Parish, S.L., Pomeranz-Essley, A., & Braddock, D. (2003). Family support in the United States: Financing trends and emerging initiatives. *Mental Retardation, 41,* 174–187.

Partington, K. (2005). What do we mean by our community. *Journal of Intellectual Disabilities 9,* 241–251.

Pearpoint, J. (1990). *From behind the piano: The building of Judith Snow's unique circle of friends.* Toronto: Inclusion Press.

Perske, R. (1988). *Circles of friends: People with disabilities and their friends enrich the lives of one another.* Nashville: Abingdon Press.

Pita, D.D., Ellison, M.L., & Kantor, E. (1999). [Psychiatric personal assistance services: A new service strategy]. Unpublished data available from the Center for Psychiatric Rehabilitation, Boston University.

Poston, D., Turnbull, A., Park, J., Mannan, H., Marquis, J., & Wang, M. (2003). Family quality of life: A qualitative inquiry. *Mental Retardation, 41(4/5),* 313–328.

Powers, K., Gil-Kashiwabara, E., Powers, L., Geenen, S., Balandran, J., & Palmer, C. (2005). Mandates and effective transition planning practices reflected in IEPs. *Career Development for Exceptional Individuals, 28(1),* 47–59.

Powers, K.M., Hogansen, J.M., Geenen, S.J., Powers, L.E., & Gil-Kashiwabara, E. (2008). Gender matters in transition to adulthood: A survey study of adolescents with disabilities and their families. *Psychology in the Schools, 45(4),* 349-364.

Powers, L.E., Deshler, D.D., Jones, B., & Simon, M. (2006). Strategies for enhancing self-determination, social success, and transition to adulthood. In D.D. Deshler & J.B. Schumaker (Eds.), *Teaching adolescents with disabilities: Accessing the general education curriculum* (pp. 235–273). New York: Corwin Press.

Powers, L.E., Dinerstein, R., & Holmes, S. (2005). Self-advocacy, self-determination, social freedom and opportunity. In K.C. Lakin & A. Turnbull (Eds.), *National goals and research for persons with intellectual and developmental disabilities* (pp. 257–287). Washington, DC: American Association on Mental Retardation.

Powers, L.E., Garner, T., Valnes, B., Squire, P., Turner, A., Couture, T., Dertinger, R., & Lawson, L. (2007). Building a successful adult life: Findings from youth-directed research. *Exceptionality, 15(1),* 45–56.

Powers, L.E., Sowers, J.S., & Singer, G.H.S. (2006). Person-directed long-term services. *Journal of Disability Policy Studies, 17(2),* 66–76.

Powers, L.E., Sowers, J., & Stevens, T. (1995). An exploratory, randomized study of the impact of mentoring on the self-efficacy and community-based knowledge of adolescents with severe physical challenges. *Journal of Rehabilitation, 61(1)*, 33–41.

Powers, L.E., Turner, A., Matuszewski, J., Wilson, R., & Loesch, C. (1999). A qualitative analysis of student involvement in transition planning. *Journal for Vocational Special Needs Education, 21(3)*, 18–26.

Powers, L.E., Turner, A., Westwood, D., Matuszewski, J., Wilson, R., & Phillips, A. (2001). Take charge for the future: A controlled field-test of a model to promote student involvement in transition planning. *Career Development for Exceptional Individuals, 24(1)*, 89–104.

President's New Freedom Commission on Mental Health. (2003). *Achieving the promise: Transforming mental health care in America*. Retrieved November 7, 2009, from http://www.mentalhealthcommission.gov/reports/FinalReport/FullReport-03.htm

Prouty, R., Smith, G., & Lakin, K.C. (Eds.). (2004). *Residential services for persons with developmental disabilities: Status and trends through 2003*. Minneapolis, MN: University of Minnesota, Research and Training Center on Community Living/Institute on Community Integration.

Pruchno, R.A., & McMullen, W.F. (2004). Patterns of service utilization by adults with a developmental disability: Type of service makes a difference. *American Journal on Mental Retardation, 109(5)*, 362–378.

Rehabilitation Act of 1973, PL 93-112, 29 U.S.C. §§ 701 *et seq.*

Rutgers University and World Institute on Disability. (1992). *Towards an understanding of the demand for personal assistance*. New Brunswick, NJ: Rutgers University.

Sands, D.J., Bassett, D.S., Lehmann, J., & Spencer, K.C. (1998). Factors contributing to and implications for student involvement in transition-related planning, decision making, and instruction. In M.L. Wehmeyer & D.J. Sands (Eds.), *Making it happen: Student involvement in education planning, decision making and instruction* (pp. 25–44). Baltimore: Paul H. Brookes Publishing Co.

Scala, M.A., Mayberry, P.S. (1997, July). *Consumer-directed home services: Issues and models*. Oxford: Ohio Long-Term Care Research Project, Miami University.

Shapiro, J.P. (1993). *No pity: People with disabilities forging a new civil rights movement*. New York: Times Books.

Shoultz, B., & Ward, N. (1996). Self-advocates becoming empowered: The birth of a national organization in the U.S. In G. Dybwad & H. Bersani (Eds.), *New voices: Self-advocacy by people with disabilities* (pp. 216–234). Cambridge, MA: Brookline Books.

Sowers, J., McAllister, R., & Cotton, P. (1996). Strategies to enhance the control of the employment process by individuals with severe disabilities. In L.E. Powers, G.H.S. Singer, & J. Sowers (Eds.), *On the road to autonomy: Promoting self-competence for children and youth with disabilities* (pp. 325–346). Baltimore: Paul H. Brookes Publishing Co.

Squire, P.N. (in press). A young adult's perspective on self-determination: A personal reflection and review of research on self-determination. *Career Development for Exceptional Individuals.*

Stoddard, S., Jans, L., Ripple, J., & Kraus, L. (1998). *What occupations are held by people with a work disability who are employed? Chartbook on Work and Disability in the United States, 1998 An InfoUse Report*. Washington, DC: U.S. National Institute on Disability and Rehabilitation Research (NIDRR).

Tecklin, S.J. (2007). *Pediatric physical therapy* (4th ed.). Philadelphia: Lippincott Williams & Wilkins.

Tritz, K. (2005). *Long-term care: Consumer-directed services under Medicaid. Congressional Research Service Report for Congress.* Washington, DC: Library of Congress.

Turnbull, A.P., Turnbull, H.R., Agosta, J., Erwin, E., Fujiura, G., Singer, G., & Soodak, L. (2005). Support of families and family life across the lifespan. In K.C. Lakin & A.P. Turnbull (Eds.), *National goals and research for persons with intellectual and developmental disabilities* (pp. 217–256). Washington, DC: American Association on Mental Retardation and The Arc of the United States.

Turnbull, A.P., Turnbull, H.R., Erwin, E., & Soodak, L. (2006). *Families, professionals, and exceptionality: Positive outcomes through partnerships and trust* (5th ed.). Upper Saddle River, NJ: Merrill/Prentice-Hall.

U.S. Department of Education. (2002). *Twenty-fourth annual report to Congress on the implementation of the Individuals with Disabilities Education Act.* Washington, DC: Author.

U.S. Department of Transportation, Bureau of Transportation Statistics. (2003). *Freedom to travel.* Retrieved May 10, 2004, from http://www.bts.gov/publications/freedom to travel/pdf/entire.pdf

Wagner, M., Newman, L., Cameto, R., Garza, N., & Levine, P. (2005). *After high school: A first look at the postschool experiences of youth with disabilities. A report from the National Longitudinal Transition Study-2 (NLTS2).* Menlo Park, CA: SRI International.

Wagner, M., Newman, L., Cameto, R., & Levine, P. (2005). *Changes over time in the early postschool outcomes of youth with disabilities. A report of findings from the National Longitudinal Study (NLTS) and the National Longitudinal Transition Study-2 (NLTS2).* Menlo Park, CA: SRI International.

Wagner, M., Newman, L., Cameto, R., Levine, P., & Marder, C. (2007). Perceptions and expectations of youth with disabilities. In *A Report From the National Longitudinal Transition Study-2 (NLTS2).* Menlo Park, CA: SRI International.

Ward, M.J. (1996). Coming of age in the age of self-determination: A historical and personal perspective. In D.J. Sands & M.L. Wehmeyer (Eds.), *Self-determination across the life span: Independence and choice for people with disabilities* (pp. 3–16). Baltimore, MD: Paul H. Brookes Publishing Co.

Ward, M.J., & Kohler, P.D. (1996). Teaching self-determination: Content and process. In L.E. Powers, G.H.S. Singer, & J. Sowers (Eds.), *On the road to autonomy: Promoting self-competence for children and youth with disabilities* (pp. 275–290). Baltimore: Paul H. Brookes Publishing Co.

Wehman, P., & Revell, W.G. (1996). Supported employment from 1986 to 1993: A national program that works. *Focus on Autism and Other Developmental Disabilities, 11(4),* 235–242.

Wehmeyer, M.L. (2005). Self-determination and individuals with severe disabilities: Re-examining meanings and misinterpretations. *Research and Practice for Persons with Severe Disabilities, 30(3),* 113–120.

Wehmeyer, M.L., Gragoudas, S., & Shogren, K. (2006). Self-determination, student involvement, and leadership development. In P. Wehman (Ed.), *Life beyond the classroom: Transition strategies for young people with disabilities.* Baltimore: Paul H. Brookes Publishing Co.

Wehmeyer, M.L., & Schwartz, M. (1997). Self-determination and positive adult outcomes: A follow-up study of youth with mental retardation or learning disabilities. *Exceptional Children, 63,* 245–255.

Westat. (1991). *A national evaluation of Title IV-E foster care independent living programs for youth: Phase 2.* (Contract No. OHDS 105-87-1608). U.S. Department of Health and Human Services. Rockville, MD: Author.

Will, M. (1984). Bridges from school to working life. *Interchange, 2–6.*

World Health Organization. (2001). *International classification of functioning, disability and health (ICF).* Retrieved December 29, 2007 at http://www.who.int/classifications/icf/en

8

Meaningful Work

Obtaining and Maintaining Employment as Youth with Chronic Health Conditions

Thomas P. Golden, Sue Swenson, Sarah von Schrader,
and Susanne M. Bruyère

Every year, more than a half million young people who have been identified as having a disability leave school (U.S. Department of Education [USDOE], 2007f). Some of these students graduate with diplomas or certificates, some move onto other postsecondary school systems, far too many drop out, some move directly into employment, and some continue or move onto income support programs such as Supplemental Security Income (SSI). All leave behind the Individuals with Disabilities Education Act (IDEA) of 1990 (PL 101-476) entitlement to free appropriate public education (FAPE) when they make the transition to what is often referred to as the adult system—at which time, they and their families must learn about various eligibility requirements, find access to the services they need and, in general, fend for themselves without assistance in navigating the more than 200 disability programs at the federal level (Government Accountability Office, 2007).

The authors acknowledge the contribution of William Erickson of the Employment and Disability Institute at Cornell University. Susanne Bruyère has been supported in part in this work by a U.S. Department of Education National Institute on Disability and Rehabilitation Research grant to Cornell University, the Employment Policy for People with Disabilities Rehabilitation Research and Training Center (Grant No. H133B040013). The contents of this chapter do not necessarily represent the policy of the U.S. Department of Education or any other federal agency, and no endorsement by the federal government should be assumed (Edgar, 75.620 (b)).

In this chapter we discuss the policies and programs that have shaped the educational system for young people with disabilities, particularly focusing on the crucial transition years (ages 14–21) leading to adult living, learning, and earning. Some of the barriers and opportunities of the current systems are highlighted and, finally, a series of practical strategies and recommendations are offered for overcoming the barriers that transition-age youth continue to face in the United States as they prepare for adulthood and valued social roles.

WHAT WE KNOW

There is considerable similarity in the goals and objectives set out in many of the policies and initiatives of the past three decades. Expansion of individualized planning, increased community-based service delivery, focus on consumer control, measurement of individual outcomes, and integrated options for people with disabilities are all evident in vocational rehabilitation, supported and self-employment, special education, and the independent living and self-determination movements, as well as in the most recent advances in education policy to support the successful school-to-work movement of youth with disabilities.

Currently, however, the United States continues to develop policies that do not recognize the intertwined experience of disability, special education, and unemployment, nor do they recognize that fragmented policies, programs, and new model demonstrations add significant and sometimes overwhelming confusion, burdens, and delays to the experience of people with disabilities and their families. Many people with disabilities, parents, service providers, administrators, and advocates have benefited from training, technical support, and outreach and are equipped to implement innovations and best practices. Others have not benefited from training and technical assistance or outreach, and they have been left behind. Systems that focus on individual outcomes may have the unintended consequence of being slow to take responsibility for people who remain unserved. Meanwhile, accountability systems might measure "inputs," such as the number of people who have been identified in diagnostic categories or who have certain functional limitations, but they do not assess the impact of the personal behaviors and outcomes of populations. It is difficult to assert that the systems that are supposed to support people with disabilities and their families are in any way systematic. This is nowhere more true than it is during the transition years between school and adult life.

The transition from adolescence to adult life can be complex for individuals with a disability and/or a chronic health condition. In school, these youth often have access to individual transition planning that addresses the individuals' goals related to training, education, employment, and independent living skills and helps them negotiate the services that are available (USDOE, 2007a). However, when entering the adult system, the complexity of regulations and services can be overwhelming, as there is no uniform system to address the needs of this diverse population (Wittenburg, Golden, & Fishman, 2002). In this section, we discuss the policies and programs that this population may encounter, particularly focusing on the transition years. Some of the barriers and opportunities of the current systems are highlighted and, finally, some recommendations are made about how we can improve on what we have.

Current Education Policies

Throughout the 1970s and 1980s, school inclusion was the centerpiece of legislation for youth with disabilities (Wittenburg et al., 2002). The Education for All Handicapped Children Act of 1975 (PL 94-142) governed the delivery of special education services to students with disabilities and required FAPE in the least restrictive environment for children with disabilities at the primary and secondary levels. In addition to the emphasis of these laws on inclusion, the Education for All Handicapped Children Act also required that an individualized education program (IEP) be developed for each child eligible for special education and related services, and that it specify specific services and supports a child needed. In 1990, the Education for All Handicapped Children Act was renamed the Individuals with Disabilities Education Act (IDEA), and the 1997 and 2004 amendments to this law (Individuals with Disabilities Education Act Amendments of 1997, PL 105-17; Individuals with Disabilities Education Improvement Act of 2004, PL 108-446) increased the emphasis on the transition planning process and services for youths ages 14–21. The 1997 IDEA amendments established transition planning requirements, which stated that beginning at age 14, the student's IEP must include transition services needs related to the child's course of study, and no later than age 16, a comprehensive transition services plan must be included in the student's IEP (PL 105-17). Most recently, new language was introduced in the 2004 reauthorization of IDEA, including a requirement that the IEP include "appropriate measurable postsecondary goals based on age appropriate transition assessments" and the transition services needed to reach these goals. According to the 2004 reauthorization of IDEA, transition services are formally defined as

> a coordinated set of activities for a child with a disability that: is designed to be within a results-oriented process, that is focused on improving the academic and functional achievement of the child with a disability to facilitate the child's movement from school to post-school activities . . .; is based on the individual child's needs, taking into account the child's strengths, preferences, and interests; and includes instruction, related services, community experiences, the development of employment and other post-school adult living objectives, and, if appropriate, acquisition of daily living skills and functional vocational evaluation. (USDOE, 2007a)

The No Child Left Behind Act (NCLB) of 2001 (PL 107-110) created a mandate for measures of system effectiveness for all students, including students with disabilities. Under NCLB, states are required to develop accountability systems that include annual targets for academic achievement, assessment participation, graduation rates, and other indicators for elementary and middle schools that include racial and ethnic groups, economically disadvantaged populations, students with disabilities, and students with limited English proficiency. The 2004 amendments aligned IDEA more closely with NCLB's state assessment and accountability system requirements to ensure that students with disabilities were being included in states' reporting of annual yearly progress measures. Some maintain that schools should not be held accountable for the performance and progression of populations of students who have typically been considered incapable of performing at higher levels. At the same time, advocates maintain that if the students are not held to the same learning standards, with accommodations as needed, their unique needs will be ignored and they will not attain successful postschool outcomes when compared to their peers without disabilities. Either way, federal policy has made it clear that no one should be discriminated against, and the NCLB provides an exceptional vehicle for ensuring that transition-age youth are measured against the same outcome standards as their peers without disabilities.

Current Employment Policies

For youth with disabilities and chronic health conditions to be able to navigate the job search and employment retention challenges that they will face in their occupational experience, it is important to understand the employment legislation that affects their access to employment support services and also may govern their employee rights and protections, once employed. The next section looks at laws that may influence how youth with disabilities and chronic health conditions look at their occupational choices, and once hired, how employers respond to their disabilities and chronic health conditions as a part of the employment process.

The Rehabilitation Act of 1973 (PL 93-112; reauthorized under the Workforce Investment Act [WIA] of 1998 [PL 105-220]; for more information, see http://www.doleta.gov/USWORKFORCE/WIA/act.cfm) requires the collaboration of the state educational agency and the state vocational agency in the transition process. Within the student's last 2 years of schooling, a student's IEP must be coordinated with their individualized plan for employment (IPE), which is required by the Rehabilitation Act. Federal regulations issued by the Rehabilitation Services Administration make it clear that state vocational rehabilitation (VR) agencies are to be actively involved in the transition planning process through outreach, consultation, and technical assistance. As a part of the state VR agency's outreach responsibilities in administering the state or federal VR program, they must inform students of the purpose of the VR program, application and eligibility requirements, and the potential scope of services available. The purpose of this requirement is to enable students with disabilities to make informed decisions on whether to apply for VR services while still in school.

Section 504 of the Rehabilitation Act ensures that a child with a disability has equal access to an education—under which the child can receive accommodations and modification as needed based on their disability. Section 504 does not require the development of an IEP, as does IDEA; however, schools may develop a 504 plan to clearly outline the child's needed support and plan for ensuring their access to FAPE. While Section 504 provides fewer procedural safeguards to youth with disabilities and their parents, many youth with chronic health conditions have benefited from the development of medical management plans under Section 504, allowing the management of their medical conditions while minimizing impact on their educational pursuits.

Beyond the implications of the Rehabilitation Act, the broader WIA holds opportunity and promise for supporting successful postschool adult outcomes of youth with chronic health conditions. The WIA consolidated workforce preparation and employment services into a unified system of support that is responsive to the needs of job seekers, employers, and communities. This law attempts both to empower customers and to provide opportunities for business and human resource professionals to focus public programs on marketplace needs. WIA created a workforce development system that encourages and facilitates one-stop service intended to serve every job seeker through a central location that provides access to numerous workforce development programs. Core services—including assessment, basic job readiness, and help with job searches—are open to a universal population. For those who require further assistance finding employment, intensive services and job training are also available. Youth leaving the entitlements of the school system behind will find a single point of entry for many services coordinated through the One-Stop Center—including access to the state VR system, benefits planners, disability program navigators, and other specialized services.

The Ticket to Work and Work Incentives Improvement Act of 1999 (PL 106-170) provides beneficiaries and recipients of SSI, Social Security Disability Insurance (SSDI), or both with the incentives and supports needed to prepare for, attach to, or advance in work (for more information on the Work Incentives Improvement Act, see http://www.socialsecurity.gov/work/abouttick et.html). The goals of this act are especially relevant to the population of youth with chronic health conditions who receive these public entitlements either prior to leaving school or as an adult. At the heart of the act was a desire by Congress to increase options available to beneficiaries of the Social Security Administration disability programs by expanding upon the existing network of service providers available and creating a more comprehensive set of supports for people with disabilities considering work. (Cornell University has developed a series of Policy and Practice Briefs on Social Security issues, including one on the Ticket program. They can be found at http://www.ilr.cornell.edu/edi/s-PPBriefs.cfm.) The Ticket to Work program permits the individual beneficiary or recipient to choose from an array of service providers (called Employment Networks), placing control over provider selection in the hands of the consumer.

The Ticket to Work Act also governs the provision of health care services to workers with disabilities and attempts to reduce disincentives to employment for people with disabilities posed by the threat of loss of health care benefits. Under this part of the act, states are encouraged to improve access to health care coverage available under Medicare and Medicaid. This is an important factor for young people with disabilities making a transition to the workforce, many of whom rely on publicly provided health coverage. O'Day, Stapleton, and Horvath-Rose (2007) found that the young work-limited population was far more likely to have public coverage (50.2% versus 8.7%) and that there has been a significant shift from private insurers to public insurers during the last 10 years. Allowing these young people to obtain employment without risk of losing health care coverage, especially coverage of their special health needs, may be crucial in making a successful transition to employment.

While typically one may not think of the Family and Medical Leave Act (FMLA) of 1993 (PL 103-3) as a critical employment policy for youth with chronic health conditions, it does provide critical support to the working parents of these children who must take unpaid leaves of absence from work, allowing them to take time off from work when their children are hospitalized or face serious health conditions that require regular medical appointments. The law's enactment was driven by concern to protect the needs of American workforces, while attending to the productivity concerns of employers. (For additional information about the FMLA, see the U.S. Department of Labor web site at http://www.dol.gov/esa/whd/fmla.) An FMLA serious health condition is an illness, injury, impairment, or physical or mental condition that involves inpatient care or continuing treatment by a health care provider. During the FMLA leave, the employer must maintain the employee's existing level of coverage under a group health plan. At the end of FMLA leave, an employer must take an employee back into the same or an equivalent job. The FMLA does not require an employer to return to work an employee who is medically unable to do his job, nor does it require modification of the job or reassignment to a new position.

Youth with disabilities seeking employment should be made aware of their protections under the employment provisions (Title I) of the Americans with Disabilities Act (ADA) of 1990 (PL 101-336). The ADA is discussed in detail elsewhere in this book, so we will not elaborate on the specifics of the law here. However, we do want to emphasize the importance of each youth understanding his or her own rights and responsibilities, as well as an employer's responsibilities to accommodate. Many employees and employers need further information to improve awareness of accommodations and nondiscrimination principles and practices to enable youth with disabilities to obtain and maintain employment.

One of the first challenges for the young job applicant will be the difficult decision whether to disclose his or her disability to an employer. If an accommodation is needed to perform the job, then disclosure will be necessary to make this request; the accommodation cannot be obtained without alerting an employer to the situation. The disclosure may make for a more supportive work environment, but it might also result in the possibility of stigma and resulting discrimination or harassment, and in loss of privacy. It is a personal decision, with both potential benefits and significant drawbacks. It will be important for young people with a disability to understand their rights and be prepared to focus on their work-related skills in presenting themselves in the job application process. This awareness will also stand them in good stead throughout their employment process, as their job requirements may change or their own disability or health condition might progress, necessitating further requests for accommodation.

OUR SUCCESS TO DATE: MOVING FROM POLICY TO PRACTICE

The previous section outlined the policy related to the movement for youth with disabilities and chronic health conditions from school to postschool activities. When put into practice, these policies have improved access to special education, integration into regular classrooms, access to formalized transition planning, and many postschool outcomes. The following section provides an overview of the impact of policy, both in school and postschool. Although the following focuses on students served under IDEA, it should be noted that not all youth with disabilities and chronic health conditions receive special education or transition planning services under IDEA. Some youth do not qualify for special education because their disability does not pose a significant barrier to learning in traditional school settings.

Individuals with Disabilities Education Act Statistics: Access and Inclusion

There are approximately 6 million (USDOE, 2007b) American students ages 6–21 served under IDEA and an unknown number of additional youth who are eligible for accommodations because they meet the definition of disability under Section 504 of the Rehabilitation Act. Since the passage of IDEA, each year the number and percentage of youth ages 3–21 enrolled in public schools receiving special education has grown. The National Center for Educational Statistics (2007) reported that in 1976–1977 some 3.7 million youth received special education services, as compared to 6.7 million youth in 2005–2006; this represents an increase from 8% to 14% of total public school enrollment. Of most interest is that during the period from 1976 to 2006, the number of children with learning disabilities accessing special education services grew threefold (from 2% to 6% in public school enrollment). Among students served under IDEA in 2007 ages 6–21, 67% were male, 1.5% were American Indian/Alaska Native, about 2.3% were Asian/Pacific Islander, 20.5% were black, 18.0% were Hispanic, and

Table 8.1. Prevalence of diagnoses among youth (ages 6–21) served under IDEA in 2007

Disability designation	Percentage
Specific learning disabilities	43.4%
Speech or language impairments	19.2%
Other health impairments	10.6%
Mental retardation	8.3%
Emotional disturbance	7.4%
Autism	4.3%
Multiple disabilities	2.2%
Developmental delay	1.5%
Hearing impairments	1.2%
Orthopedic impairments	1.0%
Visual impairments	0.4%
Traumatic brain injury	0.4%
Deaf-blindness	< 0.1%

Source: U.S. Department of Education (2007b).

57.7% were white (USDOE, 2007c, 2007d). The most common diagnoses were specific learning disabilities (43.4%), speech or language impairments (19.2%), other health impairments (10.6%), and mental retardation (8.3%). Table 8.1 presents more specific information about diagnostic prevalence.

Core to the intent of IDEA is the principle of a student receiving educational supports in the least restrictive environment. The USDOE (2007e) reported that only 56.8% of students ages 6–21 served under IDEA spent over 80% of their time in regular classroom settings. Close to a quarter (22.1%) spent 40%–79% of their time in regular classes, whereas 15.4% of students spent less than 40% of their time in regular classes, with the remainder in more restrictive settings. Although more recent educational reforms like No Child Left Behind appear to have had a positive impact on increasing least restrictive settings, many youth with disabilities still do not spend the majority of their time in general classroom settings.

The longitudinal impact of education and transition planning for youth with disabilities was documented in the National Longitudinal Transition Study (NLTS), which included more than 8,000 youth between the ages of 13 and 21 in special education within secondary schools in 1985. A subsequent 10-year study, NLTS2, is being conducted with a nationally representative sample of more than 11,000 youth who were ages 13–16 and receiving special education services in grade 7 or above in the 2000–2001 school year. These studies help to illuminate the characteristics of youth with disabilities, their educational experiences, and their postschool outcomes. The NLTS and NLTS2 were designed to allow for the comparison between the two studies, providing a useful indicator of changes over time in special education and the youth it serves. NLTS and NLTS2 statistics are weighted (in terms of disability category and kind of school district) to represent the national population of youth receiving special education; therefore, the weighted estimates of the NLTS and NLTS2 closely mirror the health and demographic characteristics of youth with disabilities nationally during the respective time periods (Blackorby & Wagner, 1996; Wagner et al., 2003).

The NLTS2 results indicate that almost 90% of secondary school students served under IDEA have an IEP in place (Cameto, Levine, & Wagner, 2004). According to school staff, transition goals tend to emphasize postsecondary education and employment, and most students have plans that include a course of study that will help them meet their goals. Most disturbing in the NLTS2 findings was that nearly 20% of secondary school students have transition programs that are only "somewhat well-suited" or "not at all well-suited" to meeting their transition goals—reinforcing the continued need to build transition services and supports at the local level that are relevant and needed by students to achieve postschool success (Cameto et al.).

School Completion, Postschool, and Vocational Rehabilitation Outcomes

Completing secondary school has an important impact on future employment. High school dropouts are more likely to be unemployed and earn less than their peers who are high school graduates (U.S. Department of Labor, 2008). Per the USDOE (2007f), of the approximately 670,000 students ages 14–21 served under IDEA who exited school, 15% dropped out, 33% graduated with a diploma, and an additional 10% received a certificate. While the numbers of students with disabilities served under IDEA graduating with a diploma or certificate has increased over the last 10 years, it is difficult to ascertain if these increases have kept pace with enrollments in special education (USDOE, 2007g). The NLTS and NLTS2 findings provide additional insight into completion rates (Wagner, Newman, Cameto, & Levine, 2005). The percentage of students leaving school (ages 15–19) with a diploma or certificate of completion increased from 54% to 70% between 1987 and 2003. This rate of school completion in 2003 (70%) did not differ statistically from the rate for the general population; while the rate in 1987 was much lower than that of the general population (54% vs. 76%, respectively). The rates of high school completion varied by diagnosis and were lowest for students with an emotional disturbance (56%), other health impairment (59%), and multiple disabilities (51%). The rates of completion increased significantly from 1987 to 2003 for youth with learning disabilities (56% to 74%), mental retardation (51% to 72%), and an emotional disturbance (39% to 56%). There were also increases from 1987 to 2003 for nearly every other demographic category, with statistically significant increases in completion rates for boys, low and middle income groups, and white and African American youth.

As noted above, most students have goals in their IEPs that focus on postsecondary education or employment. Analysis of the 2007 American Community

Survey demonstrates that youth with disabilities have lower rates of employment and participation in postsecondary education than their peers without disabilities. Of high school graduates ages 16–21 without disabilities, 87% were employed and/or attending postsecondary education as compared to only 69% of those with disabilities. Both types of outcomes were significantly different: 57% of those without disabilities were employed as compared to 44% of those with disabilities, while 60% of those with disabilities were attending postsecondary education compared to 44% of those with disabilities[1].

According to NLTS2 findings among those who completed high school, there were significant increases in participation in postsecondary education (23.7% to 41.3%) from 1987 to 2003 (Wagner, Newman, Cameto, & Levine, 2005). Increases in participation were seen for 2-year colleges (5.3% to 28.4%) and for 4-year colleges (2.5% to 13.4%), while participation in vocational, technical, and business school decreased (16.1% to 5.1%). High income and white youth saw the largest increases in postsecondary participation across time. Among those who dropped out, nearly a quarter participated in GED programs in both study years. Employment outcomes postschool for youth with disabilities who had been out of school for up to 2 years improved from 1987 to 2003, with 70.4% working for pay since high school in 2003 compared to 54.8% in 1987; however there was no statistical difference in employment status at the time of the interview (48.9% in 1987 versus 40.5% in 2003) (Wagner, Newman, Cameto, & Levine, 2005).

In 2003, among employed youth, 39.2% reported working full-time and 84.6% percent reported earning more than the federal minimum wage. In both studies, youth with learning disabilities and speech or language impairment were more likely to report being employed (Wagner, Newman, Cameto, & Levine, 2005). As noted above, there was variance in postschool outcomes by impairment and demographic characteristics (Blackorby & Wagner, 1996; Wagner, Newman, Cameto, & Levine, 2005). However, in general, comparison of NLTS and NLTS2 highlights positive changes in postschool outcomes during the period from 1987 to 2003; particularly encouraging are increased school completion rates and increased participation in postsecondary education.

The Rehabilitation Act mandated the participation of VR in transition planning under IDEA and required a formal interagency agreement outlining roles and responsibilities of VR and public school systems in transition planning. In 1999, approximately 135,000 transition-age youth (defined as less than 25 years old) participated in VR and nearly two thirds received special education services in high school; most of these youth were referred to VR by their educational institution (Hayward & Schmidt-Davis, 2000). However, it is not easy to gauge the number of youth with disabilities and/or chronic health conditions who are eligible or could benefit from VR services. Results from the NLTS2 indicate that the VR agency is contacted for 38% of students engaged in transition planning (more

---

[1]Based on analysis of the 2007 American Community Survey (ACS) Public User Microdata Sample (PUMS), William Erickson, Cornell University, StatsRRTC. *Note:* Definitions of disability under ACS and IDEA are not the same.

than any other organization outside the school); this percentage increases to 56% percent by the time the students are 17–18 years old and near graduation (Cameto, Levine, & Wagner, 2004). Among transition-age VR consumers, studies have indicated that around 60% achieved an employment outcome as a result of services (National Council on Disability, 2008). When controlling for other factors, Hayward and Schmidt-Davis found that receipt of specific VR services was strongly associated with achieving an employment outcome and entering competitive employment; however, receipt of public financial assistance was negatively related to entering competitive employment for VR participants.

BARRIERS AND OPPORTUNITIES

Although the policy and practice movements highlighted previously sought to achieve improved postschool outcomes for youth, at the same time several other important policies and practices may be posing barriers to success. The following sections discuss these challenges and suggest ways to address them.

Supplemental Security Income and Means-Tested Cash Transfer Program Barriers

In 2006, there were 1.1 million SSI recipients under the age of 18 (SSA, 2007). The number of children receiving SSI has grown exponentially over the past two decades. Three major policy enhancements in 1990 expanded eligibility for SSI for youth with disabilities, potentially inducing youth to not enter the workforce (Wittenburg & Maag, 2002). The Zebley Decision (*Sullivan v. Zebley,* 1990) reversed SSA's policy of holding children to a stricter eligibility definition than adults. This was followed by regulations promulgated by SSA that expanded eligibility criteria for youth who did not meet or equal SSA's medical eligibility requirements, by affording a secondary eligibility evaluation focusing on functional assessment, as well as additional regulations that expanded the mental impairment listings for children to include additional developmental, behavioral, and emotional disorders.

Subsequently in 1992, SSA modified the parent-to-child deeming rules by reducing the amount of family income deemed against the child. While SSA administrative data initially documented a 250% increase in the number of children receiving SSI as a result of these changes, the Personal Responsibility and Work Opportunity Reconciliation Act of 1996 (PL 104-193) retracted the secondary functional assessment and instated an age 18 redetermination for youth to ensure eligibility for SSI under the adult disability standard, which resulted in a decrease in child enrollments (Wittenburg & Maag, 2002).

The induced entry into means-tested cash transfer programs and the long-term dependence they foster is hard to negate. At a time when schools and other community providers are trying to make a case for the importance of developing human capital as it relates to postschool movement, certain federal policies do not provide incentive. The Ticket to Work and Self-Sufficiency program is an example of a relatively new federal policy that held promise for supporting the postschool movement of youth with disabilities who receive SSI—however, the potential of this program was never realized, as only individuals who have been redetermined under the adult disability standard are considered eligible for the program. Further, individuals under the age of 18 are not entitled to participate. The decision to not provide a Ticket to Work to school-age youth at a point when they need transition support the most is irresponsible at best, in providing youth the critical supports they need for adult success.

This policy oversight is further compounded when one considers that, according to the Social Security Advisory Board (2006), between 1996 and 2004 more than 400,000 child SSI recipients completed age 18 redeterminations, with one third resulting in benefit termination following the appeal process. Ironically, in the Social Security Advisory Board's response to the 2006 Annual Report on SSI it went on to recommend that SSA place more emphasis on equipping education stakeholders in understanding the age 18 redetermination process and that action be taken to inform them of this process as early as age 14 to allow them opportunity to engage in activities to develop the student's postschool capacities. The report, however, does not mention the potential utility of the Ticket to Work program as a vehicle for developing employment and postschool capacities— providing SSI youth with a Ticket as early as age 14 would allow a student to begin working with the Employment Network of their choosing to support career planning and employment. The Ticket to Work and Work Incentives Advisory Panel since its inception has urged the president, Congress, and the SSA to ensure that Ticket eligibility criteria be changed to include child SSI recipients (Ticket to Work and Work Incentives Advisory Panel, 2001).

Further, for those children facing an age 18 redetermination who likely will not meet the adult disability standard, Congress and the SSA established a transition planning incentive commonly referred to as Section 301 or continuation of benefits following medical recovery. A child completing an age 18 redetermination who does not meet the adult disability criteria is considered to have medically recovered. Section 301 is a transition planning work incentive, providing an important safety net for children not redetermined eligible but who are receiving vocational rehabilitation services and actively engaged in an individualized plan for employment that is expected to increase their self-sufficiency or result in their removal from the benefit rolls. Children who meet the eligibility criteria for Section 301 would continue to receive their benefits until they complete their formal plan—providing not only an important incentive for remaining in school but also completing a formal transition plan to adulthood.

The No Child Left Behind Act and High-Stakes Testing

NCLB was designed to help schools, districts, and states understand and close achievement gaps by monitoring student proficiency on state- or district-specific standards. Although the testing mandated by NCLB does not necessarily have high stakes for individual students, the stakes are high for schools and districts whose students do not make adequate progress. Also, many states use high-stakes tests (e.g., promotion or graduation tests) to fulfill NCLB requirements. With the passage of NCLB and other high-stakes testing or state-specific standards reforms came increasing concerns that the drop-out problem would be exacerbated. It has been reported anecdotally that large numbers of students have not fared well on these high-stakes assessments, resulting in decreased interest in school completion, and that several factors beyond academic achievement influence individual student ability to pass these assessments.

In 2004, Orfield, Losen, Wald, and Swanson went as far as to suggest that the high-stakes performance measures placed on states have potentially resulted in an unintended consequence of disengaging low-performing students (e.g., minority populations including youth with disabilities) or pushing them out so as not to affect their school-wide performance levels. The report further suggests that currently available drop out data are suspect and that the scope of the problem is much greater than reflected in current nationally available data sets— specifically, states rarely disaggregate their graduation rates by race or socioeconomic status, meaning that the extremely low graduation rates for racial and ethnic minorities, students with disabilities, low-income students, and students with limited English proficiency are rarely identified or targeted for specific intervention. Thurlow, Sinclair, and Johnson (2002) documented that accurate identification of the disability, provision of needed accommodations, and educational supports that make learning possible regardless of disability-related factors have played a primary role in influencing student performance on these assessments and must be considered to ensure the successful participation of students with disabilities in achieving higher academic standards.

As management of school systems adjusts to systems measures imposed by NCLB, careful analysis of the "logic model" is recommended. Logic models show, at a systems level, how inputs such as populations of students and resources may be transformed into results through planned programs, and how these results may achieve outcomes (and unintended outcomes) that lead to a desired system-wide impact. Promising practices identified in demonstration studies can be brought to scale if resources are carefully planned in accordance with the actual wants, needs, and decision behaviors of salient populations of children, bearing in mind the twin imperatives of results and equity. If no child is to be left behind, then no child must be left out, either.

Preparing for Increased Participation in Postsecondary Education

The large increase in participation in postsecondary education is very encouraging, as it has been shown that lifetime earning is closely linked with educational attainment (Migliore & Butterworth, 2008; Price-Ellingstad & Berry, 1999/2000; Weathers et al., 2006). Students with disabilities have increasing options for postsecondary educational experiences. Effective counseling aims to help youth plan early for the options they want to pursue. Without it, students can leave high school without the prerequisites they need for postsecondary study. When students have access to effective learning support and when they have access to the general education curriculum, they can expect to earn a high school diploma. They are thus eligible for admission to postsecondary options including community colleges, vocational training and trade schools, and 4-year colleges.

Students and their parents face system expectations in postsecondary settings that are significantly different from those of IDEA programs in high schools. First, IDEA guarantees a FAPE to all children with disabilities, but postsecondary programs are not designed to meet the needs of all students. Nevertheless, otherwise qualified and admissible students with disabilities may not be excluded from or denied admission to a postsecondary opportunity based on their disability. The U.S. Department of Education advises prospective students that they must disclose their disability to their postsecondary educational program in order to gain the needed "academic adjustments" or accommodations. The student and the school agree on specific appropriate academic adjustments based on the student's disability and individual needs.

According to the U.S. Department of Education,

> Academic adjustments may include auxiliary aids and modifications to academic requirements as are necessary to ensure equal educational opportunity. Examples of such adjustments are arranging for priority registration; reducing a course load; substituting one course for another; providing note takers, recording devices, sign language interpreters, extended time for testing and, if telephones are provided in dorm rooms, a TTY in your dorm room; and equipping school computers with screen-reading, voice recognition or other adaptive software or hardware. (USDOE, 2002)

More programs are providing learning supports to students with more complex intellectual disabilities in college settings as well, although the level of supports are often a function of the capacity of the institution (Sharpe & Johnson, 2001). A leader in the development of such programs is the Canadian province of Alberta, which has offered on-campus support to students with intellectual disabilities for more than 20 years (Bowman & Weinkauf, 2004). Currently, 200 such students are enrolled in nondegree programs at universities across Alberta; another 60 people are supported in new programs in British Columbia (B. Salisbury, personal communication, April 23, 2009). At the time of this report, several states publish resource lists that help students with disabilities locate postsecondary supports, but to date there is no evidence of any state taking a statewide approach similar to Alberta's.

Issues Related to Chronic Health Conditions

Students who meet the disability standard under the IDEA have an IEP that guides their educational transition. Many of these youth have special health care needs that are not addressed in the IEP. However, a successful transition to employment, postsecondary education, and independent living requires that individuals are able to meet their health care needs in the adult-oriented system. The American Academy of Pediatrics (2002) laid out critical steps to ensuring successful transition to adult-oriented health care, including developing a written health care transition plan by age 14 that includes services needed, who will provide them, and how they will be financed. However, analyses of the data for 4,332 adolescents in the 2000–2001 National Survey of Children with Special Health Care Needs indicated that 50.2% of parents reported discussing the transition issues of their adolescent with their doctor and only 16.4% of respondents had developed a plan for addressing transition needs (Scal & Ireland, 2005). Even if a plan is developed by a health care provider, a youth's health care needs should be still considered when setting employment and other goals. Further, health-related goals that could affect an individual's successful transition, (e.g., moving toward independently managing health issues) should be incorporated into an IEP.

Inadequate Interagency Collaboration

There is a need for interagency collaboration in order to improve outcomes of the transition process, for example, between educational agencies and VR agencies. However, thus far, formal agreements between VR agencies and schools are relatively rare, with many states reporting that coordination efforts have not begun (National Council on Disability, 2008). Beyond formal agreements between agencies, many states have funded transition coordinators to help students and other stakeholders better understand the opportunities available through various agencies. There is little, if any, empirical research to support the outcomes related to such collaborative efforts (Cobb & Alwell, 2007). However, without such efforts to inform parents and other key stakeholders in the transition process of services and supports available outside of the school, it is much less likely that these services will be utilized to improve postschool outcomes. Beyond VR, it is important that representatives of other agencies that govern important resources related to health care, SSI benefits, and transportation are involved in the transition process. Because there are already pathways for communication in place, it is logical for school staff to coordinate and share information with parents and students about postschool services. According to NLTS2, school staff report that information about postschool services have not been provided to a quarter of parents of students with disabilities ages 17–18 who are about to leave high school (Cameto, Levine, & Wagner, 2004).

Lack of Family Involvement

Increased involvement of families in the transition planning process is another important method for improving the quality of transition programs. In synthesizing the results of several qualitative studies, Cobb and Alwell (2007) note the important influence parents have in career planning and ultimately finding a job, especially for youth with mild to moderate disabilities, perhaps overshadowing the influence of school vocational experiences. However, many of these same studies report lack of active participation by both students and parents, and disinterest and anxiety associated with the IEP process were cited reasons. According to NLTS2, 85% of parents or guardians are involved in the transition planning process; while most are satisfied with their involvement in decision making, one third of parents would like to be more involved (Cameto, Levine, & Wagner, 2004). Preparing parents or guardians to be active participants in the IEP process may increase parental and other agency involvement and improve the quality of the youths' identified postsecondary goals (Boone, 1992). To increase chances of active participation of families in the transition process, it is important that families fully understand the transition process and the resources available. Every effort should be made to include the parent or guardian in IEP meetings and to prepare them to be active contributors in the transition planning process.

PRACTICAL STRATEGIES FOR OVERCOMING BARRIERS

If federal policymakers are to address seriously the postschool success and community contributions and participation of youth with disabilities, then further policy reform in both the education and employment sector is needed. Extensive efforts must be undertaken to braid together the programs, services, and supports of the more than 200 currently existing U.S. disability programs—removing unintended consequences through careful and sophisticated strategic planning. Better data sets and stronger research investment will be required to support such planning. Following is a series of proposed education and employment policy solutions to support the successful transition to adult living, learning, and earning of youth with chronic health conditions.

- Children receiving SSI should have access to the Ticket to Work program as early as age 14 to provide them an additional resource to build their economic self-sufficiency and human capital. This would also allow them continued access to health insurance through Medicaid and access to the Medicaid Buy-In program in states with this option.

- A campaign must be undertaken to increase stakeholder knowledge regarding the age 18 redetermination process, the Ticket to Work Program, and utilization of Section 301. Also, a social marketing campaign should target the value of work, reach out to potential employers and investors, instill disability pride, hope, and aspiration in young people and their families, and help recipients of means-tested programs to understand that the programs are a stepping stone to greater financial independence and self-sufficiency. Relevant data studies will be needed to support planning for social marketing.

- Extensive interagency collaborations and integration will be required, even though these terms may have been the administrative nightmares of recent decades. Data improvement projects will be required to support integrated planning and reporting, and disparate programs should be aligned in more systematic ways, replacing complication with complexity and rigidity with simple fluidity.

- National efforts to build electronic health records should be aligned with educational data improvement efforts so that families of children with disabilities and young people with disabilities can access and manage their own records and take responsibility for their own documentation and accommodations to the maximum extent possible.

- People with developmental disabilities and their families from the United States should be supported to participate in appropriate internationally recognized organizations for people with disabilities (e.g., Inclusion International) to the same extent as adults with other disabilities are supported to participate in such organizations (e.g., Disabled People's International, Rehab International, The World Federation of the Blind).

- Congress, states, and communities should consider whether and how to create or advance community-based, non-Medicaid, non-Social Security, non-stigmatizing supports for youth making transitions and family supports for their families.

- Publicly funded universities should have training and technical assistance available to them to support the inclusion of youth with a broad range of abilities on campuses, in degree-granting and nondegree programs.

- Some youth will find that they may need accommodation in a future environment that was not identified in any transition planning process. In addition, a significant number of students who do not experience particular disabilities during school will acquire disabilities in their young adult transition years due to accident, injury, armed conflict, or processes secondary to their original disability, among other causes. Others will become parents of children with significant disabilities during their young adult transition years. For these reasons, the National Consortium on Leadership and Disability for Youth has called for universal adoption of disability awareness and civil rights curricula in American schools. Young leaders with disabilities have begun a process of lobbying for local adoption of effective curricula with the more than 13,000 local school districts in the United States.

CONCLUSION

The purpose of this chapter has been to provide an overview of the challenges and opportunities available for youth making the transition from secondary educational settings to employment and postsecondary education. There has been historically a decided disconnect between these systems, which has led to significantly lessened opportunities for full participation by youth with disabilities and chronic health conditions. Lack of an integrated set of supporting policies and programs to provide transition services has meant that many of these youth will not realize their potential in the adult world and rightfully take their places alongside their peers in the workplace of the future. This tragic loss of opportunity for both the youth themselves and for the American workforce must be addressed. Dramatic changes in public policy are needed immediately to bring about the needed profound systemic alterations that will assure that youth with disabilities and chronic health conditions are afforded a seamless transition to the opportunities of adult life and in fulfilling valued social roles.

REFERENCES

American Academy of Pediatrics. (2002). A consensus statement on health care transitions for young adults with special health care needs. *Pediatrics, 110,* 1304–1306.

Americans with Disabilities Act (ADA) of 1990, PL 101-336, 42 U.S.C. §§ 12101 *et seq.*

Blackorby, J., & Wagner, M. (1996). Longitudinal postschool outcomes of youth with disabilities: Findings from the National Longitudinal Transition Study. *Exceptional Children, 62(5),* 399–413.

Boone, R.S. (1992). Involving culturally diverse parents in transition planning. *Career Development for Exceptional Individuals, 15(2),* 205–221.

Bowman, P., & Weinkauf, T. (2004). Implementing SRV: Post-secondary education as a pathway to socially valued roles [Electronic version]. *International Journal of Disability, Community and Rehabilitation, 3(1).*

Cameto, R., Levine, P., & Wagner, M. (2004). *Transition planning for students with disabilities. A special topic report of findings from the National Longitudinal Transition Study-2 (NLTS2).* Menlo Park, CA: SRI International. Retrieved November 2, 2009, from www.nlts2.org/reports/2004_11/nlts2_report_2004_11_complete.pdf

Cobb, B., & Alwell, M. (2007). *Transition planning/coordination interventions for youth with disabilities.* Retrieved May 13, 2009, from http://www.nsttac.org/pdf/what_works/2c_full_text.pdf

Education for All Handicapped Children Act of 1975, PL 94-142, 20 U.S.C. §§ 1400 *et seq.*

Family and Medical Leave Act (FMLA) of 1993, PL 103-3, 5 U.S.C. §§ 6381 *et seq.,* 29 U.S.C. §§ 2601 *et seq.*

Government Accountability Office. (2007). *Modernizing federal disability policy.* Washington, DC: GAO. Retrieved May 13, 2009, from http://www.gao.gov/new.items/d07934sp.pdf

Hayward, B.J., & Schmidt-Davis, H. (2000). *Fourth interim report: Characteristics and outcomes of transitional youth in VR.* Chapel Hill, NC: Research Triangle Institute. Retrieved November 2, 2009, from http://www.ilr.cornell.edu/edi/lsvrsp/ PublishedResearchFiles/RTI_4thInterim_Report.pdf

Individuals with Disabilities Education Act (IDEA) of 1990, PL 101-476, 20 U.S.C. §§ 1400 *et seq.*

Individuals with Disabilities Education Act Amendments (IDEA) of 1997, PL 105-17, 20 U.S.C. §§ 1400 *et seq.*

Individuals with Disabilities Education Improvement Act (IDEA) of 2004, PL 108-446, 20 U.S.C. §§ 1400 *et seq.*

Migliore, A., & Butterworth, J. (2008). *Postsecondary education and employment outcomes for youth with intellectual disabilities.* DataNote Series, Data Note XXI. Boston, MA: Institute for Community Inclusion.

National Center for Educational Statistics. (2007). *The condition of education.* Washington, DC: U.S. Department of Education. Retrieved November 2, 2009, from http://nces.ed.gov/programs/coe/2007/section1/indicator07.asp

National Council on Disability. (2008). *The rehabilitation act: Outcomes for transition aged youth.* Washington, DC: Author. Retrieved May 13, 2009, from http://www.ncd.gov/newsroom/publications/2008/doc/RehabilitationTransitions.doc

No Child Left Behind Act of 2001, PL 107-110, 115 Stat. 1425, 20 U.S.C. §§ 6301 *et seq.*

O'Day, B., Stapleton, D., & Horvath-Rose, A. (2007). *Health insurance coverage among youth and young adults with work limitations.* Ithaca, NY: Cornell University, Rehabilitation Research and Training Center on Disability Demographics and Statistics.

Orfield, G., Losen, D., Wald, J., & Swanson, C.B. (2004). *How minority youth are being left behind by the graduation rate crisis.* Washington, DC: The Urban Institute. Retrieved May 13, 2009, from http://www.urban.org/UploadedPDF/ 410936_LosingOur Future.pdf

Personal Responsibility and Work Opportunity Reconciliation Act of 1996, PL 104-193, 42 U.S.C. §§ 211 *et seq.*

Price-Ellingstad, D., & Berry, H. (1999/2000). Post secondary education, vocational rehabilitation and students with disabilities: Gaining access to promising futures. *American Rehabilitation, 25(3),* 2.

Rehabilitation Act of 1973, PL 93-112, 29 U.S.C. §§ 701 *et seq.*

Scal, P., & Ireland, M. (2005). Addressing transition to adult care for adolescents with special health care needs. *Pediatrics, 115,* 1607–1612.

Sharpe, N.M., & Johnson, D.R. (2001). A 20/20 analysis of postsecondary support characteristics. *Journal of Vocational Rehabilitation, 16,* 169–177.

Social Security Administration. (2007). *SSI Monthly Statistics, December 2007.* Baltimore, MD: Office of Policy, Social Security Administration. Retrieved January 30, 2007, from http://www.ssa.gov/policy/docs/statcomps/ssi_monthly/2007-12/index.html

Social Security Advisory Board. (2006). Statement on the Supplemental Security Income Program. In *2006 SSI Annual Report.* Retrieved January 30, 2008, from http://www.socialsecurity.gov/OACT/SSIR/SSI06/board.html

Sullivan v. Zebley, 493 U.S. 521 (1990).

Thurlow, M.L., Sinclair, M.F., & Johnson, D.R. (2002). *Students with disabilities who drop out of school—Implications for policy and practice: Issue Brief, 1(2).* Minneapolis, MN: Institute for Community Inclusion.

Ticket to Work and Work Incentives Advisory Panel. (2001, February 20). *Preliminary advice report.* Retrieved May 13, 2009, from http://www.ssa.gov/work/panel/panel_documents/par_final_report.html

Ticket to Work and Work Incentives Improvement Act (TWWIIA) of 1999, PL 106-170, 42 U.S.C. §§ 1305 *et seq.*

U.S. Department of Education. (2002). *Students with disabilities preparing for postsecondary education: Know your rights and responsibilities.* Washington, DC: Author. Retrieved May 15, 2009, from http://www.ed.gov/about/offices/list/ocr/transition.html

U.S. Department of Education, Office of Special Education Programs. (2007a). *IDEA regulations: Secondary transition.* Washington, DC: Author. Retrieved November 2, 2009, from http://idea.ed.gov/object/fileDownload/model/TopicalBrief/field/PdfFile/primary_key/17

U.S. Department of Education, Office of Special Education Programs, Data Accountability Center. (2007b). *Table 1-3: Students ages 6 through 21 served under IDEA, Part B, by disability category and state: Fall 2007*. Retrieved May 13, 2009, from https://www.ideadata.org/arc_toc9.asp

U.S. Department of Education, Office of Special Education Programs, Data Accountability Center. (2007c). *Table 1-19: Students ages 6 through 21 served under IDEA, Part B, by race/ethnicity and state: Fall 2007*. Retrieved May 13, 2009, from https://www.ideadata.org/arc_toc9.asp

U.S. Department of Education, Office of Special Education Programs, Data Accountability Center. (2007d). *Table 1-12: Children and students served under IDEA, Part B, in the U.S. and outlying areas, by gender and age group: Fall 1998 through Fall 2007*. Retrieved May 13, 2009, from https://www.ideadata.org/arc_toc9.asp

U.S. Department of Education, Office of Special Education Programs, Data Accountability Center. (2007e). *Table 2-2: Students ages 6 through 21 served under IDEA, Part B, by educational environment and state: Fall 2007*. Retrieved May 13, 2009, from https://www.ideadata.org/arc_toc9.asp

U.S. Department of Education, Office of Special Education Programs, Data Accountability Center. (2007f). *Table 4.1: Students ages 14 through 21 with disabilities served under IDEA, Part B, who exited school, by disability category, exit reason and state: Fall 2006-07*. Retrieved May 13, 2009, from https://www.ideadata.org/arc_toc9.asp

U.S. Department of Education, Office of Special Education Programs, Data Accountability Center. (2007g). *Table 4.3: Students ages 14 through 21 and older with disabilities served under IDEA, Part B, in the U.S. and outlying areas who exited school, by exit reason, reporting year, and student's age: 1997–1998 through 2006–07*. Retrieved May 13, 2009, from https://www.ideadata.org/arc_toc9.asp

U.S. Department of Labor, Bureau of Labor Statistics. (2008). *Employment projections: Education pays*. Retrieved November 2, 2009, from http://www.bls.gov/emp/emptab7.htm

Wagner, M., Marder, C., Levine, P., Cameto, R., Cadwallader, T., & Blackorby, J. (with Cardoso, D., & Newman, L.). (2003). *The individual and household characteristics of youth with disabilities. A report from the National Longitudinal Transition Study-2 (NLTS2)*. Menlo Park, CA: SRI International. Retrieved November 3, 2009, from www.nlts2.org/reports/2003_08/nlts2_report_2003_08_complete.pdf

Wagner, M., Newman, L., Cameto, R., & Levine, P. (2005). *Changes over time in the early postschool outcomes of youth with disabilities. A report of findings from the National Longitudinal Transition Study (NLTS) and the National Longitudinal Transition Study-2 (NLTS2)*. Menlo Park, CA: SRI International. Retrieved November 2, 2009, from www.nlts2.org/reports/2005_06/nlts2_report_2005_06_complete.pdf

Weathers, R.R., Walter, G., Schley, S., Hennessy, J., Hemmeter, J., & Burkhauser, R.V. (2006). *How postsecondary education improves adult outcomes for Supplemental Security Income children with severe hearing impairments*. Ithaca, NY: Rehabilitation Research and Training Center on Disability Demographics and Statistics, Cornell University.

Wittenburg, D., Golden, T.P., & Fishman, M. (2002). Transition options for youth with disabilities: An overview of the programs and policies that affect the transition from school. *Journal of Vocational Rehabilitation, 17*, 195–206.

Wittenburg, D.C., & Maag, E. (2002). School to where? A literature review on economic outcomes of youth with disabilities. *Journal of Vocational Rehabilitation, 17*, 265–280.

Workforce Investment Act (WIA) of 1998, PL 105-220, 29 U.S.C. §§ 2801 *et seq.*

9

Recommendations for Policy and Practice

George Jesien, Deborah Klein Walker, and Donald Lollar

T he previous chapters provided a detailed picture of issues, challenges, and
specific recommendations in areas important to the transition of youth
with special health care needs and disabilities, such as education, health,
housing, and transportation. This chapter provides a set of general guidelines, values, and recommendations to be espoused in making the transition process more
effective and more user friendly, leading to better outcomes for the emerging
adult as he or she begins to take a place in the adult world. These guidelines and
recommendations are not meant to be exhaustive, but rather to provide a point
of departure for planning, policy development, and collaborative action on behalf
of youth in the transition process. They focus on maximizing the functioning and
participation of youth and young adults in society and maintaining a preventive
orientation that is designed to minimize short- and long-term disability. Doing
this requires an integrated approach that uses resources on behalf of individuals
in a seamless way across jurisdictional sectors.

This volume highlights the complexity of the barriers to the transition from
adolescence to young adulthood for those with chronic health conditions and
disabilities. Given the varied programs, definitions, eligibility requirements, services, and systems involved, it is clear that the overarching recommendation is the
need for an integrated policy that could move this complex field forward. One
way to provide a forum for building a consensus for an integrated policy would
be a national working conference, possibly sponsored by the White House; alternatively, the secretaries of key federal departments could form a task force to

convene such a conference. In these ways, a long-term process can be initiated with both leadership and authority to establish a unified and coordinated direction for integrated policies, services, and programs. Such a conference could use this volume as a foundation for discussion among the leadership in transition across governmental sectors, and could include young people with chronic health conditions and disabilities and their families, as well as those making the policies in Congress. The degree of fragmentation is sufficient that nothing short of major attention will provide the direction needed for this important group of young people in our country.

GUIDING PRINCIPLES AND VALUES FOR TRANSITION

In order for children and youth to make a successful transition through the "critical life stage" from adolescence to young adult status, several key principles need to be addressed at the individual person level, as well as at the service and systems level for programs and policies that affect the transition. These principles are outlined in this section.

At the Individual Person Level

- *Address individual needs and choices.* Just as services from early childhood throughout the school years for children with disabilities and chronic health conditions have been individualized based on the needs of the child and preferences of the family, transition services should extend the principle of individualization into adulthood. Each adolescent has specific health, education, and career needs that should be addressed if transition to adulthood is going to be successful. The evolving adolescent has the additional need of learning to grow and cope with an ever-increasing array of choices before him or her. Providing a menu of options from which to choose gives the adolescent opportunities to practice and acquire decision-making skills as well as provides for a more individualized approach to meet specific and unique needs.

- *Support for growing independence and self-determination.* The developmental progression to independence has been a difficult one for many adolescents with special health care needs or disabilities. Parents and service systems may have been overprotective, limiting the opportunities to decide under the guise of concern over safety and expressions of caring. The trajectory to independent decision making arises from the gradual and developmentally appropriate assumption of responsibility by the developing youth, and includes the family. Providing the mechanisms for a youth to direct his or her own care and to obtain the needed assistance related to the individual's wants and future goals facilitates the development of self-determination that will be necessary in adulthood if the individual is going to pursue his or her own aspirations and goals.

- *Partnerships for shared accountability and action.* The goal of total independence may not be realistic or even desirable for some youth with chronic health conditions or disabilities. For youth who need assistance in the management of their health condition or have a disability that will require ongoing supports and personal assistance, a concept of interdependence and circles of support may be more appropriate and useful. With a circle of support, responsibility for acquiring the needed assistance and for guiding the intensity and structure of services is a shared responsibility. Decisions are made in collaboration, and each of the parties takes on a shared responsibility for action, follow-through, and monitoring. Partnerships are formed with family, friends, and providers that lead to coordinated action guided by the best interests of youth.

- *Equity in service access and supports from all social sectors.* Another principle that always needs to be kept in mind is that of equity in the availability and distribution of resources—financial and human. Adolescents with chronic conditions come from tremendously varied cultural and socioeconomic backgrounds. Indeed, children and youth today come from much more diverse cultural backgrounds than the adult U.S. population, and disability disproportionately affects people with fewer economic resources. Given the effects of social and cultural factors on access to and appropriateness of services, it is critical that quality, intensity, duration, and accountability are available equitably in all communities and geographic regions. The needs of individuals, including their cultural values, should determine the services received.

At the Service Level

- *Dialogue and communication across agencies with consumers and family members.* Information and decision making about choices and opportunities must be shared across all stakeholders, with the individual person with the disability or chronic condition involved as much as possible. The focus of communication needs to put the individual at the center so that the young adult with a disability is empowered to make his or her own choices. The dialogue and communication needs to evolve developmentally to reflect the changing maturational and legal status of the individual. Open dialogue and honest communication among the individual, their family, and all other players in the transition process can help to ensure a successful transition to adulthood.

- *Diversity and inclusion in individual and provider policies and decisions.* A diversity of stakeholders with their differing opinions and perspectives need to have input into provider policies, available alternatives, and the decision-making process. An ongoing dialogue of diverse perspectives that results in an array of options in services and policies assures that the individual will have real choices available from which to choose and will be able to make decisions based on individual circumstances in a community-based setting.

- *Individual choice and control over services and opportunities in the least restrictive environment.* A major tenet of a successful transition is that the individual with the chronic health condition or disability will have maximal individual choice and control over his or her services. Policies, services, and systems need to reflect this principle of individual choice and control. This principle is strongly supported at the federal level though the Americans with Disability Act (ADA) of 1990 (PL 101-336) and its 2008 amendments (PL 110-325), the Individuals with Disabilities Education Act (IDEA) of 1990 (PL 101-476) and its amendments in 1997 (PL 105-17) and 2004 (PL 108-446), and the *Olmstead v. L.C.* Supreme Court decision. Providers need to work to design their services such that respect for individual choice and control can be evident on a daily basis.

At the Systems Level

- *Family and youth leadership for action and advocacy.* Federal, state, and local systems must support youth and family leadership options for involvement in policy making, legislative initiatives, program planning, implementation, and evaluation activities to ensure that these systems are constantly monitored and accountable to assure the best options for individuals with chronic health conditions and disabilities.

- *Political will and social strategies for action.* Mechanisms for promoting the best set of policies and services for individuals with chronic health conditions and disabilities must be in place. Such organized support will help build the political will at the local, state, and federal level necessary to continually support a system of care for individuals with chronic health conditions and disabilities and ensure they are served, employed, and included in community-based systems of their choice. This will require frequent and regular access to legislators and policy makers to ensure that this important constituency is heard from and seen as a priority.

- *Ethical code of conduct for providers and systems.* The highest code of conduct and ethics must be observed at all times in the individual decision-making process as well as in the design and implementation of services, policies, and programs at the community, state, and federal levels. Accountability systems that are transparent and accessible are needed so that conduct is open to the public for review and comment.

These principles and values can be translated into critical elements for solutions and into specific recommendations. The next section outlines these critical elements, from more individual elements to services to systems elements. Examples of specific recommendations from the book's other chapters are also included with the elements.

CRITICAL ELEMENTS FOR SOLUTIONS TO OVERCOME CURRENT BARRIERS

- *Need for flexibility to address individual needs and supports for independence and self-determination of individuals.* All parts of the transition process must be consumer-friendly and provide for self-determination and choice for the individual youth with chronic conditions and/or disabilities. This is a special challenge during the transition from adolescence to adulthood for any youth who is moving away from the restrictions and protections of their parents and family toward adult independence. The transition system must foster communication among parents, family members, providers, and the youth in order to assist the youth in making his or her own decisions for employment, education, and living in community-based settings. It is important to establish services to address individual needs and support independence early in adulthood to ensure that individuals are supported appropriately in community-based settings and do not end up at risk for being placed in more restrictive settings because there are no community options in place. Several chapters in this book provide specific directions focused on individualized transitional plans to implement this element. A skilled direct support work force is another important example of an important element necessary for individual needs to be addressed.

- *Consumers make decisions and direct their resources.* One of the basic developmental progressions through adolescence is toward greater independence, self-management, and self-determination. Greater control of resources along with increased opportunity to decide among options and exercise personal choice in how resources are used should characterize systems of supports for youth in transition. A major innovation over the past decade has been the development of "money follows the person" rather than resources being programmatically assigned to a class of eligible clients. Future systems need to build on the increasing role of youth in making key decisions and directing available resources toward personal goals and aspirations. Clearly, supports from family and others will be needed and will also need to be slowly withdrawn as the youth accepts increasing responsibility and moves toward greater independence and self-management. Medicaid waiver programs are often designed to encourage this level of self-direction.

- *Standard set of services and rights for individuals regardless of geography.* Work in the area of transitions has proceeded since the early 1980s. We clearly have programs and guidance that have been gleaned from demonstration projects, research findings, and state-initiated efforts. We are approaching the time when it is necessary to "go to scale" with our efforts such that transition supports and services are based on need and not determined by a youth's zip code. Practices need to be implemented nationally to provide equal access to youth regardless of state or county of residence. Such "ramping up" of services and supports will require investment of human and financial resources at

national, state, and local levels. But only when we go beyond the demonstration and local project level of implementation will we truly begin to address
the next cohort of youth entering this critical developmental stage. Part of
implementing standardized services begins with a single point of entry and
coordination of services. Appropriate and uniform health care coverage related to standard services will be needed. Chapter 4 of this book strongly encourages the medical home as a standard service, along with the implementation
of navigator services to aid in individualized services. Both transportation and
housing alternatives need to be provided as part of integrative services.

- *Provide opportunities for developing choices, leadership, and self-advocacy.* Both
  the child and youth system and the adult system of services and supports for
  individuals with chronic health conditions and disabilities should be aligned
  to provide ongoing opportunities for individuals to express leadership and
  self-advocacy. Systems that support self-advocacy training will more likely
  ensure that individuals have maximal control and choice over options for
  employment, education, and daily living in a community setting. Chapter 7
  of this book advocates acceleration of the *Olmstead* decision to assist individuals, as functioning allows, to transition toward greater autonomy. In addition, opportunities to participate in advocacy and disability-related organizations (often called disabled persons organizations) should be encouraged so
  that self-advocacy can be encouraged.

- *Consistent definitions of chronic conditions and functional limitations.* One of
  the most imposing challenges for the future development of effective transitions is bringing together the range of definitions of chronic health conditions and disability into a more consistent framework that could be
  employed across different systems and sectors. Throughout this volume, a
  common theme is the difficulty surrounding different definitions—that is,
  who is eligible for services, what services are available, what services may be
  paid for, and the limits or criteria by which services may be stopped. A common framework would result in a consistent set of terms that would have
  similar meaning in health, education, and employment environments.
  Developing such a framework may seem like a daunting task, but further utilization of the International Classification of Function, Disability and Health
  (ICF) developed by the World Health Organization could provide such a
  common framework. Common terminology would provide a basis for communicating important information across social sectors and an understand-
  able vocabulary for professional and consumer alike. Whether it is greater use
  of the ICF or the development of another common framework, we will need
  to reform our vocabulary, terms, and definitions if we are to move toward a
  more comprehensive and unified system of supports in the future.

- *Collaboration across federal agencies, including ongoing monitoring and evaluation used for quality improvement.* Although there are some examples of efforts

that work to link two systems in the transition process, such as health and employment, school and employment, or high school and postsecondary sectors, much more comprehensive efforts are needed to bring together multiple sectors that affect the lives of adolescents. A more in-depth collaboration is needed with at least the major systems of health, mental health, secondary education, postsecondary education, employment, and community living. The federal agencies that govern and support these sectors need to find new and creative ways to collaborate and to share resources and information to make transition a more seamless process. By sharing data on outcomes, a more accurate picture of progress and barriers can be obtained and hopefully addressed. Since the late 1990s, interagency coordinating councils have been a popular way to bring federal agencies, consumers, and constituency groups together for the purposes of collaboration and policy development. This may be an opportune time to consider a multisector council focused on the issues of transition for youth with special health care needs and disabilities. This council—similar to others that have been formed around urgent needs in this country, such as early intervention councils in the mid-1990s or, more recently, the Interagency Autism Coordinating Committee—would have high-level representatives from the leading federal agencies, foundations, advocacy organizations, and consumers to provide overall direction for policies, research, and provider training that will be needed in the future to adequately address the needs of youth with disabilities and special health care needs as they transition into adulthood.

- *Shared accountability across sectors with clear lead responsibility for all sectors.* Both the child and adult systems can only succeed when there is a clear "shared accountability" for all services and supports for the individuals involved. This implies that all the sectors involved (e.g., health/mental health, education, employment, housing, transportation, social services) must work together and assure that they will follow through with providing services and supports in their system. Shared accountability also implies working across public and private resources as well as the individual's and family responsibilities. Systems of care for individuals with disabilities need the resources and supports of many sectors and payers. Because there is no one system or agent that is accountable for ensuring all the components of the system work together, it is important for the individual to be empowered as a self-advocate to work with all the accountable parts of the systems. Beyond the individual empowerment, however, it will be important that a system of appeal be provided and made more efficient if services are coordinated or offered in a single setting.

- *Sustained political support for transforming the current fragmented state.* Awareness and understanding of the needs of individuals with chronic health conditions and disabilities across the lifespan must be heightened and ongoing in order that all citizens in the country are knowledgeable about the issues and can provide ongoing political support for a comprehensive, community-based quality system of care in each community. Enabling all individuals with chronic conditions and disabilities to work, go to school, and be active in community activities like those individuals without chronic conditions will benefit the entire community and society in many ways, including ensuring the United States continues to be a worldwide leader in the full participation of all its citizens in the economic and social fabric of society. There are many priorities competing for social and political support. Few, however, are more pressing than assisting a class of young people toward productive lives, both in employment and community inclusion. There is an implicit, if not explicit, recommendation in all chapters in this book that sustained attention to this issue is required until appropriate policy changes are made. The outcome of these changes would be the seamless transition of adolescents with chronic health conditions and disabilities into productive adulthood. Its focus should be on maximizing their functioning and preventing limitations and progression of their illnesses and disabilities.

To support these elements, there will be a need for data to address the needs, services provided, programs implemented, and outcomes of the adolescents as they move into young adulthood. As research is implemented to evaluate various specific services and overarching programs, stronger connections can be made between individual needs and services and programs offered. Seamless data will be needed to monitor seamless transition. Operationally, this would suggest longitudinal data that allows an understanding of the progress of adolescents to young adulthood (for all of the population) and that includes data on education, housing, health, and other aspects of young adult community participation.

Second, there will be a need for training of those professionals implementing a new network of coordinated services, including an emphasis on disability awareness and rights and focusing on maximizing functioning and minimizing long-term disability. Of course, an understanding of developmental and disability-related needs will also be required, along with a thorough knowledge of community resources. This may entail training a new corps of providers of transition services and programs.

Universal design is another undergirding principle for transition, and is explored in both Chapter 6 and Chapter 7. Finally, Chapter 7 discusses the idea of "communities for all"—the notion that inclusion into everyday life is the expectation of us all.

How these guiding principles, values, critical elements, and specific recommendations will merge is yet to be determined. The price for delay has been high and will continue to rise if we do not bring together the political will and evidence-based knowledge to work together to provide a more integrated and effective launch for the lives of this and future cohorts of emerging adults. The quality of their lives will in great part be determined by the success or failure of our efforts.

REFERENCES

Americans with Disabilities Act (ADA) Amendments Act of 2008, PL 110-325, 122 Stat. 3553, 42 U.S.C.

Americans with Disabilities Act (ADA) of 1990, PL 101-336, 42 U.S.C. §§ 12101 *et seq.*

Individuals with Disabilities Education Act Amendments (IDEA) of 1997, PL 105-17, 20 U.S.C. §§ 1400 *et seq.*

Individuals with Disabilities Education Act (IDEA) of 1990, PL 101-476, 20 U.S.C. §§ 1400 *et seq.*

Individuals with Disabilities Education Improvement Act (IDEA) of 2004, PL 108-446, 20 U.S.C. §§ 1400 *et seq.*

Olmstead v. L.C., 527 U.S. 581 (1999).

Index

Page numbers followed by *t* indicate tables; those followed by *f* indicate figures.

Policies
 community participation and, 142–144
 current program options
  children and youth, 7–9
  multiage, 11–14
  young adults, 9–11
 demographic changes and, 3–5
 educational, 167–168
 on employment, 166–171
 obstacles to success, 14–18
 overview of, 18
 transition importance and, 5–6
 on transportation, 105
Political support, 17–18, 188, 191–192
Positive behavior supports, 113
Postsecondary education
 case examples, 37, 38, 104
 health insurance and, 89
 participation rates, 174
 preparation for, 177–178
 recommendations on, 181
 special education and, 66
 university transportation at, 109
Poverty
 community living outcomes and, 141
 disability prevalence and, 57
 equity in service access and, 187
 graduation rates and, 177
 special education and, 67
 special health care needs and, 54–55
Primary care physicians, 81, 92–93, 99
Private-pay shared homes, 120–121
Program for All-Inclusive Care for the Elderly (PACE), 128–129
PSID, *see* Panel Study on Income Dynamics
Psychological/cognitive development, 24–25, 32
 see also Mental health
Public health insurance programs, *see* Medicaid; Medicare
Public transportation, 107–108, 111, 112, 113